# THE ROUGH GUIDE to

# The
# Brain

# Credits

**The Rough Guide to the Brain**
Contributing editors:
Duncan Clark & Ruth Tidball
Layout & design: Tom Cabot
Proofreading: Jason Freeman
Production: Gemma Sharpe

**Rough Guides Reference**
Editors: Kate Berens, Tom Cabot,
Tracy Hopkins, Matthew Milton,
Joe Staines
Director: Andrew Lockett

## Publishing information

This edition published June 2012 by
Rough Guides Ltd, 80 Strand, London WC2R 0RL
11 Community Centre, Panchsheel Park, New Delhi 110017, India
Email: mail@roughguides.com

Distributed by the Penguin Group:
Penguin Books Ltd, 80 Strand, London WC2R 0RL
Penguin Group (USA), 375 Hudson Street, NY 10014, USA
Penguin Group (Australia), 250 Camberwell Road, Camberwell, Victoria 3124, Australia
Penguin Group (New Zealand), 67 Apollo Drive, Mairangi Bay, Auckland 1310,
New Zealand

Rough Guides is represented in Canada by Tourmaline Editions Inc.,
662 King Street West, Suite 304, Toronto

Printed in Singapore by Toppan Security Printing Pte. Ltd.

312 pages; includes index

A catalogue record for this book is available from the British Library

ISBN: 978-1-40539-006-4

1 3 5 7 9 8 6 4 2

THE ROUGH GUIDE to

# The
# Brain

## Revised
## 2nd edition

by
## Dr Barry J. Gibb

www.roughguides.com

# Contents

# Acknowledgements

The author wishes to thank the small army of scientists, friends and specialists who responded to his pleas and requests for help, guidance and support. Without invaluable, frequent feedback from both sides of the scientific picket-fence, pinpointing the correct balance of accessibility versus hard science would have been a far more arduous task.

Bringing the right kind of sheen to the brain's many faces, through reviewing, emails, phone calls, interviews, images and general guidance have been the following: Leslie C. Aiello, President of the Wenner-Gren Foundation for Anthropological Research; Robin Dunbar of the Evolutionary Psychology and Behavioural Ecology Research Group at the University of Liverpool; Jo Power at the British Heart Foundation; Barrie Lancaster, Susan Griffin, Gary Wilson and Brijesh Roy at the Wolfson Institute for Biomedical Research, University College London; Declan McLoughlin at the MRC Centre for Neurodegeneration Research, King's College London; Chris Bird and Sam Gilbert at the Institute of Cognitive Neuroscience, University College London; Catherine Hall within the Department of Physiology, University College London; Nick Sireau; Tomas C. Bellamy within the Laboratory of Molecular Signalling, the Babraham Institute; Colin Cooper, School of Psychology, within the Queen's University of Belfast; Rob Keynes, somewhere in the Western Hemisphere; Nancy Rothwell within the Faculty of Life Sciences, University of Manchester; Peter Finegold of Isinglass Consultancy Ltd; Ken Arnold, Head of Public Programmes at The Wellcome Trust; Marina Wallace and Caterina Albano at Artakt; Igor Aleksander, Emeritus Professor of Neural System Engineering, Department of Electrical and Electronic Engineering, Imperial College; Steve Grand at Cyberlife Research Ltd; Sophie Duport at the Royal Hospital for Neurodisability; and many others I crossed paths with during my research.

Sincere thanks to Andrew Lockett at Rough Guides for his gentle encouragement and for taking a shot at such an immense subject with a first-time author. My editors, too, Ruth Tidball and Duncan Clark, deserve my heartfelt gratitude. Their laser-sharp eyes and insatiable curiosity helped craft and refine the book, the pair displaying a clarity of thinking the world could use far more of.

Thank you to my family for their unflinching support and for enduring neurological conversations for more than a year – chemistry sets and robotic toys have a lot to answer for! Finally, this book could never have happened without the piercing intellect, patience, limitless support and downright wonderfulness of my glorious wife, Charmaine Griffiths. You appear to have taken up permanent residence in all the parts of my brain responsible for happiness. But do you know where they are…

## Acknowledgements for the 2nd edition

Sincere thanks again to the team at Rough Guide, in particular Andrew Lockett and Tom Cabot, for their help and support in getting this revised book off the ground and aiding in its subsequent creation. I'd also like to thank all the scientists who took the time to respond to my persistent pleas to answer "a few simple questions" which were, of course, not simple at all.

Special thanks to Janaina Mourao-Miranda, Robert Plomin, Geraint Rees and Seralynne Vann for their time and valuable insights that resulted in the "Expert View" interviews that appear through the book.

Writing this revised edition would have been a far more arduous task without the support of The Wellcome Trust and I'd like to thank the organization for being generous with its time and the Neuroscience and Mental Health team, led by John Williams, for its frequent help.

The science of the brain is a gargantuan task for a single publication and it's only right to acknowledge the scientists across the centuries whose desire to know more about the human mind has resulted in the vast body of knowledge that I've researched and plundered for this book.

And, of course, thanks again to Charmaine, my wife and best friend for her unflinching support and inspiration.

# Introduction

Anatomically speaking, the brain is nothing more than a collection of interconnected nerve cells, a coordinating hub for our body's electrical system. Yet these 1.4 kilograms of wrinkled grey-white matter hold the key to our consciousness – the way we think and feel, our experience of fear, love or despair. The very same organ also oversees our physical selves – from blood pressure to hormone regulation. It's possible to go through life blissfully oblivious of the brain's existence. You never really need to know it's there. And yet your brain *is* you.

The brain is always active – it never shuts down, even while we sleep: zero brain activity means death. Rapidly evolving imaging techniques allow us to see this activity in real time, in ever increasing layers of detail – and it's an extraordinary sight to behold. Pulses and waves of light pass over the surface and deeper structures of the brain, with all the splendour of the aurora. Each type of mental activity elicits its own unique lightshow.

Imaging the living brain is one way that scientists have improved their understanding of the brain. Other insights have been gained by studying people who have suffered damage to specific regions of the brain – from war veterans to mental-health patients – and seeing how their skills and behaviour have been affected. Yet more insights have come courtesy of surgery. Modern surgeons can probe the exposed grey matter of a conscious patient; as the surgical baton touches the delicate tissue, speech, knowledge or sensations are triggered or diminished in real time.

Some may be fascinated by the reductionist approach science is employing to understand the Holy Grail of organs, and wondering whether it's threatening the essence of our humanity. Others may be seeking answers to questions that have long dogged them concerning how their own mind works.

Whatever your interest in the brain, this book should shed some light on this most intriguing and complex of organs. And while a week may be a long time in politics, the progression of science is built on mere moments; flashes of inspiration, sudden insights into previously impenetrable mechanisms, seized glimpses of deeper truths. Since the first iteration of this book, many such insights and ideas have flourished as scientists across the planet have enthusiastically embraced the desire to fully comprehend the brain, fusing behavioural, computational, genetic and imaging approaches.

The book begins at the beginning of life, explaining how evolution endowed our species with one of the largest and most complex brains on the planet. From there it proceeds to brain science and anatomy before looking at three key areas: memory, consciousness and intelligence. Next come brain disorders and the effects of drugs on the brain. The last three chapters cover in turn: the "unexplained brain", from the power of positive thinking to extrasensory perception; followed by an entirely new chapter, "The Technological Brain", exploring how modern living and devices interact with our brain; with the final chapter looking at the brain's future.

Each of these topics could fill many books in its own right. For those wishing to dig deeper, there's a resources section at the back covering relevant websites, blogs, books, science festivals, organizations and films.

# CHAPTER 1

# The long view

## The evolution of the human brain

The human brain is the result of an evolution stretching back through most of the history of our planet. Earth formed around 4.6 billion years ago and life emerged roughly a billion years later in the form of simple, microscopic organisms such as bacteria. These organisms each consisted of single biological cells – the basic building blocks of life. They could consume food, produce waste, reproduce and favour life-enhancing over potentially hazardous environments. But despite this sophisticated, seemingly intelligent behaviour, single-celled animals do not have brains: they simply respond to chemical and environmental cues around them, like light or food. They are unthinking, mechanical.

Things started to change some time over a billion years ago, with the emergence of the first organisms consisting of several connected cells. This step necessitated cooperation between cells and also led to some cells taking on specialized roles. One such specialized cell was the **nerve cell** or **neuron**, which became adept at organizing and processing sensory information – such as sight and smell. Logically enough, these nerve cells tended to gather in higher concentrations at the point in an animal where it received the bulk of its sensory information, a location usually close to the place where it would take food into the body.

> "The evolution of the brain not only overshot the needs of prehistoric man, it is the only example of evolution providing a species with an organ which it does not know how to use."
>
> Arthur Koestler

As evolution proceeded, nerve cells tended to coordinate themselves into **neural networks**, enabling them to communicate and work together. These concentrated masses of interlinked neurons were the first brains. Still extremely simple compared to a human brain, these early neural networks nonetheless enabled primitive animals to receive a variety of inputs from their different senses (smell, vision etc), integrate that information together, and then produce a coordinated response that would be sent back to the muscles: eat, move away, mate and so on.

## The nematode brain

One of the smallest and most studied brains belongs to a worm around 1mm in length. The diminutive *Caenorhabditis elegans* is usually found in soil-based environments, where it can feed on bacteria. But thanks to Nobel Prize-winning scientist Sydney Brenner, it became popular as a **"model organism"** in the 70s, turning up in laboratories all over the world. This worm's tiny size has allowed scientists to completely tease its biological nature apart, organ by organ, cell by cell, in the hope that discoveries made here can be translated into understanding more complex creatures, like us.

A typical worm, from end to end, is made up of 959 individual cells and, of these, 302 are neurons. Twenty of these neurons reside within the animal's pharynx, a region dedicated to the important task of eating. The remaining 282 neurons, while spread throughout the worm's length, are concentrated into several bundles, or ganglia; most of the remaining neurons are found in the head, with the remainder travelling down the worm's length, terminating in a small mass of nerve cells in the tail region. In the head region, just 68 neurons are dedicated to vital survival tasks, such as sensing the environment – through touch, temperature and proximity to chemicals and food.

In total, the neurons form around 5000 chemical synapses, points where one nerve communicates with another, a tiny number relative to the trillions calculated to inhabit the human brain. This relative simplicity has enabled scientists to determine each and every synaptic connection within the worm's nervous system, known as its **connectome** (see p.256).

dorsal cord

head ganglia
(brain)

tail ganglia

ventral cord

**The first and only connectome that has been mapped completely is that of a simple worm, *C. elegans* – it possesses just 302 nerve cells!**

## The fly's brain

Despite being mere millimetres in size, *Drosophila melanogaster* – a small fruit fly – has a complex, fully integrated central nervous system that has revealed much about the genetics and operation of nervous systems in general. The fly's brain lacks a cortex and focuses on those abilities most crucial for its survival – especially smell recognition, by way of its large **antennal lobes** and **mushroom bodies** (so named due to their appearance).

The fly's sensitive antennae possess sensory neurons which, when activated by an odorant molecule, send signals to the antennal lobe for processing. Some of this sensory information is then shunted to the mushroom bodies, a network of neurons and glial cells that play a central role in the fly's memory, for smell in particular. Genes involved in the early development of the mushroom bodies have been found to possess similarities to those expressed during mammalian forebrain development, prompting some to compare these mushroom-like structures with the mammalian cortex.

# The early days

The story of the brain begins in earnest with the **Cambrian explosion** – the metaphorical name given to a period that saw a sudden increase in the diversity of life on Earth. The "explosion" lasted around 40 million years, occurring between 570 and 530 million years ago. Prior to this time, evolution had come to a relative rest: there was no great pressure on existing life forms to adapt.

But then came a period of rapid geographical transformation, with Earth's tectonic plates moving ten times faster than they do today. These shifts tore apart ecological systems that had evolved within specific conditions, changing every habitat, neighbour, climate and food source. In this period of geological turmoil, life became dispersed and the pulse of evolution quickened to approximately twenty times its normal rate. As a consequence, almost all of the animal groups inhabiting Earth today emerged.

Following the Cambrian explosion, large brains with elaborate sensory systems appear to have evolved twice, independently: once among the **cephalopods**, of which a modern example is the octopus (see box on p.6), and once among our fish-like, backboned ancestors, the **chordates**.

The chordates developed a sophisticated sense of smell, allowing them to detect prey and danger, communicate with each other chemically, and identify and "map" locations.

## Reptilian brains

Stripping a human brain down to its barest components would leave you with the **brain stem**, located where the spinal cord enters the skull. This is probably the oldest region of the brain and controls various basic functions (see p.32). The region is also known as the **reptilian brain**, since it's roughly equivalent to the simple brains found inside the skulls of reptiles.

Broadly speaking, reptiles' brains have a tripartite structure. Towards the front, the forebrain is responsible for such abilities as smell and taste. Behind the forebrain, the reptilian midbrain deals with vision (rather than the rear of the brain, as in mammals) and hormonal regulation. At the back, the hindbrain is primarily responsible for determining the reptile's ability to hear and balance, amongst other regulatory and motor functions.

As with a human, the brain of a reptile possesses a **pineal gland** – an important structure linking the Earth's day/night cycle to a range of physiological processes. Unlike the human gland, however, the pineal gland of a reptile does not detect light levels via the eyes. Frequently, the gland is located near a thinner region of the skull, towards the top, allowing it to interface almost directly with the outside world.

# The rise of mammals

A vital stage in our brain evolution was escaping the oceans. Water is a supportive, stable environment – the temperature doesn't fluctuate much. Being on land is a very different matter – temperatures can soar during the day, plummet at night, and there's no buoyancy, necessitating a stronger supporting frame and limbs.

Around 370 million years ago, the first **amphibians** (ancestors of modern frogs and newts) arrived on land, exposing themselves to this unstable environment. Cold-blooded, these creatures were completely dependent on the local ambient temperature for their own body temperatures. This meant that every chemical process within the amphibians' bodies – including the brain – was dependent upon the weather. Egg-laying **reptiles** then burst onto the scene, adapted to spend most of their time on land. But reptiles are also cold-blooded, their brains tightly bound to the climate (see box above).

Approximately 290–245 million years ago, the reptilian evolutionary tree branched, forming three new lineages: one that would lead to the dinosaurs, birds and modern reptiles (the *diapsids*), one that would become the turtles (the *anapsids*), and one that would lead to the large-brained, warm-blooded mammals (the *synapsids*).

Towards the end of the Permian period, around 250 million years ago, following 100 million years of relative stability, life was almost eliminated from our planet in less than 100,000 years – incredibly fast in terms of geological time. Estimates of the loss of life during this period, known as The Great Dying, are as high as 96 percent of all sea-dwelling animals and 75 percent of all land animals. Various theories exist as to why this dramatic extinction occurred, from prolific volcanic activity to dynamic tectonic shifts. But NASA-funded scientists, such as Luann Becker at the University of California, are confident that the geological evidence most likely pinpoints the tipping point as rapid climate change caused by the arrival of a formidable asteroid somewhere in the region of between 6 and 12 km in diameter – imagine a rock around the size of Mount Everest – travelling at terminal velocity.

One group of mammal-like reptiles was able to adapt to these tempestuous times: whiskered descendants of the synapsids known as **cynodonts** (from Greek, *kuon*, dog, and *odous*, tooth). With better-fitting, more specialized teeth, the cynodonts were able to chew food more efficiently, reducing the burden on the digestive system. With this improved digestion came a faster, more immediate supply of nutrients to the body – and to the brain.

The cynodonts had another evolutionary advantage in the form of **homeostasis**: physiological regulation of the body, including its temperature. This liberated them somewhat from the shackles of their environments and also had a major impact on brain evolution, because big brains require a stable temperature. However, big brains also require lots of energy – and so does homeostasis. These twin energy demands would have made it almost impossible for young cynodonts to feed themselves sufficiently well to survive infancy. This is why the dawn of **parenting behaviour** was such a major advance towards larger brains, freeing the young to simply grow, with all nutrition supplied by the mother's milk (from glands adapted from sweat glands). Over time, these adaptations allowed cynodonts to evolve into the first true mammals.

## Sound improvements

By two hundred million years ago, the pinnacle of brain evolution was possessed by the **eucynodonts**, a collection of animals ranging in size from shrew to dog. Eucynodonts were covered in hair and benefited from excellent ears (for tracking prey with unprecedented accuracy and speed) in addition to sharp teeth (for rapid digestion). With these tools, a female eucynodont could gain enough nutrition to feed both her own power-hungry brain and her young.

There's speculation that eucynodonts' exceptional hearing, which was sensitive to high frequencies, may also have opened new lines of communication between mother and child. If so, this would have been a kind of ultrasonic signalling system, much like that used by ground squirrels today, allowing them to communicate in frequencies out of the range of predators and prey.

Eucynodonts developed the crowning achievement of brain evolution: the **cortex**. Unique to mammals, this rippling outer layer was the last part of the brain to evolve. The nascent cortex was what allowed eucynodonts to become such excellent predators, enabling them to collect and integrate visual, olfactory and auditory information, and to plan and remember where the best prey, or the most dangerous predators, might reside.

# (Another) mass extinction

Sixty-five million years ago, another vast meteorite crashed into Earth, causing an explosion that shook the planet. In 2010, a team of scientists pored over the wealth of available data and concluded that a rock,

## The octopus brain

Regarded as the most intelligent living organism without a backbone, the octopus is a mollusc capable of learning and memory. Clearly this is a creature with a sophisticated brain, yet one of the most remarkable qualities of the octopus nervous system is how it interacts with the creature's skin. While a portion of the complex brain of the octopus is protected by a cartilaginous cranium, many of the animal's nerves extend throughout its eight arms. These are used to aid jet propulsion, dismantle food, and probe and analyse the environment by means of suckers and chemical sensors.

Within the skin resides the animal's ace card – **chromatophores** – specialized cells possessing coloured or reflective pigments. The chromatophores, directly linked into the octopus nervous system, allow the animal to alter its colours and patterning in the blink of an eye. This dramatic interaction of vision, brain and chromatophores works almost instantaneously, providing camouflage against almost any background.

But this remarkable ability is not used only for providing cover; it also affords the octopus an excellent form of communication with others. Like a ship's flag, the colours and patterns generated by an octopus can alert others to its state of mind or intent: anger, fear or arousal.

A gravity anomaly map of the Chicxulub impact crater which may have caused the death of the dinosaurs 65 million years ago. A gravity anomaly occurs where the local gravitational field is different from the expected value. The 180-km wide crater (at centre) has a negative gravity anomaly because it is filled with low-density impact debris and sediments.

somewhere in the region of between 10 to 15 km across, had collided with Earth resulting in the Chicxulub crater, which NASA estimates as anywhere between 180 and 300 km in diameter. The crater is located within Mexico's Yucatan Peninsula, better known for its beautiful white sand and crystal clear waters. Skies darkened as debris spewed into the atmosphere, the temperature dropped and countless species, including the dinosaurs, died. Thankfully, our ancestors already possessed a number of adaptations

## The dolphin's brain

Dolphins are mammals that returned to the sea, and they use their unusually large brains to thrive in the oceans of the world. The brain of a bottlenose dolphin weighs in at 1.5–1.7kg, slightly more than that of a human (1.3–1.4kg). Being mammals, dolphins have a large cortex – actually considerably larger than the human cortex – but it's organized very differently, making it difficult to draw meaningful comparisons.

Dolphins devote ten times less brainpower to visual processing than humans, but nearly ten times more to processing sound, an adaptation allowing them to "visualize" their surroundings by creating, and listening for echoes of, high-frequency clicking sounds.

In addition to their colossal cortex, dolphins appear to be self-aware. Project Delphis, initiated in 1985 by Don White and Dexter Cate, tested this using two different techniques: one involving mirrors (does the animal recognize its reflection as itself?), the other involving CCTV (does it understand that the live image on a screen is of itself?). In both cases, the behaviour demonstrated by the dolphins was indicative of self-awareness.

**Human 1350g**

**Chimpanzee 400g**

**Orangutan 400g**

**Macaque 100g**

**Brain weights of humans and primates.**

allowing them to stand a fighting chance in this hostile environment – such as fur, warm blood and nocturnal habits, all of which would have made them less sensitive to the lower temperatures and reduced daylight. With the less-able dinosaur predators wiped out, the early mammals were suddenly able to move into and dominate new environments.

After around ten million years of breeding and natural selection, the primitive primates, or **prosimians**, emerged. Resembling the modern lemur, these creatures dwelled predominantly in tropical environments and had highly developed visual capabilities. Facing forwards, their two eyes gave them so-called binocular vision, enabling them to perceive depth more effectively: to judge their own position relative to other objects in space. Prosimians also developed specialized cells allowing them to discriminate motion, contrast, light, shapes and forms more efficiently – something tied to a large expansion of the area of the brain known as the **visual cortex**. All of this made our ancestors much more effective predators.

Improvements didn't stop there. A large degree of brainpower is needed for tasks we take for granted today. For instance, when walking or running, our eyes remain trained on the subject of interest rather than bobbing up and down in unison with our body and creating a nauseating shanty. Many creatures can't do this: birds, for instance, have to move their entire heads to redirect their line of sight. Our ancestors' brains developed the processing power to form seamless links between the eyes, the muscles controlling the eyes within their sockets and the movement of the entire body.

Another development was the emergence, through genetic mutation, of three-colour (trichromatic) vision, which replaced the two-colour (dichromatic) sight of our earlier ancestors. In an evolutionary instant, the world exploded into colour, and with this came both the ability to reap greater rewards from the environment and a concomitant higher demand for processing ability within the visual cortex. One result of greater perception of colour was the ability to spot ripe, and therefore easy-to-digest, fruit. This in turn allowed the development of a speedy metabolism, which is exactly what's required by large, energy-hungry brains.

Our ancestors' visual cortex became ever-more expansive and elaborate, and so too did their ability to map and plan the environment. This included temporal **memory**: those more able to remember not just *where* the best foods were, but also *when*, would be most likely to survive.

Even today, primates that eat fruits have a larger, more rippled cortex than those favouring leaves, which demand far more work from the digestive system but less planning when it comes to finding food.

## Human ancestry

It isn't clear exactly when our ancestors branched off from the apes, but a skull discovered in Chad in 2001 suggests it could have been seven million years ago or more. The species in question, *Sahelanthropus tchadensis*, was relatively human-like but had a brain of only 350cc (cubic centimetres), around three times smaller than that of a human. For the next five million years or so, brain size didn't change a great deal, though various other developments unfolded.

One notable example was **bipedal locomotion**, the ability to walk upright on two legs. This freed hands for the manipulation of objects, enabled standing to scan the horizon for predators or prey, and allowed new types of movement. Each of these behaviours demanded increased brainpower to be fully exploited. Manipulating objects with the hands, for example, requires a high degree of refinement in the motor systems linking the muscles and nerves of the hands and eyes with the brain. And walking itself, essentially a controlled fall, demands an ever-present

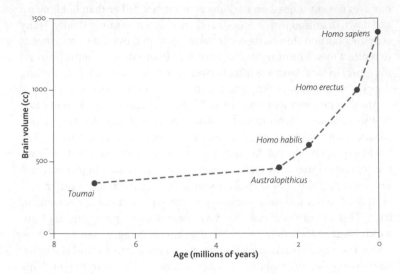

**The growth of brain size over the past eight million years, as measured in cranial capacity.**

system of sensory feedback to avoid toppling over. Despite this, the biggest brains around 2.5 million years ago, possessed by the so-called *Australopithicines*, were just 400–500cc.

Then, after roughly five million years of slow growth, brain size started to shoot up. Between 1.5 and 2 million years ago, hominids such as the "handyman" (*Homo habilis*) arrived, with brains as big as 600cc. Soon after, *Homo erectus* emerged, with a skull capacity of around 1000cc. In the last half-million years, craniums swelled even faster to the human average of 1400cc.

## Communities and language

What prompted the initial burst of brain growth after millions of years of inertia? One theory, the **social hypothesis**, suggests that a primary cause was that our ancestors began to live in larger communities. These bigger, more complex social groups would have encouraged more sophisticated interactive behaviour, from cooperative hunting to grooming. It seems likely that this more complicated social existence may have favoured larger brains – and, indeed, there is a strong correlation between the size of an animal's cortex and the size of the social group within which it lives. With increasing community size came ever more elaborate systems of communication – such as facial and hand expressions, body language and vocal interaction.

It seems likely that increased collaboration and communication would have enabled our ancestors to become more effective hunter-gatherers, allowing us to consume a more high-energy diet, which, in turn, provided favourable conditions for further brain development. These and other factors eventually led to the emergence, at some point during the last half-million years, of **language**, which was to prove pivotal in the final stage of our brain evolution. As language evolved, humans could converse not only about a tool they had crafted, for instance, but also about one which did not yet exist. Imagination became communicable, allowing ideas to be shared and ever more efficient hunting and survival skills to evolve.

Language reached its zenith with our own species – *Homo sapiens* – which emerged around a quarter of a million years ago. (Neanderthals, which had similarly large brains, appeared at a similar time, but died out around 30,000 years ago, and no one knows exactly how developed their language skills were.)

With their large brains and highly developed language, humans brought about a cultural explosion, beginning approximately 40,000 years ago, and eventually came to dominate the planet. The brain evolved to help us thrive in a hostile world, but became so powerful that today we have the dubious luxury of shaping the world to suit our whims.

So has the brain stopped evolving? Of course not. To find out what the future might hold, turn to Chapter 12.

## Chris Frith FRS FBA
*Emeritus Professor of Neuropsychology, Leopold Müller Functional Imaging Laboratory*

**What is your favourite part of the brain and why?** The medial prefrontal cortex. This region of the brain becomes active when we interact with other people and think about mental states, but no one knows precisely what it does. It is one of the regions of the human brain that is greatly expanded compared to other animals.

**What scientific breakthrough helped us to understand the brain the most?** The discovery of neurons (nerve cells) and the realization that they transmit information, rather than energy.

**What's the next big thing in neuroscience?** A computational model of brain function.

Drawing, 1489–92, of vertical and horizontal sections of the human head by Leonardo da Vinci, erroneously linking vision with the ventricle system.

# CHAPTER 2

# Exploring the mind

## The story of brain science

Our understanding of the human brain is far from complete. As we'll see later in this book, the science of memory, consciousness, intelligence and many other areas is full of unknowns. However, things have come a very long way since the days of ancient Egyptians, who thought the heart, not the brain, was the centre of intelligence and emotion. The brain, not being seen as particularly significant, was unceremoniously removed from the skull during mummification.

Around 450 years BC, the Greek physician **Alcmaeon** was among the first to recognize the brain's significance, but his view wasn't universally accepted. A hundred years later, Aristotle reasserted the dominance of the heart, suggesting the brain may be little more than a cooling system. This idea was comprehensively discredited another half-century later, after thorough dissection of the human body in Alexandria and the discovery of the nervous system.

From the first century BC for more than a millennium, the standard view of the brain was that of Greek physician **Galen**, who suggested that the organ contained and controlled the four "humours". These four liquids – blood, phlegm, yellow bile and black bile – had been seen as key to health and personality since the time of Hippocrates. This theory was nonsense, of course, though Galen did succeed in recognizing the brain's role in memory, emotion and processing of the senses.

> "If the human brain were so simple that we could understand it, we would be so simple that we couldn't."
>
> Emerson M. Pugh

## Trepanation

Trepanation, a surgical operation in which a hole, or **burr hole**, is drilled into the skull, is a practice stretching back over 7000 years. Curiously, the technique seems to have arisen independently in different cultures, from Europe and Africa to South America (where pre-Incan civilization used both bronze and sharpened obsidian rock to drill into the skull). The operation, which was used to treat everything from headaches and epilepsy to mental illness, was often seen to have religious and magical significance – a way of releasing an evil spirit from the head.

In modern-day medicine, trepanning (from Greek, *trepa*, hole) is rare but still used in certain circumstances – for example, as a means of reducing pressure on the brain when there is bleeding inside the skull. The patient receives a general anaesthetic, a flap of scalp is cut and folded back and a motorized drill removes a small circle of skull. (The World Health Organization recommends, sensibly enough, that doctors use "little pressure when cutting the inner table to avoid plunging through into the brain".)

Even today, however, a few people still advocate non-clinical trepanning as a means of quite literally opening up the mind. The International Trepanation Advocacy Group (www.trepan.com) claims that this can provide a permanent state of "natural high", enhanced concentration and greater blood flow to the brain, supposedly restoring our childhood creative energies. Do not try this at home.

**Hieronymous Bosch's *The Extraction of the Stone of Madness* (c.1485).**

The progress of brain science in the Middle Ages was slow, largely thanks to a Church ban on human dissection. Things started picking up in the Renaissance era, when artists and thinkers such as Leonardo Da Vinci took an interest in the subject. Indeed, among Leonardo's prolific output of the late fifteenth and early sixteenth centuries are a series of anatomical studies – including some of the brain. In one drawing he explores the brain's structure layer by layer, conjuring a tangible sense of discovery. His depictions reveal a clear awareness of the major nerves – detailing points of entry for those associated with vision and hearing, amongst others.

Leonardo was also the first person to use a solidifying material – in this case, wax – to reveal the complete three-dimensional form of the brain's internal structures. In yet another inspired moment, Leonardo injected hot wax into the **ventricles** (a series of interconnected "spaces" within the brain, usually occupied by cerebrospinal fluid) of an ox's brain, then let it harden. Once the brain tissue was removed, Leonardo could examine the internal structure of these ventricles (which in his time were thought to house certain higher functions, such as memory and reasoning).

## The birth of neurology

Despite the advances of Leonardo and others, neurology only really started to flourish in the seventeenth century, largely thanks to Englishman **Thomas Willis** (1621–75). Willis studied at Oxford University and became involved with a group of intellectuals known as the Virtuosi, whose ranks also included architect, scientist, artist and mathematician Christopher Wren (with whom Willis would later become a founder member of London's Royal Society).

Working at a time when many people still believed nasal phlegm was a brain waste product, Willis was the first to examine the organ with real scientific rigour. In 1664, after years of research, he published

**Thomas Willis.**

his ground-breaking *Cerebri Anatome*, complete with detailed drawings by Wren. The book was a masterpiece, providing the first complete descriptions of the major brain regions, cranial nerves and vasculature. Willis also laid the basis of brain-science terminology, coining words such as neurology, lobe, reflex and hemisphere. One important brain area – the "circle of Willis" – bears his name to this day.

Willis correctly linked **memory** and **higher functioning** with the cerebral hemispheres. This insight was achieved by examining the brains of other animals and noting their relative smoothness (the more cortex an animal has, the more wrinkled its appearance, since it folds to fit inside its skull). He also noticed poor development or damage to the rippled surface of the brain in people with "weak intellect".

Another breakthrough was Willis's proposal that the liquid-filled spaces deep inside the brain, the **ventricles**, served no significant purpose. Previously, many respected individuals had believed the ventricles to be the home of various higher brain functions, such as reasoning and imagination. Willis challenged this claim on the basis of his observations – and he was right.

The ventricle system, first modelled by Leonardo and first understood by Willis.

Willis also looked at a brain region known as the **corpus striatum**, a kidney-shaped structure hidden underneath the hemispheres, roughly in alignment with the ears. This region takes it's name from its stripey interior, made up of alternating bands of white, fatty myelin (see p.31) and unmyelinated grey matter. Observations on dogs and the post-mortem brains of people who had suffered from movement difficulties allowed Willis to correctly propose that this striped area was important for voluntary movement. And, indeed, the corpus striatum is the region affected in Huntington's chorea (in which it degenerates) and in Parkinson's disease (in which it fails to receive signals from elsewhere in the brain – see p.181).

Next, Willis turned his sights on the **cerebellum** (see p.33), a large appendage at the back of the brain, at its base. The presence of this structure in all but the simplest of brains indicated to Willis that its function must be very basic and uniform throughout all brained animals. This led him to conclude that the cerebellum was most likely responsible for involuntary movement, a requirement all animals need to carry out the various basic life functions, such as breathing. He was, in this rare instance, wrong: the cerebellum is responsible for involuntary skeletal-muscle movement, but not for other involuntary behaviours such as heartbeat and digestion.

# Divide and conquer

Willis had succeeded in associating certain brain areas with specific bodily functions but it was Swedish scientist **Emanuel Swedenborg** (1688–1772) who first suggested that even the regular-looking cortex may consist of discrete areas with different roles. Way ahead of his time, Swedenborg also had insights about brain activity being tied to breathing (as opposed to heartbeat) and the brain's control of voluntary movement. Sadly, his work lay undiscovered for decades, and the idea of specific brain regions controlling specific functions didn't really take off until the end of the eighteenth century, through the work of **Franz Joseph Gall** (1758–1828).

## Lumps and bumps

In Gall's time, **physiognomy** was popular: the idea that there was a tight correspondence between facial features (for example, the distance between the eyes) and character (for example, criminality). Gall developed a similar theory for the brain, suggesting in 1792 that highly localized portions of the cortex – areas he referred to as "cerebral organs" – could be linked to specific behavioural traits. He claimed that the surface features of the skull were a direct correlate of the underlying structure of the cortex, with bumps suggesting an expansion of a specific brain region and a corresponding change in behaviour.

Gall believed that almost any trait, or mental illness, could be linked to a particular combination of bumps. His practice of matching skull shape with brain functions – **cranioscopy**, as he called it – became immensely popular, and as his collection of skull casts grew, so did his reputation. However, Gall's theory, later to be called **phrenology** (the

> "I never knew I had an inventive talent until Phrenology told me so. I was a stranger to myself until then!"
>
> Thomas Edison

**Franz Joseph Gall's cranioscopy diagram, showing the 27 areas he associated with:**

1  impulse to propagation
2  tenderness for the offspring, or parental love
3  friendly attachment or fidelity
4  valour, self-defence
5  murder, carnivorousness
6  sense of cunning
7  larceny, sense of property
8  pride, arrogance, love of authority
9  ambition and vanity
10 circumspection
11 aptness to receive an education, or the memoria realis
12 sense of locality
13 recollection of persons
14 faculty for words, verbal memory
15 faculty of language
16 disposition for colouring, and delighting in colours
17 sense for sounds, musical talent
18 arithmetic, counting, time
19 mechanical skill
20 comparative perspicuity, sagacity
21 metaphysical perspicuity
22 wit, causality, sense of inference
23 poetic talent
24 good nature, compassion, moral sense
25 mimicry
26 theosophy, sense of God and religion
27 perseverance, firmness

study of the mind), was deeply flawed: he had never taken time to look below the skull and see whether bumps on the surface really were direct evidence of greater cortical development beneath. The Academy of Sciences of Paris disapproved of his unscientific approach and asked experimentalist Marie-Jean-Pierre Flourens to determine once and for all whether there was any validity to the new science. Ironically, some of Flourens' own experiments were badly designed, but he had little trouble discrediting Gall's work.

## Doctor Broca and Mr Tan

The discrediting of Gall's work elicited a renewed resistance to the idea that the outer cortex could be mapped onto specific areas with specific functions. It took another individual, French-born Paul Pierre Broca

(1824–80), to turn things around. A respected surgeon, Broca provided the first truly compelling evidence of cortical specialization in a famous case involving a patient called Leborgne. A middle-aged man, Leborgne had spent much of his adult life in hospital after losing his ability to speak in his early thirties. Despite being able to comprehend the conversations of others, Leborgne could only say one word: "tan", which soon became his nickname. Tan died soon after coming into Broca's care, giving the surgeon a chance to perform an autopsy. As Broca had expected, he found damage towards the front of the brain – in the left hemisphere near the temple, a region now known as **Broca's area**.

Further research led Broca to believe – correctly – that the frontal lobes were also key to intellect, judgement, abstraction and reasoning. But one thing troubled him: why did speech problems appear to be linked primarily to damage on the *left* side of the brain? The answer was **cerebral dominance**: the fact that the two apparently identical halves of the brain are far less similar than they appear. This realization was made independently by Broca and Gustave Dax, a physician from the south of France, and by the mid-1860s it had become accepted that the two halves of the brain focused on different tasks.

But if the left hemisphere was controlling language, what was the right half doing? Were these two mounds of flesh interacting with each other in harmony or were they each struggling to gain the upper hand? The idea of two distinct personalities struggling to cohabit within one cranium

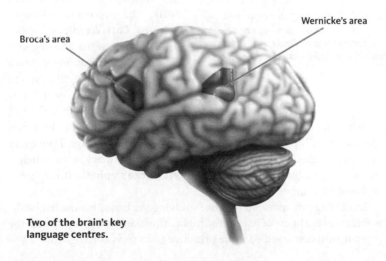

Wernicke's area

Broca's area

**Two of the brain's key language centres.**

## Dr John Williams
*Neuroscientist and Head of Clinical Activities/Neuroscience and Mental Health, Wellcome Trust*

**What is your favourite part of the brain and why?** The hippocampus – for sentimental, aesthetic and scientific reasons. The sentimental because it's the brain area I did my thesis on and it will always be associated in my mind with an important time in my life as I grew into adulthood. Aesthetic because its layered structure (think Victoria sponge) is both distinctive and receptive to a variety of stains that reveal form and hint at function. Scientifically it has been a treasure trove of both specific and generic information about neuronal and circuit function.

**What scientific breakthrough helped us to understand the brain the most?** The recognition that nerve cells communicated by means of specialized structures called synapses. The work of the anatomists Cajal and Golgi, and the physiologists Langley, Dale and others was key.

**What's the next big thing in neuroscience?** On a horizon that we can see, it will be our ability to manipulate the function of brain circuits using optical technologies.

was explored soon after in Robert Louis Stephenson's *The Strange Case of Dr Jekyll and Mr Hyde*, published in 1886.

Across the English Channel, back in England, a prolific British neurologist, John Hughlings Jackson (1835–1911), was to advance the idea that the right hemisphere endowed us with the power of **spatial awareness**. Deficits in spatial awareness (or spatial perception) can be seriously debilitating, as in the case of Jackson's patient Elisa P., who, due to damage to the right hemisphere of her brain, was unable to locate a park that she had lived near for thirty years, even when she was standing at the gates. She was no longer able to recognize her own position relative to the park's.

Following on from Broca's work, the precocious German scientist **Carl Wernicke** (1848–1905) added to the growing evidence for localization of brain functions. In 1874, the young physician, anatomist, neurologist and psychiatrist published work in which he identified a region of the left hemisphere, further back and distinct from Broca's area, that was also involved in language. Damage in this area resulted in the patient being perfectly fluent, but in meaningless nonsense – a condition now known as **Wernicke's aphasia** (from Greek *aphatos*, meaning speechless).

Increasingly, it appeared to those studying the brain that the left hemisphere was the home of reasoning, higher functions and speech whilst the right hemisphere handled more primitive tasks such as navigation.

# Experimentalism

By 1881, when the Royal Institution of London held a large meeting of medical clinicians, the hesitancy to associate brain areas with specific functions was gone. At the meeting, an ambitious Scot named **David Ferrier** (1843–1928) made significant suggestions about how the cortex might be organized. In addition to proposing that there was an area dedicated to processing information from each of the five senses – vision, hearing, smell, taste and touch – Ferrier also spoke about a discrete cortical region set aside for voluntary movement.

Ferrier's brain research began in Yorkshire a decade or so earlier, when he started expanding upon work published in 1870 by two Germans: **Gustav Fritsch** (1838–1927) and **Eduard Hitzig** (1838–1907). Working as a doctor during the Prusso-Danish War of 1864, Fritsch occasionally had to treat wounds that had left regions of brain exposed. He noticed that accidentally touching the exposed brain could elicit twitching movements from the soldier.

Along with Hitzig, Fritsch started to explore this phenomenon using dogs as subjects – exposing their cortical surface to minute electrical currents. By gently touching various regions of exposed brain, they discovered an area towards the front of the cortex that resulted in movement of the forepaw, hind-paw, face and neck.

Ferrier performed a series of similar experiments on a variety of other animals, leading him to share most of Fritsch and Hitzig's conclusions – in particular, that they had identified the region of the brain required for voluntary movement.

## The cortex and personality

Our knowledge of the brain owes a great debt to a large number of unfortunate individuals, and there's no better example than Phineas P. Gage (1823–60). An American railroad foreman, Gage had the role of packing explosive charges into the ground to clear the way for new tracks. One day in 1848, as Gage was doing just this with the

**Phineas Gage: holding the iron bar that travelled through his brain.**

THE ROUGH GUIDE TO THE BRAIN

## The rise and fall of the lobotomy

Few surgical procedures are as notorious as the **lobotomy**, the neurosurgical operation made famous in the closing section of *One Flew Over the Cuckoo's Nest*. The technique, which is no longer in use, was designed to ease mental illness by irreversibly damaging a specific part of the brain. This type of surgery has its origins in the late nineteenth century, when Swiss psychiatrist **Gottlieb Burckhardt** deliberately damaged the brains of six mentally ill patients. In that instance, one patient died immediately following the operation and another was found dead in a river soon after.

Brain surgery became more honed in the 1930s, when scientists discovered that performing a "prefrontal leucotomy" – severing the connections between the prefrontal cortex and regions involved in motivation and emotion – had a calming effect on monkeys. Portuguese neuropsychiatrist **António Egas Moniz** applied the same approach to sufferers of severe mental illness, a move that led to him sharing the Nobel Prize for Physiology or Medicine in 1949.

However, it was American physician **Walter Jackson Freeman** who turned lobotomy into a cure for everything from schizophrenia to extreme childhood misbehaviour. Freeman developed a speedy "ice-pick" version of the operation, which involved putting an ice pick through the skull above the tear duct and wiggling it around to destroy the brain tissue – a procedure deemed, curiously, as "minimally invasive". Touring the US in his so-called Lobotomobile, Freeman performed his rough-and-ready operation on around 3500 people. He also zealously promoted his approach to other doctors, helping pave the way for more than 40,000 lobotomies in the 1940s and 50s.

Lobotomies generally succeeded in "calming" patients, but often at the cost of attention span, planning skills, creativity, decision-making and social behaviour – all functions associated with the prefrontal lobe. In the worst

aid of a tamping iron, the explosive charge blew prematurely, sending the iron rod (109cm long and 3cm wide) directly through his head. The rod entered his skull below the left eye, continued through the front left region of his cortex and soared out the top of his head, landing some twenty metres behind him.

The first physician on the scene seems to have been one Edward H. Williams. Brain exposed, the freshly traumatized Gage apparently ceased chatting to his fellow workmen for long enough to deliver the line, "Doctor, here is business enough for you."

The next doctor to tend Gage back in town, John M. Harlow, documented his experience in a now classic paper, "Passage of an Iron Rod Through the Head":

cases, the result could be a nearly complete mental standstill or side effects such as epilepsy. As such, the approach became viewed as unethical and dangerous, and it was phased out with the emergence of **antipsychotics** (see p.206) – a case of surgical intervention being replaced by chemical intervention.

**Walter Freeman administering a lobotomy in 1949. The operation was often carried out without general anaesthetic.**

I am informed that the patient was thrown upon his back, and gave a few convulsive motions of the extremities, but spoke in a few minutes. His men (with whom he was a great favorite) took him in their arms and carried him to the road, only a few rods distant, and sat him into an ox cart, in which he rode, sitting erect, full three quarters of a mile, to the hotel of Mr. Joseph Adams, in this village.

Gage's remarkable lucidity was short-lived, however, and there followed weeks of coma and meningitis. He recovered, but not entirely: his personality had changed. Once popular and friendly, Gage was now foul-mouthed and erratic. Despite living for another eleven years, Gage was never again to become his former self. Years later, in the 1870s, Ferrier

## Neuromarketing

Aside from all its various medical functions, brain imaging may also have a future in marketing and product design. In a development that many will see as the invasion of our last true dominion of privacy – the mind – companies have started using imaging technology to gauge the neurological impact of their brands.

One recent example – described in a 2004 article by Dr P. Read Montague of Baylor College of Medicine, Houston – involved the brain scanning of people taking the "Pepsi Challenge". When the subjects were given two unmarked drinks – one Pepsi and one Coke – and asked to pick their favourite, the result was a roughly equal selection of the two. The associated brain scans revealed activity in the **prefrontal cortex** – a region involved in determining preferences based on sensory information.

However, when the subjects were given two identical drinks (both Cokes) and told that one was Coke and the other Pepsi, far more people picked the former. In this instance, the scans showed extra activity in other regions of the brain, including another part of the prefrontal cortex, implicated in working memory and biasing behaviour, plus the **hippocampus** – key to memory formation and retrieval (see pp.35, 67). The subjects, it seems, were accessing their knowledge of Coke, with all of the branding and feelings that went with it, and this was biasing their decision in Coke's favour. Pepsi, by contrast, left these brain regions relatively inactive, suggesting that the company's advertising campaigns have some way to go to reach the parts that its competitor is accessing already.

speculated that the very region destroyed in Gage's brain was responsible for higher intellectual functioning.

More breakthroughs came in 1889, when **Santiago Ramon y Cajal**, the father of modern neuroscience, published his *Manual of Normal Histology and Micrographic Technique*, one of the greatest scientific texts ever written – and drawn. Cajal showed that the brain and nervous system consisted of discrete cells – **neurons** (see p.29) – and his publication described the nervous system with unparalleled clarity, beauty and detail. He received the Nobel Prize for Medicine in 1906.

The amassed work from the previous several hundred years laid a solid foundation for the twentieth century, when serious research into this area proliferated. In 1932 Sir Charles Scott Sherrington and Edgar Douglas Adrian won the Nobel Prize "for their discoveries regarding the functions of neurons", further refining the work of Cajal (whom Sherrington had met). This feat was further added to by Sir John Carew Eccles, Alan Lloyd

Hodgkin and Andrew Fielding Huxley, who received the Nobel Prize in 1963 "for their discoveries concerning the ionic mechanisms involved in excitation and inhibition in the peripheral and central portions of the nerve cell membrane" – put simply, how neurons communicate with each other, the absolute foundation of mental functioning.

As a consequence of these breakthroughs, scores of observational studies, surgical techniques and drugs to remedy brain dysfunction were developed. Perhaps the greatest advance of all, however, was that of observing the activity of the living brain.

## Brain scanning

The first major step towards scanning the human brain in real time was taken on 6 July 1924, when **Hans Berger** used his electroencephalograph to measure human brain-waves. Berger laid the groundwork for future research which came into its own in the 1970s with the rise of **computerized axial tomography** (CAT or CT) and **positron emission tomography** (PET).

CAT scans, which won Godfrey Newbold Hounsfield and Allan McLeod Cormack the Nobel Prize in Physiology or Medicine in 1979,

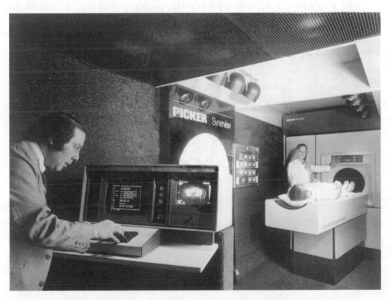

**The dawn of brain imaging: an early CAT scanner in action, April 1978.**

employed the computing power of the day to turn numerous two-dimensional x-rays of the target body into a three-dimensional image for further analysis. PET scans, by contrast, employ radioactive "tracer" substances, which are injected directly into the human body. The tracer gradually collects inside the major organs, all the while emitting positron radiation – the presence of which is indirectly detected by a sensor.

A more recent and less invasive scanning technique is **functional magnetic resonance imaging** (fMRI), which makes use of a magnet weighing several tons. The technique, which won physicist Peter Mansfield and chemist Paul Lauterbur the 2003 Nobel Prize for Physiology, relies on the magnetic charges of metal ions in our blood. Human blood is full of such ions, including those of iron (which, as in rust, produce the red colour). The magnetic properties of the iron change with the presence or absence of oxygen, allowing the magnet to "see" fresh, richly oxygenated blood as it gets delivered to the various regions of the brain. This in turn reflects brain activity, since the harder a region of the brain is "working", the more oxygen and nutrients it demands and (within a few seconds) receives. The information gathered by an fMRI scanner is processed by a powerful computer to construct a two- or three-dimensional image of brain activity.

fMRI enables scientists to observe the global behaviour of the brain during all kinds of activities, such as mental arithmetic, piano playing or thinking of a loved one. It's being employed to understand everything from neurological conditions to the way in which fizzy drinks affect our thinking.

For those interested in a more detailed history of brain science, turn to p.287 for recommended further reading.

# CHAPTER 3

# A brief tour

## Inside the brain and nervous system

As we've seen, the human body, like all other living organisms, is composed of cells: the fundamental building blocks of life. A human body consists of an unimaginable number of cells – around a hundred trillion. To put that vast figure in perspective, if every person on the planet supplied 15,000 cells, you'd have enough to make a human. Cells come in a vast array of shapes and sizes, each performing a particular role. Kidneys, heart, eyes, brain – each component in our bodies is made up of myriad specialized cells working in unison.

The cells that form the basis of the brain and nervous system are known as **neurons** – aka **neurons** or **nerve cells**. These cells are specialists in communication. They process, relay and store information. There are more than fifty types of neuron, each focusing on a given area, from movement, pain, vision and smell to memory, planning and speech.

This chapter explains how neurons work and then takes a look at the brain's various regions. First, however, let's put the brain into its wider context within the nervous system.

## The big picture: the human nervous system

The brain is the control centre of the nervous system – a complex network for receiving sensory data, making decisions, controlling movement and generally managing the body. The system consists of two parts: the **central nervous system** and the **peripheral nervous system**.

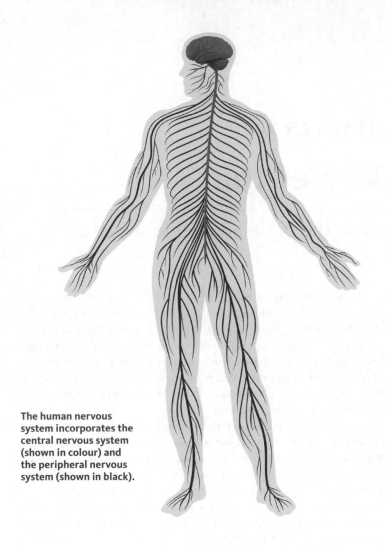

**The human nervous system incorporates the central nervous system (shown in colour) and the peripheral nervous system (shown in black).**

The central nervous system includes the brain itself and the **spinal cord**, a thick nervous tract, more than 40cm long, which acts as the conduit between brain and body. The central nervous system is heavily fortified. Most obviously, it's encased in bone: just as the brain is safely enclosed in the skull, the spinal cord runs down the inside of the back-bone. Further protection is afforded by the **blood–brain barrier** (see p.188) which stops certain substances passing into the central nervous system from the rest of the body.

The **peripheral nervous system** consists of neurons stretched out into nerve fibres, which connect the spinal cord with the rest of our bodies, right down to the toes and fingertips. Some such neurons stretch over surprisingly long distances – in the case of the sciatic nerves, for example, individual cells run the entire length of our legs.

In the peripheral nervous system, **afferent neurons** (also called afferent nerves), carry sensory information *towards* the central nervous system. In the other direction, **efferent neurons** (also known as efferent nerves or motor neurons) carry instructions from the central nervous system to our muscles or glands – instructions to move, for example.

The peripheral system feeds into 31 pairs of nerves within the spinal cord, which relay the signals to the brain. Neurons that only connect to other neurons (and no sensory organs or muscles) are known as **interneurons**. These are predominantly found within the brain and spinal cord.

Surrounding all of the various neurons are **glial cells** (from the Greek word for glue). Outnumbering their neuronal counterparts by ten to one, these are the cells that, amongst many other functions, hold the entire matrix of the brain in place.

# How neurons work: the action potential

The nervous system constitutes a communications network of extraordinary complexity. The central nervous system alone contains around a hundred billion neurons – if each was the size of a brick, that would be enough to pave 500 square miles. Each of these is capable of receiving signals from thousands of others in varying regions of the brain. The result is an almost limitless number of data pathways.

The place at which any two neighbouring neurons come together is known as a **synapse**. This comprises a minute gap – the **synaptic cleft** – through which one cell can send chemical signals to the other. But how does one neuron decide when to send a signal to its neighbour? The key is the **action potential** – a term coined in 1939 by A.L. Hodgkin and A.F. Huxley. Here's how it works.

## From the leaves...

Neurons typically have a tree-like structure and pass signals in one direction, from the leafy top section, down via the trunk to the roots.

Dendrites

Cell body

Axon

Synaptic terminals

Neurotransmitters

The leafy section consists of a mass of branching structures known as **dendrites** (from the Greek *dendron*, tree). Each branch reaches out to neighbouring neurons and uses sensory proteins to detect chemical signals emitted by those neurons.

The information is harvested by dendrites and sent (now in the form of charged ions) down to the neuron's control centre, the **cell body**. (The cell body also determines the overall properties, shape and behaviour of the neuron by producing proteins in accordance with DNA-issued instructions.)

The cell body pools together the data from each branch of the dendrites to create an overall signal, which is passed to an area known as the **axon hillock**. The hillock, brimming with charge-sensitive proteins, determines whether or not the cell will "**fire**". When at rest, the inside of the neuron possesses a negative charge, while the exterior is positive. But if – and only if – the overall charge from the dendrites reaches the critical threshold value for the neuron in question, the cell becomes depolarized and the situation is reversed for a few milliseconds, the interior suddenly flooding with positive charge.

The result is a burst of electrical activity being sent down the cell's "trunk": the **axon**.

## ... down the trunk

Axons, also known as **nerve fibres**, vary widely in width and length (in the case of a giraffe's neck, they can be many metres long), but they always serve to transfer the charge from one end of the cell to the other.

The firing of a charge down an axon is less straightforward than the flow of electrons down copper wires, but the two are analogous. Electrical activity is simply the movement of charge from one place to another, and the brain is brimming with charge in the form of molecules known as **ions**.

Just as copper wire is often insulated with plastic, many axons have a covering of biological insulation known as a **myelin sheath**. These fatty sheaths, which give the brain its whitish appearance, reduce the risk of short circuits caused by other nearby axons. They also help speed the charge on its way and ensure that it doesn't fizzle out en route.

Myelin sheaths are broken up, every millimetre or so, by small gaps known as **Nodes of Ranvier** (after the French physician Louis Antoine Ranvier, who discovered myelin sheaths in 1878). The nodes are free from myelin but

# Scott Waddell

*Professor of Neurobiology, Centre for Neural Circuits and Behaviour, University of Oxford*

**What is your favourite part of the brain and why?** I don't have a favourite part because I don't work directly on the brain itself. However, when I talk to people that do, there's something interesting about every piece someone cares to look at. It's just that some of it gets way more press and attention than the rest. Neurons are I guess my favourite part of the brain!

**What scientific breakthrough helped us to understand the brain the most?** Do we understand the brain? Nevertheless, there have been lots of breakthroughs and it's hard to say which one has helped the most. One of my favourites is the discovery of the hypocretin receptor mutation in narcoleptic dogs. I think that was profound and has had major implications for subsequent study and understanding. Another would be the actions of leptin in the brain – of huge significance. Lastly, the use of genetic technology to manipulate small groups of neurons along with the new generation of genetically encoded tools, that allows the visualization and manipulation of these neurons, are of major significance in research... and, of course, are in vogue at the moment.

**What's the next big thing in neuroscience?** The next big thing!? I think everything is big in neuroscience because I think it remains a frontier of biology... and, umm... the new edition of *The Rough Guide to the Brain*.

packed full of proteins, allowing the electrical signal to recharge and continue to the next node, and so on. This process, known as **saltatory conduction** (from Latin *saltere*, to jump), results in a reliable electrical signal that can travel in excess of one hundred metres per second.

Multiple sclerosis causes the destruction of myelin around neurons, which in turn causes the various symptoms of that disease (see p.151).

## ... to the roots

The axon delivers the charge to the roots of the neuronal tree: the **synaptic terminals**. These contain an abundance of tiny spheres called **vesicles**, which in turn contain special chemicals, **neurotransmitters**, whose task it is to amplify or modulate electrical signals being passed to neighbouring neurons. There are various types of neurotransmitter, including some familiar names such as dopamine (mainly involved in emotion and movement) and serotonin (memory, temperature regulation and sleep, among other functions).

The arrival of an action potential signals a burst of activity, with vesicle after vesicle merging with the neuron's outer membrane and delivering its chemical contents into the synaptic cleft – the tiny space separating the neuron from the dendritic branches of its neighbours. Depending on the receptors in each receiving cell, the arrival of a neurotransmitter can either add to or detract from the overall signal that determines whether or not it, in turn, will fire and pass a signal onto the next neuron in line.

And so the cycle continues through the next neuron, and the next... and so on. Working through our endlessly variable neuronal data channels, action potentials set our brains alight in a storm of electrical activity that lasts from the moment our neurons form in the womb until the day we die.

# Brain regions

As we saw in Chapter 2, it took centuries to gain even a rudimentary understanding of the brain's various regions and their respective functions. Today, although there's still a huge amount that we *don't* know about the brain and nervous system, we do have a good knowledge of the basic anatomy and function of each region. So, which bit does what?

## The brain stem

The junction between the top of the spinal cord and the brain is called the **brain stem**, which comprises around ten percent of the central nervous system. Also known as the "reptilian brain" (see p.4), the brain stem stretches from the base of the skull into the centre of the brain, roughly in line with the eyes.

midbrain

pons

**The brain stem**

medulla
oblongata

Responsible for governing some of the body's vital functions, the brain stem consists of three parts. At the bottom, connecting to the spinal cord, is the **medulla oblongata** (which roughly translates as "elongated inner-section"). This part is essential for involuntary functions such as breathing, digestion, heart rate and blood pressure. Sitting immediately above the medulla, like a ripe cherry, is a more swollen region called the **pons** (from the Latin for bridge). This has a hand in some of the same functions as the medulla but also directs movement-related information between the cortex and the cerebellum (more on these later).

Crowning the brain stem is a smaller, curving structure referred to as the **midbrain**, located at the organ's centre. This is responsible for controlling and coordinating many of the body's sensory and motor functions, such as eye movements.

## The cerebellum

The **cerebellum** ("little brain") is found behind the brain stem, to which it is connected. Split into two hemispheres, it has a convoluted surface that makes it look somewhat like a giant walnut. The cerebellum was one of the earliest brain regions to evolve, and the human version is comparatively similar to those in other animals.

Despite occupying only one tenth of the brain's volume, the cerebellum accounts for around half of the total number of neurons. Its primary functions are movement and balance. Receiving and processing a range of

The cerebellum

inputs from the eyes, ears, balancing systems and cortex, the cerebellum despatches instructions back through the brain stem to other regions of the brain.

## The diencephalon

Found above the midbrain and between the large cerebral hemispheres is the **diencephalon** region, which contains several important substructures, including the thalamus and the hypothalamus.

The egg-shaped **thalamus** is essential in the gating, processing and transfer of almost all the sensory information (except from the nose) entering the brain. More than a simple relay, the thalamus appears to

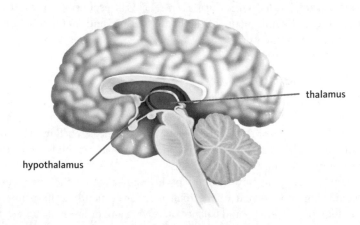

thalamus

hypothalamus

decide whether or not the various inputs merit being sent to the cortex for conscious consideration. Information from the cerebellum is also sent to the thalamus for processing, along with signals from the other brain areas involved in movement.

Sitting beneath the thalamus is the **hypothalamus**, where a multitude of critical functions are controlled and regulated. Connected to almost every other part of the brain, the hypothalamus is essential to motivation, including the seeking out of activities that the person finds rewarding, like sex and music – or even drugs. As a regulator of hormone release, the hypothalamus is also involved in everything from homeostasis and eating to maternal behaviour. It also manages the body's daily cycle: the **circadian rhythm**.

## The basal ganglia, amygdala and hippocampus

In addition to those discussed above, there are three further major brain structures buried deep beneath the folds of the cortical hemispheres.

Connected to the cortex and thalamus, the swollen structures comprising the **basal ganglia** resemble the head of some beast with formidable, swept-back horns. Receiving most of their input from the cortex, the ganglia are vital in the coordination of fine movement. Parkinson's disease provides a powerful example of what happens when this area becomes damaged (see p.181).

At the end of the ganglia "horns", beneath the hypothalamus, is the **amygdala**. This term comes from the Greek for almond – a reference to the size and shape of this small but significant component. The amygdala plays a significant role in generating emotional responses such as fear and desire, and also affects the way we relate to the world and others around us.

basal
ganglia

amygdala

hippocampus

## The developing brain

How do we get from the union of a female egg and a male sperm to an organ with the unparalleled complexity of the brain? Once the egg and sperm unite, a new single-celled embryo is formed and proceeds to go through successive rounds of cellular multiplication and division. At a stage when the embryo resembles little more than a tiny triple-layered sausage, brain development begins in earnest. A specific part of the outermost layer of the embryo folds in on itself, pinching off to form an inner **neural tube**. This is where the central nervous system starts to form, one end continuing down a path that makes the spinal cord and the other forming a series of swellings that become the brain.

Inside the embryo, the precise location of each cell determines which chemical signals it will be exposed to from various others. These signals gradually alter the receiving cell's nature, making it more or less sensitive to other signals and causing it to develop in a specific way. This process causes the cells in the neural tube to become neurons.

Each embryo produces far more neurons than is ultimately required, the excess being culled through a process known as **apoptosis**. Those that survive use chemical signals to communicate to future neighbours. Responding to these signals, a cell's **growth cone** (the tip of its axon) burrows through the nervous system like a mole rat, seeking out its partner.

Sometimes the relationship between two new partner cells weakens and sometimes it strengthens, a phenomenon referred to as **plasticity**, which is essential for learning and memory (see p.61).

Emotions and memories are tightly interwoven. Close to the amygdala is the **hippocampus**, which takes its name from its seahorse-esque shape. It's here that memories are forged: awake or asleep, the hippocampus is responsible for turning experiences into new neural pathways that are stored for future reference. Turn to Chapter 5 for more on memory.

The amygdala, hippocampus and basal ganglia, together with various other structures, make up the **limbic system**, which is key to the brain's processing of emotion and motivation.

## The cortex

The crowning achievement of brain evolution, both literally and figuratively, is the **cerebral cortex**. This is the rippling outer layer (the term roughly translates as "brain bark") that gives the human brain most of its unique powers.

**The cortex stretches right across the brain and is responsible for many higher-level functions. It consists of four sets of lobes.**

The cortex grew a great deal over a comparatively short time frame (see p.9). To accommodate this growth, evolution favoured an approach in which the cortex became increasingly folded. Were you to take a typical human cortex and spread it out flat, it would be somewhere between two and four millimetres thick and cover around 1.5 square metres – enough for a reasonable picnic blanket.

The grey surface of the cortex is due to a vast network of specialized neurons, six layers of which travel down towards the underlying **white matter**. Here, they form a staggering number of connections with other neurons – both within the cortex and in other brain regions. This vast, coordinated matrix allows swift intercommunication, facilitating our powers of thought.

The cortex is clearly divided into two **hemispheres**, which are themselves divided, by particularly deep grooves, into four major "lobes": the frontal, parietal, occipital and temporal.

The **frontal lobe**, directly beneath the forehead, is involved in what are collectively termed "higher functions": attention, planning, language and movement. It's like a master control unit that helps to integrate information and govern what the rest of the brain does. Behind it, at the top of the head, the **parietal lobes** process lots of sensory information, allowing us to perceive the world and our place within it.

At the back, the **occipital lobes** deal primarily with vision; it is here that signals from the eyes become transformed into a useful visual representation. Finally, the **temporal lobes** down each side of the brain focus on sound and language, and, by way of their connection with the hippocampus, memory formation and retrieval.

## The corpus callosum

The brain's two hemispheres are held together by the **corpus callosum** ("thick body"). This is the largest bundle of nerve fibres in the body and the main channel through which information flows from one side of the brain to the other – as it must for the whole thing to function properly. If the corpus callosum is severed, it can cause some curious symptoms (see p.89).

# CHAPTER 4

# Inputs and outputs

## How the brain reads our senses and directs our bodies

Whenever we're awake, signals are constantly flowing into and out of the brain. The main incoming signals are dispatched by our five senses – touch, vision, hearing, taste and smell – which deliver information about the outside world. The brain processes all this information and chooses appropriate responses. Some of these responses are voluntary, such as going to the shop, while others are involuntary, such as the pupils dilating if the lights dim. But they all involve the brain taking stock of what's required and sending out instructions to the relevant body parts.

## The senses

Our senses are the gateways between our brains and the outside world. Receiving signals from skin, eyes, nose, tongue and ears, the brain seeks out patterns in order to create a representation of the world. This representation is so intrinsic to the human experience that, as far as we're concerned, it *is* the world. But in reality hearing, vision and other sensory impressions occur *inside* the brain, created from variations in the chemicals, light, air and physical forces we're exposed to.

Sensory experiences start with **sensory receptors**, cells whose sole purpose is to detect specific stimuli (cold, bright, salty, loud etc) and convert them into an electrical signals that can be sent to the brain for processing. Only once that processing is done can the brain visualize a scene, say, or hear a sound.

Interestingly, sensory information is processed by the opposite side of the brain from the side of the body from which it comes. For example, the right side of the brain processes signals from the left ear and left-hand field of vision.

## Touch

The sensory receptors for our sense of touch are known as **mechano-receptors**. These are built into our skin and are most sensitive on the hairless parts of the body: fingers, palms, lips and the soles of the feet. The tips of fingers, in particular, are swarming with receptors, organized into the ridges that create our unique fingerprints.

Mechanoreceptors are actually a type of neuron, possessing special **stretch-sensitive gateways** (proteins known as channels) at their surface. If, say, a raindrop hits the skin, it briefly and subtly alters its shape. This causes the mechanoreceptors buried in the skin to open their stretch-sensitive gates. The more the skin is deformed, the more gates open up. The opened gates enable the receptors to start firing electrical signals down their length, towards the brain.

The sensation of **temperature** adds another level of sophistication to our sense of touch. This is achieved thanks to **thermoreceptors**, which

### The basics of pain

From an evolutionary perspective, pain is good – it's what causes it that's bad. Pain is the body's way of making sure we're aware of potentially dangerous stimuli, such as extreme hot or cold, strong physical pressure, dangerous chemicals or extremes of light and sound.

Pain is possible thanks to special sensory cells known as **nociceptors** (from the Latin *nocere*, to injure). There are various categories of these cells, each of which responds to one or more types of stimuli. When activated, they release a range of chemical messengers into their immediate environment. These bind to, and activate, nerves in the skin that exist specifically to transmit pain information to the brain. The signal is received in the thalamus, which in turn passes it on to the cerebral cortex, where a response is created.

Though pain usually serves its defensive purpose very well, it can also cause unhelpful suffering. This can be combated either via drugs (see p.212) or through the power of the mind (see p.225).

feature a protein that varies their degree of activity according to the heat they're exposed to. "Cold receptors" fire signals most frequently at 25°C, whilst "warm receptors" are most active at 45°C. If skin is exposed to potentially dangerous temperatures – in excess of 50°C or close to freezing – the pain-creating nociceptors kick in (see box opposite page).

The information harvested by the skin, including pressure, temperature, pain and **proprioception** (the position of the body), is sent to the brain's cortex via the spinal cord and thalamus. Here, it's processed in a **sequential map** of the human body by nerve cells specializing in analysing texture, shape, orientation, temperature and other factors.

# Vision

The eye analyses light, allowing the brain to create a three-dimensional model of the world. The conversion of light to electrical signals begins at the surface of the retina, at the back of the eyeball. The retina is covered with **photoreceptors**, specialized neurons called **rods** and **cones**. Named after their shape, rod cells (around 120–125 million per eye) perform better in dim light conditions, while cone cells (between six and seven million per eye) perform better in brighter environments.

The retina possesses three types of cone cells, each adapted to detect a specific slice of the visible light spectrum: red, green or blue. An almost infinite selection of hues and shades can be detected by interpreting the relative levels of these three colours (the same three used to create images on a computer screen). By contrast, there is only one type of rod cell, explaining why our night vision is low on colour.

The colour detectors inside cone cells are called **photopsins**, each of which consists of a light-sensitive chemical called retinol (made from dietary vitamin A) sitting snugly inside a shell of opsin protein.

 9 8 7 6 5 4 3 2 1

**The brain does a great job of automatically filling in visual blanks, so that we never even realize they're there. The above diagram provides an example. Close your right eye. With your left eye, scan quickly from right to left and you probably won't get any sense of the picture being incomplete. But now look at each number in turn, starting with 1. The face should disappear when you arrive at 4 and reappear when you get to about 7. Experiment with the distance between your head and the page.**

The red, green and blue versions of these detectors each have a slightly different type of opsin, ensuring they only absorb light of a certain wavelength. When the absorbed light hits the retinol, the latter changes its molecular shape, which in turn causes the enveloping opsin to change shape. This sets in motion a biological domino effect resulting in activation of the nerves leading to the optic nerve – a bundle of neurons running from the back of the retina into the brain.

Routing via the thalamus, the optic nerve terminates at the **occipital lobe**, right at the back of the cortex. This is where "seeing" actually occurs. As with the sense of touch, the visual cortex possesses a cortical representation of the retina – a **retinotopic map** – with cells that are phys-

**The right and left visual fields are each processed by the opposite side of the brain.**

ically close together on the retina activating neurons in close proximity within the cortex. But there isn't just one map: there are separate ones for motion, depth, form and colour.

The signals from the eyes need some clever processing before the brain can work out what's actually being seen. For example, a person on safari may stop the car to observe some lions. The person's eyes, capturing light reflected off the animals and surrounding grassland, send a two-dimensional pattern of retinal stimulation back to the primary visual cortex. With help from the temporal lobe, the brain then builds a three-dimensional picture and separates and recognizes the different components of the scene ("big cat", "empty land", etc). From the way the signal changes over time it can also detect any movement – both speed

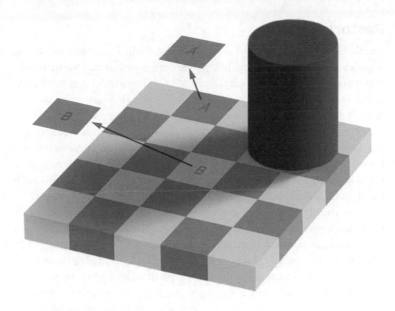

Optical illusions demonstrate that our visual system is based on mental interpretation rather than simple eyesight. In this example, created by Edward H. Adelson of MIT, our brains are so aware of the chequered pattern and compensate so effectively for the shadow of the cylinder, that it's pretty much impossible to believe that square A is printed in exactly the same tint of grey as square B.

and direction – of each of the scene's components. This data processing works at such speed that we remain totally unaware of it.

Clues to how the brain processes sight have been gleaned by the study of individuals with **visual agnosia** – problems with vision that stem from the brain rather than the eyes. A classic example is "the man who mistook his wife for a hat", made famous in a book of the same name by clinical neurologist Oliver Sacks. Despite being an excellent pianist and music teacher, the patient, Dr P., could no longer recognize objects by sight and once tried to place his wife on his head when intending to put on a hat.

Dr P. is just one example in a host of clinical cases. Other visual agnosia sufferers are unable to correctly perceive depth, say, or faces. Agnosia can affect the other senses, too, rendering people unable to differentiate smells or sounds, for example.

## Restoring vision

Impaired vision, or blindness, is usually the result of damage occurring somewhere along the visual pathway – the cornea or lens may fog up reducing optical clarity, the retina may degenerate or the visual cortex itself, right at the back of the brain, may suffer damage through injury or stroke. But current advances in the biological, engineering and technological sciences mean there are an increasing number of options open to those who are losing, or have lost, their vision. Stem cells, in particular, continue to provide hope for a large variety of medical conditions, including impaired vision, thanks to their inherent ability to become *any* cell a scientist desires – with the right biological coaxing that is, a major feat in itself.

If the usually transparent cornea becomes opaque through injury or disease, it's surgically possible to remove the damaged surface cells and graft a new layer of fresh corneal cells (from a donor eye) into place. While effective, such transplants carry a risk of rejection or of simply degenerating over time. Corneal stem cell grafts can bypass these limitations in two ways. By their very nature, these stem cells will become a living part of the cornea, continuously replenishing old corneal cells as they age and die. To prevent rejection, the originator stem cells are often obtained from the patient, frequently from their remaining healthy eye (but scientists are exploring other sources when this choice doesn't exist), or from a close relative. Once harvested, the corneal stem cells are first grown into a delicate sheet of cells within a lab, just one cell thick, then into a more sturdy multilayered sheet of cells, by way of a support matrix that encourages structured growth. This new tissue is then grafted into place.

Computer artwork of a biomedical chip (coloured square, centre right) implanted just under the surface of the retina in a human eye. Retinal implants are being developed so that they may one day be able to provide a usable form of sight to people suffering from degenerative retinal diseases.

Restoring vision at this level is, intellectually, quite straight forward – the engineering equivalent of cleaning a window, allowing more light to pass through into the main visual arena, the retina. Bypassing retinal damage (caused, for example, by macular degeneration) at the rear of the eye's interior, creates larger technical challenges. The cells in the retina are the direct interface between light and the nerve cells carrying visual information deep into the brain by way of the optic nerve. Again, stem cells appear to be showing incredible promise, with a team in Japan having succeeded in using mouse stem cells to grow not just a few retinal cells, but the actual structure that develops into the retina, the optic cup.

While the implications of such work for human visual restoration are probably years distant, retinal implants are being used to help restore vision today. A form of **neuroprosthesis**, a common type of retinal implant, known as an epiretinal implant, is composed of three main components working together to restore a type of vision: a camera to capture light, a video processor to interpret the incoming video signals and convert them into electrical signals and finally the retinal implant itself.

The user wears a discrete external camera, usually mounted into a pair of glasses, that captures the wearer's immediate environment. In this form, the video information is useless to the person, so it's shunted to the video processor where the video signals are

## Dr Liam Drew
*Psychiatry Department, Columbia University, New York*

**What is your favourite part of the brain and why?** My favourite part of the brain is usually the part I'm working on at the time! What constantly astonishes me is the way in which all the many subsystems of the brain are perfectly coordinated to create a unitary perception and memory of the world as we interact with it. Another beautiful example of brain regions interacting perfectly is the way that the signals which drive the constant motion of one's eyes are accounted for by the visual system so that the world appears still despite a constantly shifting retinal image.

**What scientific breakthrough helped us to understand the brain the most?** There are so many, but I will go with Hodgkin and Huxley's description of the action potential. In determining how action potentials are generated by the orchestrated opening of different ion channel types, Hodgkin and Huxley demonstrated how a complex cellular phenomenon could be explained by the behaviour of a system of individually simple but beautifully integrated molecular components.

**What's the next big thing in neuroscience?** I think the fusion of computational studies and neurobiology will be huge over the coming years. This discipline is in its infancy but to understand how all the electrical currents and spewing chemicals we are familiar with actually represent information is the gigantic challenge ahead of us. Whether the maths will prove to be horrendously impenetrable, or will eventually be reducible to something simple and elegant, we'll have to wait and see.

reinterpreted as electrical signals: as in normal vision, light has been converted to electrical signals, but those signals still need to get to the brain's visual cortex. The electrical interpretation of the video signal is now transmitted wirelessly to a receiver located within the eye itself. The receiver completes the final stage of the visual journey – it is connected to the retinal implant itself, an array of minute electrodes embedded within the retina, in direct contact with the cells leading to the optic nerve. The implant's electrodes send their signals off towards the visual cortex but a wearer doesn't experience vision in the usual way. Instead, they see patterns of light and dark that, over time, they learn to interpret and give meaning to.

Also being trialled by a team at Germany's University of Tübingen are smaller, more discreet sub-retinal implants suggestive of a major break-through in restoring vision. Sitting underneath the retina, these new devices possess 1500 light sensors able to directly capture natural light entering the eye and convert it to electrical signals, sending them straight down the optic nerve. As such, they completely bypass the need for any external hardware. Initial results are promising, with newly fitted people quickly gaining the ability to see shapes and describe objects, including letters.

# Hearing

Without our sense of hearing, there would be no speech and no music, and survival would be much more difficult. Our ears provide a complete 360-degree sensory field from which the brain can tell not just the volume and pitch of a sound but the direction and distance of the source, and if and how fast the source is moving.

The shell-like outer section of the human ear has the task of directing air vibrations down the ear canal. Here, the vibrations are picked up by the **tympanic membrane**, better known as the eardrum, and passed on to three minute bones: the malleus ("hammer"), incus ("anvil") and stapes ("stirrup").

The stirrup in turn connects with the **cochlea**, a spiral-shaped shell (the term derives from the Greek for snail) containing three fluid-filled cavities. A soft part of the cochlea's shell – the so-called oval window – is driven in and out by the piston-like stirrup, causing the fluid inside to move around.

This movement is detected by **hair cells**, which are somewhat like microscopic brushes. Each one is capped off with between twenty and three hundred hair-like (but rigid) protrusions known as stereocilia, arranged

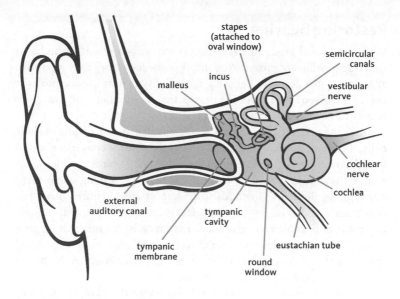

**The parts of the middle and inner human ear.**

in a wedge from small to large. The joints between the stereocilia and the main body of the hair cell are flexible, which means that vibrations in the surrounding fluid nudge them around like grass in the wind. This movement causes mechanical gates (protein channels) in the hair cell to open, which results in chemical signals being released to surrounding nerve cells, creating the all-important electrical signals destined for the brain.

The arrangement and size of hair cells down the coiled length of the cochlea is such that only sounds of particular frequencies reach or affect individual hair cells – a setup known as a **tonotopic map**. Each hair cell can activate around ten nerve fibres, passing along information about the sound itself and the direction and movement of the source. The nerves carry the signals to the brain stem, essential for targeting the sources of sound, and from there on to the cortex for further analysis. The temporal lobes take a closer look at the sound information, with low frequencies analysed towards the front and higher ones towards the back.

Both temporal lobes perform sound processing but the left lobe – home to Broca's and Wernicke's areas (see p.19) – is particularly critical for language, both speaking and understanding. Damage to this region can lead to serious linguistic problems, such as losing the ability to understand words altogether.

# Restoring hearing

While few would argue that restoring vision is contentious, attitudes to restoring hearing are mixed. Proponents of "deaf culture" have a positive attitude towards deafness, believing the inability to hear is not a problem that needs "fixed". An interesting perspective and reminder of how quick society can be to negatively label differences.

By far the greatest cause of hearing loss is damage to, or loss of, **hair cells**, the biomechanical intermediaries responsible for converting sound into electrical signals. Unlike some animals, such as birds or fish, mammals are unable to reproduce hair cells as they die, leaving scientists to develop ingenious new methods to replace or create entirely new hair cells from scratch. Taking the biological route to new hair cells affords two paths of possible recovery, one via **stem cells**, the other using gene therapy, both at the bleeding edge of research. While a more engineered approach, the cochlear implant, bypasses hair cells altogether. First, let's take a brief look at the biological approaches.

Stem cells are malleable and controllable – with the right coaxing they can be persuaded to become whatever a scientist wants them to, including auditory hair cells. A team at Stanford University, led by Stefan Heller has managed to make "hair cell-like cells" in a dish using stem cells from mouse embryos. By exposing the stem cells to a highly specific biological environment, they eventually took on the characteristics of immature hair cells, forming clusters of cells with protruding cilia which, when touched, were able to respond by producing electrical signals. While full of promise, there's still a scientific gulf between mouse cells in a dish and healthy human hair cells in one's ear.

Another approach, again using mice, has tried to bridge this gulf using stem cells from an adult's olfactory cells; in essence using nose cells to repair hearing cells. The nose's layer of mucosal epithelium is a source of natural stem cells with the inherent ability to create more as required. By taking these cells and introducing them into the ears of mice with failing hearing, the researchers found that, one month later, the hearing in those mice was better than control mice who had not received the stem cells. While the new stem cells didn't actually integrate into the cochlear tissues, they did provide the remaining hair cells with the appropriate biological signals needed to survive. This approach provides valuable insights into stem cells also being used as supporting cells, rather than necessarily replacement cells.

**Gene therapy** utilizes an entirely different approach to making more hair cells. Instead, as the name of the technique suggests, it's all about genes. Like all great ideas, it's actually quite simple – find a gene that causes a desired effect, isolate it, amplify it and deliver it to where it's needed. In the case of hearing, one mammalian gene being used to explore gene therapy approaches to restoring hearing is called **ATOH1** (named after its Drosophila fly equivalent, "Atonal homolog 1"). Normally, this gene makes a protein known as a "transcription factor", a protein capable of turning other genes on and off. The reason it's garnered interest is because ATOH1 is essential for making certain types of cells, amongst them hair cells. Scientists believe – and there is evidence to support their thinking – that the artificial reintroduction of ATOH1 to the inner ear should create the right environment to stimulate a fresh tide of hair cell development. Delivering the gene in the right amounts and to the right location is, in itself, an art form with today's methods largely relying on specially engineered **attenuated viruses** to achieve the task. Whilst potentially surprising, in many respects, a virus is the perfect delivery vehicle: highly adapted to coexist within a human, capable of self-replication and able to produce one's desired gene in concentrated amounts. If such biological approaches can be made to work in humans, restoring hearing could eventually become a routine matter

## Cochlear implants

At the engineering end of hearing restoration lies the cochlear implant, in many respects the auditory twin of the retinal implant used to restore a semblance of vision. Unlike a hearing aid (which amplifies sound, boosting it up to perceptible levels for a sub-par hearing network), an implant is capable of bringing sound to someone who was born, or has become, completely deaf.

Sitting behind the ear is the external portion of the device, housing a microphone and speech processor. Whilst the ability to hear everything might sound good in principle, it's the sounds forming human speech that are given priority; this is what goes on inside the speech processor, filtering out unnecessary frequencies (such as wind) and homing in on those mostly found in the human voice. Once analysed, the resulting information is transmitted to a receiver sitting underneath the person's skin – this further converts the audio information into representative electrical impulses. As in the retinal implant, a point is reached where environmental information, whether light or sound, is converted into more brain-friendly electrical impulses.

This electrical information is finally shunted on to the actual cochlear implant itself, a tiny electrode array surgically embedded within the cochlea. The implant receives these impulses and uses them to directly

**A section through the outer and inner ear showing a cochlear implant. Sound from an external microphone (behind external ear, top left) is transmitted, via wires, to electrodes (white dots) that are implanted into the cochlea (coil, centre right) of the inner ear.**

stimulate differing parts of the auditory nerve, entirely bypassing the need for hair cells. While recipients still don't enjoy a full range of sound, such as that found in music, such technology enables many to perceive more facets of their environment and, importantly, the voice of another.

## The chemical brothers: taste and smell

Taste and smell are two of the most evolutionarily ancient senses, so tightly linked to human evolutionary success that it's difficult to overstate their significance. It's also hard to separate these two senses, not just because they operate in similar ways but because they are so co-dependent (with a clothes peg shutting off the nose, it's possible to mask the taste of a raw onion). Taste and flavour are more than simple stimulation of the tongue's taste buds. When eating, the tongue gets its share of stimulation, but airborne molecules from the food also travel up to the nose, stimulating nasal sensors. Together, this combination of sensory stimulation reaching the brain informs it whether something tasty or foul is being consumed.

Deep inside the nose is a sheet of tissue, the **olfactory epithelium**, where several million olfactory neurons reside. These varied chemical sensors are very short-lived, surviving for only thirty to sixty days. Because of this short lifespan, unusual for nerve cells, they are constantly being replaced by a sheet of **stem cells** close by, cells that wait in line to become part of the next generation of nose sensors. At one end of these nerve cells sit between five and twenty little projections, not unlike those on the hair cells of the ear. These projections, known as **cilia**, protrude out into the nasal cavity, protected from drying out by a thin layer of mucous. The mucous also serves to dissolve and present smell-bearing chemicals – odorants – in the environment to the cilia, aiding detection.

The human nose can distinguish a huge range of different smells. Remarkably, it seems we possess as many as a thousand separate olfactory neurons, each one tuned to a highly specific odorant molecule. When one of these olfactory neurons comes into contact with, and binds to, its specific odorant partner, it results in the neuron firing an electrical signal down its axon. These axons project straight up through a porous bit of the skull, the cribriform plate, and straight into the brain's olfactory bulb where analysis of the signals can begin. Passing through the thalamus, these signals end up in the temporal lobe's olfactory cortex, a series of five major cortical regions.

Smell, a powerful sense, is capable of stirring up old emotions and memories – a phenomenon known as the Proust Effect:

> When nothing else subsists from the past, after the people are dead, after the things are broken and scattered … the smell and taste of things remain poised a long time, like souls … bearing resiliently, on tiny and almost impalpable drops of their essence, the immense edifice of memory.
>
> Marcel Proust, *The Remembrance of Things Past*

The reason this happens is because the pathways analysing smell are strongly connected to parts of the brain involved in emotion and formation and retrieval of memories (the amygdala and hippocampus respectively).

Working together with the nasal passages, the tongue is home to sensory cells with the relatively simple task of discriminating between just a few types of taste: bitter, sweet, salty, sour and umami (savoury). These sensory cells are responsible for taste and are found all over the tongue, within the taste buds. A single bud consists of a small opening into which around a hundred **taste cells** project their very own small projections, or **microvilli**. Each of the different types of taste cell is present in buds all over the tongue – not, as was once thought, localized to specific regions. Chemical signals from these sensory cells are once again converted to electrical signals and sent into the cortex, passing through the thalamus as they go. Once the odorant and taste information derived from millions of individual receptors has been analysed, the information is transformed into a unified perception – taste.

**A nerve connecting with a skeletal muscle.**

# Voluntary movement – I think, therefore I move

From walking and talking to playing a musical instrument, our movement is entirely controlled by the brain, which sends the signals that tell each muscle how and when to contract or relax. This is a complex job, since even a relatively simple physical task – turning a page in this book, say – requires a whole series of twists, turns and changes in force to be strung together in a seamless biomechanical flow. The senses, especially touch and sight, form a feedback system through which the brain can see how the task is progressing in real time, allowing it to correct any part of the operation that's going off-track. If each piece of the action had to be consciously planned, analysed and executed, we would quickly grind to a halt. No wonder that many "simple" tasks are still beyond the latest robots.

Skeletal muscles are the workhorses of voluntary movement. There are more than six hundred of them, covering almost the entire skeleton and accounting for between forty and fifty percent of body weight. Irrespective of their size, all skeletal muscles are composed of the same building blocks: thousands of **muscle fibres**, or **myocytes**, ranging in

## Learning in motion

When we learn a new physical skill – driving, for example – the supplementary motor area works hard to assimilate the new movements. But once we've mastered the new collection of motor skills, the primary motor cortex takes over and the supplementary area ceases to be involved.

Perhaps the most efficient way to learn a new action, be it a keep-fit move or heart-surgery process, is to watch someone else do it first. In this type of learning, the brain calls on specialized cells called **mirror neurons**, which are found in a region of the parietal lobe, and also found in Broca's area. Here, it seems, we mentally assimilate the movements in an attempt to understand and mimic them in the real world.

length from one millimetre to tens of centimetres. These fibres, each of which consists of thousands of individual muscle cells fused together, can exist in just two states: relaxed or contracted.

The brain tells the muscle fibres when to contract via nerves known as **motor neurons**. A single muscle has as many as a hundred of these nerves reaching out to it from the spinal cord, each of which splits into hundreds of branches that connect to the muscle at different points. This way, when the nerves fire off their signals, the entire muscle can contract swiftly and in harmony.

When we're born, our muscles and motor neurons are all in place, but the brain hasn't yet had a chance to learn how to use them – there are no pre-programmed instructions, even for basic tasks such as crawling or walking. With so many individual muscles and the almost infinite permutations in which they can be combined, it's little wonder that it takes years of trial and error for a baby to develop from a biological rag doll to a walking, talking individual.

In later life, some people continue to develop their motor skills in complex activities, such as painting or typing, dancing or martial arts. No matter which movements we favour, similar regions of the cortex are involved.

## Movement and the cortex

When the brain decides to initiate a simple voluntary movement – raising an arm, say – the process is controlled by the **primary motor cortex**, a narrow strip running down from the very top of the brain to the left and right. As with other parts of the cortex, this part of the brain is organized somatotopically – into a "map", with adjacent regions

Primary motor cortex

Posterior parietal cortex

Supplementary motor cortex

Premotor cortex

## Motor neuron disease

**Motor neuron disease** is a devastating condition in which the motor neurons in the brain and/or spinal cord cease to function. The person afflicted is still perfectly lucid but is unable to communicate with their musculature. Movement – including breathing – becomes progressively difficult, and the muscles soon start to waste through disuse. Eventually, even breathing can become impossible, at which point the disease becomes life threatening.

There are various types of motor neuron disease, the best known being amyotrophic lateral sclerosis, also called Lou Gehrig's disease, after the famous baseball player who was killed by the condition. Physicist Stephen Hawking is another high-profile figure affected by the disease.

of the body controlled by roughly adjacent regions of the cortex (see p.36 for more information on the relative areas of cortex devoted to each body part).

To plan and execute more precise movements, the primary motor cortex recruits the help of additional regions of motor cortex. These include the **premotor** area, which sits to the front and focuses on controlling core

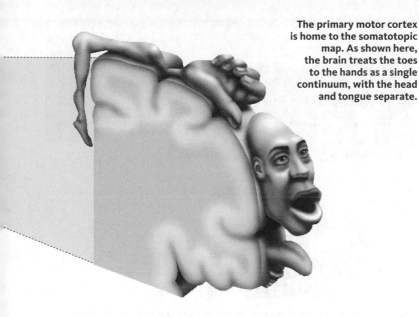

The primary motor cortex is home to the somatotopic map. As shown here, the brain treats the toes to the hands as a single continuum, with the head and tongue separate.

muscles such as those of the trunk, and the **posterior parietal cortex**, which sits to the rear, behind the somatosensory cortex, and helps create movement based on visual data coming in from the eyes.

A fourth key area is the **supplementary motor area**, located at the top and front of the motor cortex. This is the region that allows us to *plan* movements prior to making them – a dancer imagining a routine before a performance, for instance. When we imagine an action in this way, it triggers the same patterns of activity in the cortex as if we were actually performing the actions. The supplementary motor area is also involved in two-handed coordination and learning new physical skills (see p.53).

To make things as efficient as possible, the motor cortex is situated just in front of the part of the cortex receiving information from the body's touch and positional sensors – the somatosensory cortex – facilitating rapid communication between the two areas. After all, there's little point being able to detect that something is dangerously hot, say, if you can't quickly let go of it.

What we *do* can have a direct impact on the motor cortex itself. Just as a muscle adapts to regular activity in the gym by becoming larger, the motor cortex will assign more processing power to those body parts being used the most. If you are a footballer, the amount of motor

**The BrainGate Neural Interface system consists of a sensor that is implanted onto the motor cortex of the brain and a device that measures and interprets brain signals and translates these signals into useful computer control.**

cortex your brain devotes to the legs will be larger than the equivalent area in the brain of a trombonist, whose brain will give more space to the manipulation of the lips and hands. It is this remarkable quality of **plasticity** that allows people to relearn how to use a limb, for example, after the relevant area of the motor cortex has been destroyed by some form of brain damage.

All motor areas eventually send their instructions, in the form of firing nerves, down through the brain stem to the spinal cord, where the various signals are consolidated and sent to the target muscles.

## Brain–computer interfacing

In Paul Verhoeven's 1987 movie, *Robocop*, a murdered police officer, Alex Murphy, becomes an unwilling participant in a new research programme designed to eliminate crime through the use of weaponized cyborgs. The scientists take little more than Murphy's central nervous and digestive systems and he is reanimated within a new body; largely human in appearance but armoured, armed and extremely deadly.

Whilst clearly science fiction (so far), the principles of brain–computer interfacing are here – the creation of communication pathways between the central nervous system and external, synthetic devices or machines.

Whilst implants used to restore hearing or sight do come under the general umbrella of brain–computer interfacing, here we're specifically exploring implants that are directly connected to the grey matter of the brain itself and are being developed to return voluntary movement to the human body. Such research has been ongoing for decades, largely helped by using primates; the reason being that in order to fully understand what is going on inside the brain when one grips an object, the subject must both be a relative of *Homo sapiens* and be capable of gripping.

Significant advances in this area have been made by people such as Brazilian scientist Miguel Nicolelis, Co-Director of the Center for Neuroengineering, Duke University. An experiment that caught the media's attention occurred in 2008 when Nicolelis and his team were able to use the thoughts of rhesus monkeys in North Carolina to control the walking motion of robotic legs in Japan. By using electrodes to directly measure the activity of neurons within the motor and sensory cortex of the monkey's brain, the teams were able to translate the brain's flurries of electrical activity into precise mechanical movements in the remote device. Intriguingly, even when the monkey stopped walking, she was still able to make the robotic legs in Japan move, suggesting that just *thinking about* walking is sufficient to create patterns of brain activity capable of inducing remote movement. Nicolelis hopes such work will lead to technology allowing the return of movement to humans with severely damaged nerves or even missing limbs, by bypassing the traditional nervous journey from, say, brain to foot, and transmitting the will to move directly from the brain to advanced body prosthetics.

A parallel technology, that may offer hope to those with severe motor impairment, is being developed commercially and is known under the trademarked name BrainGate. Already being trialled on humans, this technology uses a "BrainGate Neural Interface" to monitor electrical activity from the user's motor cortex using external electrodes. The technology then interprets this information and translates it into forms of action. The term "gate" is appropriate, as the resulting actions can be quite diverse. By using complex software as an intermediary between the Neural Interface and an action, it's becomes possible for a person to perform a wide range of tasks, such as control a cursor on the computer screen, play games, control household appliances or even move about using thought to control a motorized wheelchair.

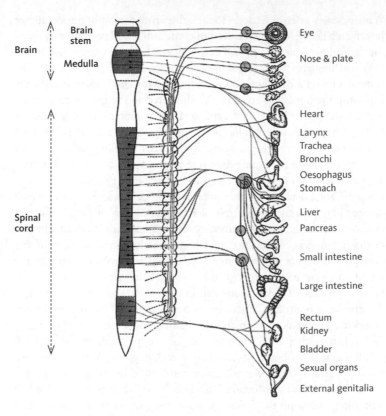

**A simplified diagram of the autonomic nervous system, adapted from *Gray's Anatomy*.**

# The autonomic nervous system

Voluntary movement is only one way in which the brain manages the body. The brain also gives out many instructions that are beyond our conscious control. After the lights dim in a cinema, for instance, the film's action-heavy opening sequence can send the pulse racing, make the pupils dilate and cause the mouth to dry.

These kinds of responses are governed by the **autonomic nervous system** (from the Greek *auto*, self, and *nomos*, law), which also controls, among other things, blood pressure, the digestive tract, hormone secretion, the bladder, penile erection and the circadian rhythm (see p.105). As with voluntary movement, these diverse biological systems are controlled via nerves travelling to the respective organs from the spinal cord.

While some parts of the autonomic system are permanently active, others respond to specific circumstances. A physical threat, for example, can cause adrenaline and other chemicals to be pumped into the bloodstream, stimulating the heart and blood flow to maximize physical and mental alertness. Other components of the autonomic system, such as breathing, take care of themselves by default but can be consciously overridden – up to a point, at least.

The eyes are also autonomically governed, both in terms of pupil dilation/contraction and focusing (imagine just how cumbersome vision would be if it was necessary to consciously *decide* whether you wanted to focus near or far, or let in more or less light). Our pupils change size in order to regulate the amount of light entering the retina – like altering the aperture on a camera to avoid over- or underexposure. Interestingly, this particular part of the autonomic system is also keyed in to our emotional state. Fear or the sight of a loved one can be enough to open up the pupils wider than normal. In Philip K. Dick's 1968 novel, *Do Androids Dream of Electric Sheep?*, such involuntary emotional responses are used to differentiate humans from androids.

## The hypothalamus

The autonomic system is governed by a series of interconnected brain structures known as the **central autonomic network**, at the centre of which sits the **hypothalamus**. Weighing in at a mere four grams – just 0.3 percent of the brain's total mass – the hypothalamus is nonetheless a hugely significant component, an ever-watchful eye monitoring every aspect of the body's condition via numerous connections to the amygdala, cortex and brain stem.

The hypothalamus acts like a conductor holding sway over an orchestra, seeking to impose a set of ancient biological rules that describe optimal physiological conditions. If the body gets low on salts or sugars, for example, the hypothalamus triggers the need to seek out the right sorts of food. If the body gets too warm, the hypothalamus initiates heat loss through processes such as sweating and diverting blood to the surface of the skin, and simultaneously creates the desire to seek out shade and water. Sexual urges are also part of the hypothalamus's remit.

It was an early version of the hypothalamus that was responsible for liberating our early ancestors from the water and the night (see p.4).

A portion of the hippocampus from a "Brainbow" transgenic mouse: researchers have manipulated neurons in mice to light up in a rainbow of fluorescent hues, creating a powerful tool for mapping out the brain's complicated wiring plan.

# CHAPTER 5

# Memory

## How the brain records and recalls experience

Thanks to memory, the brain is constantly travelling through time, pulling fragments of the past into the present. This ability is key to our entire existence. Without long-term memory you'd have no idea who you are, where you're from, who you know, or the difference between a safe and a dangerous situation. Short-term memory is just as important. Without it, there would be no point reading this paragraph – by the time you'd reached the end, you'd have forgotten what it said at the beginning.

Over the course of a single life, each person accumulates a huge matrix of memories, all of which are unique to their perspective. These memories are mostly based on genuine experience, but the brain can create false memories to embellish its version of reality – just as it can suppress memories of events it found unpalatable.

But what *is* memory? It's the brain's ability to encode, store and retrieve thoughts and sensory experiences. But unlike the heart that pumps inside the chest – a discrete mechanical organ whose workings are well understood – memory does not reside in one specific area. Rather than having a large single repository of information in, say, the left temporal lobe, memory is like a complex web spread across the entire brain.

To understand this fascinating topic, it's best to delve into memory's workings one step at a time, beginning at the edges of perception, within the senses, and ending with long-term memory...

# Sensory memory

Most of our memories are based on sensory input such as sight and sound. However, before this kind of raw input can become part of even our "short-term" memory, it first gets briefly stored in unprocessed form within our **sensory memory**. This super-short-term repository – which typically holds information for less than a second – is also known as iconic memory (for sight) and echoic memory (for hearing).

## Iconic memory

In 1740, a Slovak German scientist called Johann Andreas Segner carried out an experiment that gave an early insight into our iconic memory. He created something akin to a Catherine wheel, attaching a piece of glowing coal to the rim of a cartwheel, which he then spun, faster and faster. Once the wheel was rotating fast enough, the trail of light behind the lit coal started to look like a complete circle. Segner found that this happened when each revolution was completed in approximately one tenth of a second, suggesting that visual information is stored for at least this length of time before being more fully processed. (The effect, known as **persistence of vision**, also relates to theories of how the human brain perceives moving images from a series of static frames on television or cinema screens.)

Curiously, iconic memory allows us to *perceive* lots of visual information but not to *recall* it. Cognitive psychologist George Sperling elegantly demonstrated this phenomenon in 1960 by flashing grids of letters – three rows by four, for example – at test subjects. Sperling found that, given a flash lasting one twentieth of a second, subjects could typically remember four or five of the twelve letters – around forty percent. This raised a question: was the flash too quick for the subjects to see all the twelve letters in the grid, or were they seen and quickly forgotten? To answer this, Sperling used a cue to tell the subject which row he wanted them to specifically recall after the flash – top, middle or bottom. Under these circumstances, the subjects remembered three out of four letters from any given row – a 75 percent success rate, suggesting that the brain is capable of perceiving much more than it's able to recall.

One form of **subliminal messaging** plays on this phenomenon: images flashed up on TV or cinema screens for such short periods that they are, supposedly, registered by iconic memory but not consciously processed. The effectiveness of this technique is debated, however, and the most famous case – subliminal cinema advertisements in the late 1950s that supposedly boosted sales of popcorn and Coca-Cola – was discredited soon after the story came to light.

## Echoic memory

The sensory memory used for hearing – **echoic memory** – lasts longer than iconic memory, at around four seconds, allowing us to remember the last few items read out to us from a list, for example. Echoic memory also lets us work out the direction a sound is coming from. We do this by subconsciously calculating the difference between the time when a sound is registered in one ear and the time when it's registered in the other. Echoic memory stores the two signals while this calculation is under way.

# Short-term memory

Short-term memory is the component of memory we use to store small amounts of information for short periods – up to around 30–45 seconds. This is the type of memory used when, for instance, a person looks up a phone number and then walks across a room to dial it. Short-term memory, which only came to be accepted as a distinct system in the 1970s, can be likened to the RAM inside a computer, designed for temporarily holding information that's relevant to the present, rather than long-term storage and retrieval (which is more akin to a computer's hard drive).

By default, the information in our short-term memories quickly disappears, but there are a few simple tricks that help us keep a memory ticking over in the short term for longer than usual. With a phone number, for example, we might use **rehearsal**, which involves repeating the number over and over, either mentally or out loud. We might also employ so-called **chunking**, combining numbers into groups that are easier to remember than their constituent parts: for example, 1984–2001 instead of 1, 9, 8, 4, 2, 0, 0, 1.

Short-term memory is also known as **working memory**, though the latter term is often used specifically to describe short-term memory being used to help **manipulate** information, rather than passively storing it. For instance, if a person was asked to mentally multiply 25 by 12, they might first multiply 25 by 10 to reach 250. This figure would be held in the working memory while a second calculation is made – 25 multiplied by the remaining 2, resulting in 50. The two interim solutions could then be added together to produce the final answer of 300.

Or take the example of one person receiving directions to a new café from a friend over the phone. As the route is described, the listener might plot each leg of the journey in a mental map, enabling him or her to look out for shortcuts.

Working memory can hold several chunks of information simultaneously. But how does it actually work? One common theory considers it to be primarily the result of the two systems discussed below – the phonological loop and the visuo-spatial sketchpad. These two systems, the theory goes, are allocated tasks by the so-called **central executive system** – a region towards the front of the brain, within the prefrontal cortex.

## Écoute et répète: the phonological loop

The **phonological loop** is the working memory's way of holding onto spoken sound. It's thought to work by "rehearsing" (repeating) the relevant words, numbers or syllables to avoid the memory fading away to nothing. It's no surprise, then, that techniques such as functional magnetic resonance imaging have revealed the involvement of the brain's language centres – Broca's and Wernicke's areas (see p.19) – in this looping system.

A good demonstration of the loop is the fact that if similar-sounding words are presented to a subject in written form, the subject recalls them poorly relative to when the words have dissimilar sounds – the loop system gets muddled up because the words sound the same when repeated over and over.

The loop system's capacity varies according to what's being remembered. A typical person will be able to remember a sequence of seven numbers, but fewer words, especially if the words are long and therefore take longer to repeat.

The phonological loop is key to, and may have evolved to support, language acquisition. A poor or damaged loop system is perfectly possible to live with as an adult but would hamper children learning to speak – or, indeed, anyone trying to learn new words or languages.

In 2011, a team based in Edinburgh found a gene that appears to be intimately associated with the phonological loop. The gene in question, **ROBO1**, is responsible for producing a protein called **Roundabout homolog 1**. Found on a specific region of chromosome 3 (chromosomes are neatly catalogued and labeled precisely to help scientists with this sort of work), the team discovered that deficits in the loop system, manifesting themselves as various types of human language impairment, are associated with small genetic variations within this gene. Prior to this discovery, the role of this protein was thought to be limited to guiding axons within the nervous system; now, however, it appears we have a firm handle on the genetic basis of language evolution and acquisition.

## Picture this: the visuo-spatial sketchpad

The **visuo-spatial sketchpad** is a grand name for a temporary store for the manipulation of visual information. If you hear the word "lion", for example, you'll quickly conjure up a relevant image in your mind. This won't be a flat, static image, but something closer to an interactive 3D model: you could zoom in to see the animal's teeth, out to see its mane, rotate it in space, and so on. This internal representation of a lion is created by the sketchpad, which greatly enhances our working memory by adding a visual component. Words such as "abstract", which are less likely to elicit a specific image, can be harder to hold in the short term memory.

The sketchpad isn't just to do with memory, however. It also has a role in eye–hand coordination, as several brain-damaged casualties of World War I demonstrated. Such patients could happily identify an object placed on a table in front of them but, when asked to pick it up, would reach out in the wrong direction. One soldier, given a bowl of soup and a spoon,

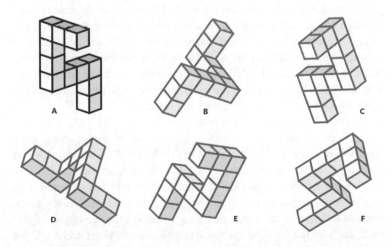

**Which coloured shape pairs with the grey one? Mental exercises such as this call on the visuo-spatial sketchpad. For the correct answer, see overleaf.**

would struggle to put the two together. Their visual sense and their ability to gauge their own physical position had become dissociated.

Cognitive neurologists test the ability of a person's sketchpad with mental rotation exercises. A typical task might show an image of a three-dimensional shape, along with a selection of similar-looking shapes rotated into different positions. The aim is to pick out the shape from the selection that is identical to the original. To find the answer, the person being tested must rotate each image mentally to see which one matches. In such a task, it seems the occipital lobe (at the back of the cortex) is mostly responsible for generating the internal image, whilst regions of the parietal lobe (nearer the top of the brain) deal with the spatial manipulation.

# Long-term memory

Sensory and short-term memory are all well and good when we're focusing on the present and last few seconds, but for storing and recalling information over longer time periods – anything from a minute to a lifetime – we need to use **long-term memory**. For a memory to be "promoted" from short term to long term, it first has to be encoded: i.e. associated in a meaningful way with information already present. At this stage in memory formation, the information is still vulnerable – easily lost or interfered with. To become more stable, the memory must be consolidated and stored. During this process, which seems to happen largely when we're asleep, neurons undergo potentially permanent change.

Long-term memory doesn't work like a library or database with thousands of discrete records. Rather, it's a complex, interconnected web. In general, the more associations the brain can make between memories, the more successfully they can be stored and retrieved.

When we come to recall a memory, we navigate this web, exploring connections to reach what we're looking for. For example, if the police asked where you were on the night of the 15th, you might answer that you were at the cinema with a friend. But in order to reach that conclusion, you might first recall that the 15th was your friend's birthday and only then remember that you went to the cinema to celebrate. As the brain accesses this store of information, it's highly likely other details will flood back, such as the weather on the day, the present you purchased, the mobile phone that rang halfway through the film… and so on.

The neuronal web that constitutes long-term memory is spread across

Page 65 answer: correct pair: A–F

the brain rather than based in a single region. However, the **hippocampus** (see p.35) is important in the creation of new memories, a fact reflected in the case of Clive Wearing. Following a viral infection, Wearing's hippocampus was seriously damaged, leaving him conscious of only the last few minutes at any time. Traces of the past remain: his musical abilities are intact, and people and places he knew before the illness are still familiar, to an extent. But nothing new can register. Should Wearing's wife, Deborah, leave the room for several minutes and return, she is met with tears of joy, as if being reunited after years of separation. (See interview with Seralynne Vann, p.70.)

## Implicit and explicit knowledge

The long-term memory store has two major knowledge categories. **Implicit knowledge** includes actions or procedures – driving or dancing, for example – that we have internalized and don't need to actually "recall" as such. **Explicit knowledge**, by contrast, includes such things as facts and scenes from our past.

Explicit knowledge can be further divided into two smaller categories. The first, **semantic knowledge**, includes facts, objects, concepts and words – the things we traditionally think of as "knowledge". The second, **episodic knowledge**, is autobiographical, encompassing events remembered from day-to-day existence, such as how well or badly a game of chess went.

# Making memories

Memory is at the cutting edge of brain research, with cognitive, neurological, biochemical and molecular scientists all straining to comprehend what happens when the brain records and recalls thoughts, facts or experiences. Modern imaging techniques show us the swarm of neurological activity that occurs when the human brain is required to remember something. But much of our specific understanding of how memory works has been gleaned from animal studies.

One key piece of research involved the sea slug, or **Aplysia californica**. This simple creature is an ideal subject for studying memory, since it demonstrates **learned behaviour** (the property of modifying actions in accordance with previous experience) and its 20,000 neurons are large enough to be individually monitored.

Scientists subjected the slug to small physical prods and observed its so-called siphon-and-gill withdrawal response, a natural defensive reflex that protects its delicate parts. When prodded, sensory cells in the slug fire, triggering a chain of communication between neurons that eventually reaches and stimulates muscle cells, which pull the slug's delicate structures away from the stimulus.

After continued gentle prodding, however, this reflex diminishes until the prods are ignored altogether. What scientists discovered is that this is due to the sensory neurons in question sending less neurotransmitter chemicals to their neighbours, hence reducing the chances of the signal being passed on. This kind of diminishing response to a harmless stimulus is known as **habituation**. A human equivalent might be a person initially reacting with shock and fear when the wind unexpectedly causes a window shutter to slam against the wall, but then getting used to it and ultimately ignoring it.

The opposite phenomenon was also observed. If the prod touching the slug gives a small but undesirable electric shock, there will come a point when simply touching the slug with the prod will result in an extreme withdrawal reflex – even in the absence of any electrical shock. This is due to **sensitization**, which is caused by a temporary increase in neurotransmitter release, making the adjacent neurons more likely to fire.

In both cases, the slug has altered its brain biochemistry and remembered the stimuli.

## Plasticity

What do temporary changes in sea-slug behaviour have to do with human memories? Everything, because, as with the slug's changing responses, our memories are founded on **synaptic plasticity** – the varying of the strength of signal between two neurons, across a synapse.

Donald Olding Hebb (1904–85) was an influential Canadian psychologist who, in 1949, proposed the following fundamental hypothesis about how plasticity works:

> When an axon of cell A is near enough to excite a cell B and repeatedly or persistently takes part in firing it, some growth process or metabolic change takes place in one or both cells such that A's efficiency, as one of the cells firing B, is increased.

In other words, if one cell consistently causes another to fire, the pair develop a relationship whereby it's even easier for the same thing to hap-

The beautifully rich neural network of the hippocampus, a deep region of the brain central to the formation and retrieval of memories.

pen again. Committing a piece of information to memory, then, involves creating a new, relevant network of strengthened neuronal connections. When the brain recalls a memory, it's causing this specific network to re-fire in the brain once again, allowing the information contained therein to enter consciousness.

As life proceeds, some connections and pathways get stronger, some get weaker, and new ones are formed. This is how practising a new activity helps make us better at it – repeated physical interaction with the outside world is being transformed into strengthened interactions between the relevant neurons inside the brain. As we initially fumble around, trying to get some new skill "hard-wired" into the brain – driving, for instance – the senses are sending repeated signals coursing through a specific pattern of neurons. After one lesson, little will probably occur in the brain to keep that knowledge intact. But after continued firing of the "learning to drive pathway", a critical threshold is eventually reached and the neurons physically change.

**Expert view**

*Dr Seralynne Vann is a Wellcome Trust Senior Research Fellow within Cardiff University's School of Psychology. Here she discusses her work, what's exciting her most in the field and what new challenges memory research faces in the coming years.*

My main interest is the neural basis of episodic memory and memory formation; looking at the different brain systems that support episodic memory. Episodic memory is memory for a specific event and it's quite a detailed memory, not just a, "I remember doing something" in a vague sense but a very rich memory which also provides you with context. It can be thought of as mental time travel, as Endel Tulving (a renowned psychologist and neuroscientist) put it.

### What parts of the brain do you think are the most important in your work?

Well I'd be stupid if I didn't say the hippocampus because the hippocampus is obviously a key brain region for memory, there's no way it isn't, but I think that everyone's become very closed-minded with respect to the rest of the brain and that if anyone mentions memory all most people think of is the hippocampus – even my mum knows about the hippocampus and spatial memory. No other brain structure seems to exist as far as the world's concerned and I think that's a little bit naïve. Thinking that one brain structure on its own is responsible for dealing with the most massive part of who we are, namely memory, defies reason. I don't understand how evolution would work that way. The hippocampus isn't an island, it's connected to a lot of other brain structures that I think all contribute something. Although you sometimes don't get as clear effects as you do with the hippocampus in a lot of cases you can find very specific memory impairments associated with damage in other parts of the brain. And, in the case of the rat, the hippocampus is huge; it takes up nearly half the size of the brain. So if you lesion it (introduce a discrete, specific injury), it's not that surprising that you end up with a memory deficit. Some of the brain structures that I'm working on are tiny and you make these tiny little lesions and you get these really quite profound memory impairments.

Frontal brain areas are also important, although their involvement is likely to be more to do with the organization of memories. My research focuses on a small brain structure called the mammillary bodies (part of the limbic system); it was the first brain region to be clearly implicated in memory, at the end of the nineteenth century, even before the hippocampus. Then the hippocampus came along and kind of brushed everything else out of the way, but in terms of Korsakoff's syndrome (see p.158), the mammillary bodies are consistently implicated and that's where they got the original link between mammillary bodies and memory – from looking at Korsakoff patients. That was fifty years before HM (Henry Gustav Molaison, 1926–2008) came along.

HM was a neuropsychological phenomenon. He was the first patient that really brought the hippocampus to light. He had severe epilepsy and they carried out a bilateral temporal lobectomy, which resulted in severe amnesia. He died a few years ago but his brain has been sliced and studied in tremendous detail (thebrainobservatory.ucsd.edu). HM was amazing; for any psychologist he's basically the go-to case for amnesia.

## What excites you about what's going on in the field today?

In one way I don't know; it's a cross between excitement and a completely overwhelming sensation. What's exciting is that there's so much going on at every single level. At the cellular level, for example, there are a lot of new candidates for long-term memory formation and maintenance such as PKM zeta (protein kinase M zeta). Work on this has caught the media's attention; people have been bandying it around in terms of post-traumatic stress disorder treatments and as a potential "memory-wiping" drug – which isn't why neuroscientists are really interested in it at this stage – but it does seem to be very important for the maintenance of long-term potentiation. So, when the memory is formed, even if it's not actually being used or activated, a PKM zeta inhibitor can still disrupt the memory. This isn't the kind of thing we've really thought of in memory before – you usually think that if a memory is activated (in a labile, changeable state) then it might be possible to modulate it, but if it's not being activated and is stable, it's safe. The work with PKM zeta seems to suggest that that's not the case.

There's also CaM kinase II ($Ca^{2+}$/calmodulin-dependent protein kinase II) which is also important for synaptic plasticity and involved in long-term potentiation. So in terms of the molecular changes that are necessary for long-term potentiation, lots of things are being discovered but then getting from this molecular level to the systems level, I think that's quite difficult. At each different level we're acquiring more and more knowledge, but we still seem far away from completely understanding how complex memories are formed, how they are stored and how we can retrieve them.

## What do you feel have been some of the biggest findings over the last few years?

A lot of Eleanor Maguire's (Professor of Neuroscience at University College London) research is very interesting, such as when she demonstrated that black-cab drivers have different shaped hippocampi (thought to be due to their heightened need to successfully navigate central London). Also, using scanning technology, Eleanor Maguire and her colleagues have shown they can identify what people have been thinking about depending on what populations of neurons have become activated. Being able to read minds sounds very science fiction, almost Orwellian, but you have to appreciate that it was a very controlled scenario, where volunteers were repeatedly shown video clips which they were then asked to vividly recall while being scanned; the scientists then looked for specific patterns of brain activation. They're not using this approach to find out what people are thinking, but to show how different cell assemblies within the hippocampus and surrounding structures support memories and to demonstrate that these patterns are stable – so that the same patterns of activation can be seen each time a memory is reactivated.

I think a lot of the most exciting progress is to do with the technology we have available as neuroscientists; the advances in technology are allowing us to do things that I never dreamed would be possible when I started my PhD. For example, the advances in neural recording technologies mean that we can study populations of neurons in different brain areas simultaneously.

In the same way, advances in functional magnetic resonance imaging technology means that we can resolve brain activity with much higher resolution. Both these approaches help us to look at how several brain regions work together to support memory and, again, help get us away from solely focusing on the hippocampus.

### What do you think are the big hurdles to understanding how memory works?

In some ways it feels like we haven't advanced very far at all, particularly in terms of understanding how we remember things, how we can conjure up a memory in a split second – it's absolutely amazing how our brains work! As I said, we're understanding more and more at each different level of the brain but putting these levels together is a major challenge. For example, we've learnt how neurons work, how they form connections and communicate within networks, and how even a single event can modify these connec-

The change involves a number of the cell's machine-like proteins becoming activated, one of which is called **CREB** (cyclic adenosine monophosphate response element-binding protein). CREB is akin to a tactical response unit within the neuron. Once activated, CREB journeys from its usual peripheral location within a neuron towards the nucleus, the home of the cell's DNA. Once there, it binds to other nuclear proteins, and to the DNA itself, resulting in specific genes (small, functional stretches of DNA) within the neuron's genetic code being "switched on". The wheels are now in motion, this cascade of new gene activation leading to the formation of new proteins with a new set of tasks. One result of this hive of activity is the tions. At the same time, we are gradually assembling our knowledge about how the different brain structures work together and the types of contributions individual brain structures make to memory. But how we bring all that information together to produce a multilevel model of memory which would then enable us to "fix" someone's memory when it goes wrong – I wouldn't know where to start, quite frankly.

**Where do you actually see the future of memory research going?**

There's a lot going on at the moment. New techniques in recording what's happening in the brain are providing us with fascinating data. The field has advanced from single cell recording, which was ground-breaking and has told us lots about how neurons work but focusing on single neurons is always going to be limiting. I think we need to learn more about how groups of neurons both within and across brain structures work together to support aspects of memory.

**What is it about memory that fascinates you?**

I think the same thing that fascinates everybody about memory; in many ways our memories define who we are and how we behave. Working with my patients with memory impairments has really made me appreciate the importance of our memories and just how devastating the effects can be when memories can no longer be accessed or new memories can't be formed. If you have nothing but your memories you've still got something, I guess.

**Do you have a favourite memory?**

[Laughs] My memory's terrible... I guess childhood ones like playing spaceships with my sister in my Nan's garden and others that are associated with summer, ice cream and beaches...

growth of new synaptic connections between partnering neurons. It's as if, instead of just brushing fingers, the two neurons are now firmly holding hands.

# Long-term storage

In 1973, Terje Lømo and Timothy Bliss published experimental evidence for a type of synaptic plasticity – **long-term potentiation** (LTP) – that is now considered fundamental to the cellular basis of long-term memory in humans. Lømo and Bliss discovered that when a certain group of nerves in the hippocampi of anaesthetized rabbits were stimulated,

## Extreme memories

The idea of a photographic, or **eidetic**, memory is an alluring one. It seems almost like a superhuman power – the ability to recall every shred of information that streams into the brain. Of course, perfect memory does not exist, but some individuals do have the ability to recall complex information in the form of images (or sounds) with extreme clarity.

A person with eidetic memory can look at a picture of some intricate scene for several seconds and, once removed, describe the picture in a great deal of detail, as if the image was still before them. They can travel back in their mind to a particular moment and relive the flood of sensory information as if they were back in the past. This ability, which some call **picture thinking**, seems to be more common in children.

Children live in a predominantly visual world; their early life is dominated by observation and experience. In such a world, it's a great help to have a powerful visual memory. However, as we get older, our brains usually develop more sophisticated methods of information storage and retrieval. As such, eidetic memory is sometimes associated with learning deficiencies.

For instance, people with **Asperger's syndrome** (also known as "higher functioning autism"), often display eidetic memory. Individuals with this condition typically have a normal to high IQ and are often precocious children. As they get older, however, certain characteristics emerge, including obsessive focus on particular subjects, trouble with certain social skills, such as reading body language, and a liking for routine. Asperger's was only recognized as a clinical condition in the 1970s, after which time many historical figures have been re-evaluated in its light. **Leonardo Da Vinci** (1452–1519) is believed by some to have had the syndrome, which could have helped him to visualize his incredible inventions in their entirety before committing them to paper.

**Wolfgang Amadeus Mozart** (1756–91) and **Claude Monet** (1840–1926) are two artistic giants widely associated with eidetic memory. Mozart had the remarkable capacity to memorize entire symphonies in his mind for days or longer before committing them to paper. One possible explanation is that a photographic memory allowed him to men-

future stimulation of the same neurons resulted in a much bigger synaptic response. The communication between these sets of neurons was becoming stronger – an effect that could last anywhere from several hours to more than a year.

tally gaze upon his finished work in its entirety in the same way we might look upon a score or a painting. Monet's memory allowed him to continue to paint and repaint scenes from his past even after his sight failed him completely. Similarly, mathematician **John von Neumann** (1903–57), who at the age of six could divide eight-digit numbers in his head, is said to have demonstrated something close to "total recall" – the ability to remember nearly everything he learned or experienced.

More recently, a few individuals have dazzled the public with extraordinary feats of memory. In 1987, for example, **Hideaki Tomoyori** recited the value of pi to 40,000 decimal places (a record subsequently broken). And, in 2002, *The Guinness Book of Records* logged the achievement

Mozart was able to hold whole pieces in his mind before committing them at great speed to scores (opposite), while von Neumann (above) is said to have remembered practically everything he ever learned.

of **Dominic O'Brien**, a British man who memorized and recited back the order of 2808 playing cards – 54 packs. How is it possible to achieve such feats? The key is the combination of an excellent memory with a good strategy and plenty of discipline. In Hideaki's case, he took the 40,000 digits and broke them down into groups of ten. He then associated the sound of each number (in his native Japanese) with a specific word, allowing him to create sentences that, in turn, provided him with a more easily memorable image. O'Brien's strategy wasn't dissimilar: he converted cards to memorable people that go on a journey, the order of places visited providing the correct sequence.

These kinds of **visual mnemonics** can be applied in day-to-day situations to help improve our chances of remembering something. For instance, on being introduced to someone called Rebecca Taylor, you might try to lodge in your mind the image of her as a "red tailor". Such improvised hooks can significantly increase our ability to recall information in the future.

Theories about LTP are far from proven, but it seems that the process has two phases – "early" and "late". The early phase seems to be entirely independent of the need for new proteins. Lasting several hours, this phase relies on the post-synaptic neuron (the one receiving rather than sending a neurotransmitter) supplying more existing receptors to its surface. This means when the neurotransmitter arrives from the neighbouring neuron, it can pack more punch.

The late phase of LTP requires repeated nerve stimulation to get going but, once it does, can last from hours to years. This phase is reminiscent of what occurred in the learning-to-drive example above. A veritable task force of proteins, including CREB, become engaged in the pursuit of enhanced neuronal stimulation. Genes are turned on, new proteins are made and neurons are modified, resulting in new, long-lasting, tightly organized structures inside the brain.

Some scientists believe there is also evidence to support two-way information flow at the synaptic junction. The hypothesis goes like this: neuron A releases a neurotransmitter into the synapse between it and neuron B. Neuron B receives the neurotransmitter, inducing LTP. Neuron B signals back to neuron A to inform it that LTP has been successfully initiated. Both the existence and the possible chemical make-up of this so-called **retrograde signal**, however, are hotly debated.

Less contested is the role of a protein known as protein kinase M zeta (PKMζ). This solitary protein appears to be all that stands between knowledge and oblivion; responsible for the maintenance of our long-term memories, it appears to keep them safe until needed. Made exclusively within neurons, particularly those in the forebrain, PKMζ never rests; where other proteins require some form of transient signal to "switch them on", once PKMζ gets going it's locked into a lifetime of activity, a permanent busy bee within the architecture of the mind.

It's difficult to overstate the elegance of the biological system that has led to the brain's ability to store experiences. Prior to PKMζ's existence as a protein, it must first exist as a stretch of messenger RNA (mRNA), the nucleic acid intermediary between DNA and protein. Most proteins, once at the mRNA stage, then progress rapidly to the protein stage – but not that encoding PKMζ, whose mRNA contains a biological block. Rather, its mRNA is transported to the dendrites of neurons and simply waits. Sitting at the centre of a biological symphony, PKMζ's mRNA waits until the right combination of signals, activated by LTP, acts upon its mRNA, releasing the block and allowing the mRNA to be processed. At last, amidst this biological melody, PKMζ is formed but not until it encounters yet another protein does it become fully "on". PKMζ now remains permanently active throughout its lifetime, affecting the behaviour of other proteins in its environment, keeping memories alive.

# Memory failure

Amazing though human memory is, it doesn't function perfectly. Forgetting things, or remembering things incorrectly, is part of day-to-day life, while amnesia can cause a total breakdown of certain memory functions.

## Forgetting

There can be few people in the world who don't sometimes wish they had a more powerful memory. Names, facts, faces, anniversaries… they can all easily be forgotten, either temporarily or permanently. Most forgetting occurs within an hour or so of learning or experiencing the thing being forgotten. This may happen because we didn't really pay much attention in the first place, or because no associations can be made with existing memories. If someone is introduced to lots of people at a party, for instance, their names are likely to be quickly forgotten. Even if a name gets consciously processed, it's unlikely to stick unless it's repeated or can be pinned to some other memory (brother of colleague, shares a name with a friend, and so on).

One thing seems clear: the more a memory is recalled, the more likely it, and its associations, will be remembered. A frequent online shopper, for example, may be able to rattle off their 16-digit credit-card number. But such memories are not carved in stone – their availability for recall may be neither consistent nor permanent.

One explanation for the brain's imperfect ability to recall memories forms part of **interference theory**. This states that information is not lost from the brain. Rather, other information, old or new, prevents a person from being able to retrieve the memory in question. Interference falls into two categories: retroactive and proactive.

**Retroactive interference** is when new memories affect our ability to recall older ones. One of the main reasons for this may be the similarity between the memories. For instance, a couple who go to a different country each year on holiday are likely to enjoy relatively clear recall of the distinct trips. But if two people go on holiday to the same resort, year after year, then it's probable the memory of Bournemouth 2007 will start to interfere with accurate recall of Bournemouth 06, 05 and 04. A shorter-term example is a mischievous friend shouting out random numbers whilst you're trying to recall a telephone number. Working memory gets reined into a battle

## *Eleanor Maguire*
*Professor of Cognitive Neuroscience and Wellcome Trust Senior Research Fellow*

**What is your favourite part of the brain and why?** The hippocampus – it is a structure deep within the brain's temporal lobes, and is central to supporting memory. Without memory, we are trapped in the present. We can't recall the past, learn about the present, or plan for the future. It also affects our decision-making, and we can't navigate around in the world. Damage to just the hippocampus compromises all of these functions. Finding out how the hippocampus supports our ability to mentally "time travel" is key to unravelling cognition.

**What scientific breakthrough helped us to understand the brain the most?** I can only speak at the level of cognitive neuroscience. I suppose the opportunities permitted by the development of magnetic resonance imaging (MRI), in particular functional MRI, are manifold and still becoming apparent. For the first time we can peer into the workings of the brain in humans in vivo. I think the best discoveries from fMRI are still to come, but without it, cognitive neuroscience probably wouldn't have flourished as well as it has.

**What's the next big thing in neuroscience?** I think, perhaps unfashionably, that cognitive neuroscience will be driven forward by clever ideas that look at the big entrenched questions in new ways that are not run of the mill or predictable, daring to challenge current theories, and thinking about fundamental mechanisms. I know this seems very vague and a bit hand-wavy, but the best discoveries come from experiments where you look at them and say: "how deceptively simple; wish I'd thought of that!"

between the old and the new – the brain tries to fit the new information into its existent tapestry and the similarities make recall much harder.

**Proactive interference**, by contrast, is when older memories affect one's ability to create new ones (as in the phrase "You can't teach an old dog new tricks"). This is ably demonstrated, in the short term, by experiments in which people have been asked to learn lists of one particular item – fruits, for example. The subjects find this much harder than memorizing a list that starts with fruits and moves onto, say, professions. The reason is that in a fruit-only list, there's more scope for interference between the items listed.

Another example: imagine that you drive to work to find your usual parking space taken, forcing you to park elsewhere. After work, when you're trying to leave, you might return to your normal space, only to discover someone else's car there. This happens because the established memory of your regular parking space interferes with the more recent memory of parking somewhere else today.

The unnerving aspect of proactive interference is that it suggests that what we know directly affects what new information we can learn and therefore affect how we see the world. Should a child be born into a household with myriad prejudices, for example, it's likely the developing mind will "inherit" some of these biased patterns of thinking as they age. To accuse such people of "only remembering what they want to" may be an oversimplification; the information stored inside their brain could be directly interfering with their ability to assimilate other points of view.

## Amnesia

Forgetting is a normal part of life and doesn't compare with **amnesia**, the general term given to the temporary or permanent malfunction of some part of the memory system. Such malfunctions can be caused by disease, head injury, trauma or even prolonged alcohol abuse. They can be **anterograde** – as with Clive Wearing, who was unable to remember anything after his illness – or **retrograde**, with existing memories being lost. Typically, amnesia affects episodic memory, the autobiographical network of one's life experiences, by disrupting or damaging the areas that link the frontal and temporal lobes.

Korsakoff's syndrome, which is typically caused by a vitamin B deficiency brought on by chronic alcoholism, is a debilitating form of amnesia that can cause both anterograde and retrograde amnesias in addition to a condition known as **confabulation**. The latter affects the ability to place new memories within a context, making it hard to distinguish between imagination and reality. For example, a sufferer might see a soap opera in which Bruce dumped Marge and later mistake a recollection of the

## Hangover amnesia

Aside from the severe, long-term damage that years of heavy drinking can do to the memory system, alcohol can also affect our ability to lay down memories on a much shorter timescale. Indeed, many people have woken up after a heavy night to find themselves suffering not only a hangover but also a complete inability to recall the latter stages of the previous evening. In fact, it doesn't take much alcohol to start to interfere with memory creation – even a couple of drinks will have some effect. Push the levels of alcohol in the blood above a critical threshold, however, and a kind of artificial anterograde amnesia kicks in. Sensory and short-term memories continue to function relatively well, but information ceases to be passed to the long-term store. The reason this happens is that high levels of alcohol cause the hippocampus – one of the most important relay stations in the formation of long-term memories – to malfunction.

programme as a memory of a real-life break-up. Or they may believe that the memory of a holiday they enjoyed last summer is merely the result of their imagination.

**Traumatic amnesia** is the term applied to memory loss following an accident that damages a person's head. Usually the victim suffers from the inability to remember events prior to the accident, stretching back for minutes or even years. Fortunately, traumatic amnesia tends to be transient, with most sufferers rebuilding a near-complete reconstruction of the past given enough time and support.

## Childhood amnesia: before your earliest memory

One form of memory loss that we all suffer from is so-called **childhood amnesia** – our inability to remember experiences from our first few years of life. Indeed, most people's "earliest memory" is a snapshot of something experienced between the ages of three and four years. Earlier memories either don't exist or lie somewhere beyond reach – which is curious, considering that during our formative first few years a child undergoes an immense amount of learning, with the brain nearly doubling in size. Some people think they can remember scenes from as young as one year, but it's far more likely that photographs and family anecdotes have merged to create a false memory (more on these below).

One explanation for our inability to remember early events is brain development itself. Not until a child becomes both self-aware and able to take their first tentative steps towards language does the brain seem able to form long-term impressions. This has led to the idea that language and memory formation are intimately bound. However, even before being able to speak, a child can demonstrate that information has reached its long-term memory. Indeed, learning *is* going on, but for some reason the memories become unrecoverable later in life. One theory is that, before the capacity for language develops, the information is encoded in a way that's alien to the mature, verbal mind, making recall impossible.

## False memories

What about those instances when someone has a very distinct recollection of an event, only to be met by a room full of people with a different, but equally strong, recollection. How does the brain get it so wrong? Confabulation demonstrates that we can confuse real events with imagined, but that's a specific neurological condition. What about **false memories** in a normal, healthy mind? The brain's ability to create false memories in the short term can be demonstrated by a simple experiment. Volunteers are asked to remember a list of words that have something in common – sharp, syringe, pin, injection, thorn, prick and so on. When asked to recall the list, a significant number of people will be certain that a related but absent word – "needle", for example – was included.

False or distorted memories can also exist in the longer term, of course. We've already seen how new memories can confuse older ones (retroactive interference). Equally, going over and over an imagined situation may be enough to cause the fantasy to enter the long-term memory as part of reality, perhaps with knock-on effects for other memories. Likewise if other people repeatedly suggest that something happened.

There may also be biological causes. For example, one relatively common category of false memory – that of being abducted by aliens – seems to be tightly linked to episodes of sleep paralysis (in which the person experiences a brief period of paralysis after waking) and hypnopompic hallucinations (in which the person experiences intrusions of dream imagery into their waking consciousness). The mind tries to rationalize the strange combination of being unable to move and vivid, potentially frightening imagery and finds few explanations in earthly reality.

False memories are usually harmless enough, but if the recollections involve people engaging in illegal acts, then the costs can be high. In this more serious context, the term **false memory syndrome** is often used. A few high-profile cases involving children falsely accusing adults of sexual or ritualistic abuse have brought this issue into the public eye. In these cases, the problems seem to have sprung from **recovered memory therapy** – a form of therapy that aims to help people remember and come to terms with traumatic scenes from their past that have somehow been repressed. The risk, of course, is that the recovered memories aren't based on real experience. According to the British False Memory Society (www.bfms.org.uk), "Any therapist, no matter how highly trained, may unwittingly encourage false memory."

Another example of dangerous memory distortion is people picking out the wrong person in police identity parades ("line-ups"). Identifications made during such parades have great sway over juries, but in truth they're unreliable, with preconceptions, prejudice, mood and the passage of time all conspiring to affect a witness's accuracy of recall. Studies by Elisabeth F. Loftus, a memory expert based at Harvard, suggest that witnesses tend to pick out the person who most closely resembles their memory of the perpetrator *relative to* the other members of the line-up – even if the perpetrator is not there. Even when told the perpetrator may be absent, witnesses still provide positive identifications on a high number of occasions. Presenting suspects individually, preventing side-by-side comparison, seems to reduce the chance of false identifications.

## Age

The brain of an ageing person is typically less powerful – and even physically lighter – than the brain of someone in their prime. Among the causes of this decline are neurons dying and levels of neurotransmitters decreasing. Memory is one of the functions that can be affected. For example, older people may take longer to recall things and, according to some studies, they're less good than younger people at **prospective memory** (remembering to remember things).

That said, serious memory loss usually only affects people with a specific neurological condition such as Alzheimer's (see p.184). Indeed, the normal ageing process has little or no effect on many types of memory – the ability to recall semantic knowledge such as facts and words, for instance – especially among people who keep their mind active as they age. Moreover, older people simply have more memories to draw on, which explains why they're associated with that characteristic combination of experience and thoughtfulness: wisdom.

# Perception of time

When we recall a memory, we can (usually) remember not just what happened, but also *when* it happened and roughly how long it lasted. In other words, our memory system is intimately tied in with the brain's ability to perceive a time continuum. Our perception of time is also key to our physical movements – swinging a tennis racquet to hit a moving ball, for instance, requires extremely accurate calculations about the time it will take both the racquet and the ball to reach the point of impact. So it's little surprise, then, that perception of time – also known as **temporal perception** – seems to be based in the same brain areas involved in body movements.

Imaging studies and disease cases have revealed that our sense of timing can be affected by, amongst other areas, the cerebellum, basal ganglia, the supplementary motor areas and the right parietal cortex. This makes sense of the altered perception of timing experienced by sufferers of

## Déjà vu

One occasional quirk of the human brain's perception of time is **déjà vu**, or **paramnesia**: the strong and often disquieting sensation that you've experienced the current situation before. Déjà vu – which means "already seen" in French – is difficult to study, since it happens unpredictably, but it seems to occur when we briefly misinterpret the present as a recollection. That explains why we usually struggle to pinpoint the conditions under which we experienced the situation before – because it never happened.

Déjà vu highlights the fact that normal perception of time requires a healthy, functional brain. And, though most people experience the phenomenon from time to time, frequent déjà vu is associated with certain neurological conditions – including temporal lobe epilepsy and schizophrenia. This could be due to such conditions causing abnormal activity within an area deep within the temporal lobes – the **entorhinal cortex**. Essential for memory processing in its own right, this part of the brain is also located close to the hippocampus, another key component in memory formation.

Parkinson's disease (which affects the basal ganglia) and certain strokes (affecting the right parietal cortex).

Even without neurological damage, our perception of the speed of passing time isn't fixed. When we're busy, time seems to pass fast, but when there's nothing to occupy the mind's attention, the brain becomes highly aware of time and moments can stretch out before us. A more extreme "slowing down" of time is often described by people in the aftermath of a dangerous or emotionally charged situation – a car accident, for example.

Psychologist David Eagleman has created an unusual experiment to examine this phenomenon. Volunteers wearing a "perceptual chronometer" – a device that flashes LED numbers faster than normal perception can capture – are dropped from a height of over thirty metres. Preliminary results suggest that people are better at recognizing the numbers on the screen when falling than when stationary. So why is this? As with **iconic memory** (see p.62), it seems the brain perceives more than it's conscious of, since there's simply no need to be aware of every single detail going on in the immediate environment – it would overload consciousness and slow the brain down. However, danger could cause this filtering mechanism to temporarily shut down, because in a life-threatening situation there's no such thing as irrelevant information. The conscious mind interprets this boosted sensory intake as slowed-down time.

Time can even appear to briefly halt altogether thanks to a phenomenon known as **chronostasis**, which is familiar from the **stopped clock illusion**. When the eyes are rapidly cast onto a clock, it can seem to take far longer than a second for the second hand to move (or, on a digital clock, for one LED number to change into another). This effect is a consequence of the visual system avoiding blur. The movement of the eyes is **saccadic**, meaning that they move in quick bursts, darting from one point in space to another. To avoid everything in between the two points becoming blurred, the visual system between the retina and the cortex is suppressed just before such a movement takes place. When the eyes fall on a clock through one of these saccadic jumps, the brain seems to add the time it took for the eyes to reach their target to the clock's first transition from one second to the next, making it seem to take an unexpectedly long time. This addition of time happens constantly, but most objects don't change with such perfect regularity as clocks, so we rarely notice it.

More generally, perception of time seems to accelerate as we get older. Many people look back at their childhood and remember summer holidays that seemed to stretch out forever. But as we age, even years can seem to fly past. The simplest explanation for this is that the brain perceives time as a rough percentage of total life lived. For a ten-year-old child, one year represents ten percent of their existence so far – a sizeable chunk. For a sixty-year-old, however, a year represents less than two percent of total life experience, giving the impression of it passing much faster.

# CHAPTER 6

# Inner space

## Consciousness, reasoning and emotion

What does the word "consciousness" mean to you? Do you consider yourself to be conscious now? If so, why? What about those around you? Can you be sure? In this chapter we will explore the thorny subject of consciousness and how it is created in the brain. We will take a detailed look at some key aspects of the conscious mind – reasoning and emotion – before exploring what happens when we lose consciousness, through sleep or more catastrophic means such as coma.

## What is consciousness?

Few questions have proved so intractable as "What is consciousness?" Scientists and philosophers have puzzled over it for centuries but failed to agree on a definition. It is not surprising that it has proved so difficult: consciousness is a unique problem. Everything else we experience, we experience through consciousness – how do we experience consciousness itself? We can't take a step back and examine it from the outside. What's more, we only have a single example to base our understanding on: ourselves. Because consciousness is internal, available only to the individual concerned, we can't know directly about any consciousness except our own.

Perhaps, instead of asking what consciousness *is*, it is better to start with a different question: what are the qualities we look for in an organism, such that we can say "It is conscious"? There are five generally accepted criteria for consciousness:

▶ **Self-awareness** – the ability to perceive one's own existence. People tend to drift around in various states of self-awareness, sometimes totally oblivious of themselves and their surroundings. Sometimes, however, usually in situations of heightened pressure, a person can become desperately self-aware, or self-conscious

▶ The ability to perceive the **relationship between oneself and one's environment**. This amounts to a dynamic interplay between the body's senses and the brain's perception of the outside – key to survival

▶ **Subjectivity** – a uniquely personal viewpoint. Subjectivity is the capacity to formulate a personal opinion, to act as observer and narrator for surrounding objects, experiences and impressions

▶ **Sentience** – the ability to feel or perceive the environment, sensing such things as temperature, colours and smells

▶ **Sapience** – the ability to think about feelings or ideas and act upon any conclusions reached in an intelligent, knowledgeable manner

Should an organism possess all the above qualities, it will be described as conscious, to the satisfaction of most. So what entities are conscious? Are humans the only ones? There are currently no machines in existence that could be said to possess consciousness. Sophisticated "toys" such as **RoboSapien** do a satisfying job of mimicking consciousness but are merely automata – they respond to their environment via simple sensors, and as such could be said to possess a level of sentience, but no more. They will never "decide" to do something, or be aware of their own existence. (See pp.269–85 for more on artificial intelligence.) Even human foetuses, in the first weeks of development, are thought to be unconscious (this is by no means certain, however). The consensus from the Royal College of Obstetricians and Gynaecologists is that the first inklings of consciousness can't emerge until at least week 24 of pregnancy. It's at roughly this time that the foetus has undergone sufficient cortical development to allow the experience of pain, a sign that it is now capable of subjective experience. Research in this area is making an important contribution to ethical debates about abortion and the use of embryos in stem-cell research. Similarly, our growing understanding of the extent to which animals are conscious has informed debates about animal rights and the ethical treatment of animals. We use animals as a source of

Lana, a two-and-a-half-year-old chimpanzee, punches out words on a pictorial keyboard, assembling sentences (such as "Please machine, give me a piece of banana") at Emory University, 1972. Only when animals have a means of communicating can we tell much about their level of consciousness.

food, for scientific experimentation and as companions. Would we be so quick to use animals in these ways if we knew them to possess as rich a consciousness as we do?

We have found it very difficult to say for certain which, if any, non-human animals are conscious. The problem is that we can only approach the issue of consciousness from a human perspective. One of the biggest barriers to testing whether an animal is conscious, by the criteria outlined above, is language. Our primary evidence for what is going on in the minds of our fellow human beings is communication. Our limited capacity to communicate with other animals makes testing them for "full-blown" consciousness very difficult indeed. Some animals seem to be able to recognize their own reflections in a mirror, suggesting a level of self-awareness. But without communication it's impossible to know exactly how significant this is.

Where the language barrier has been broken, some startling results have been achieved. For instance, researchers have taught chimpanzees to express themselves in a remarkably complex way using pictorial keyboards. Some chimps have built up a vocabulary of hundreds of words and can assemble them into complex sentences.

## What causes consciousness?

Where does this mysterious quality, consciousness, come from? Early ideas about consciousness, beginning with the ancient Greek philosophers, revolved around the notion of a **duality**, with the physical brain and the non-physical mind existing in their own rights, as entirely separate entities. Not until **René Descartes** (1596–1650) came along was it mooted that there might be some link between the two. Descartes felt there should be a specific "point of contact" for the "soul" within the brain – a designated structure that acted as a sort of conduit between the two. He decided this structure should be the **pineal gland**. He thought that any structure with such an important function should be unique and, indeed, the pineal gland is one of the few brain structures defying the brain's usual symmetry by appearing only once. It also seemed to be a strong candidate due to its central location within the human brain. Today, we know this gland as the source of melatonin, a hormone that plays a crucial role in regulating the circadian day/night cycle (see p.105). But although he may have been wrong about the details, Descartes had made an important step forward by linking the brain and the mind.

Today, most scientists and philosophers agree that, rather than being an essentially separate entity tethered to the brain via a small structure such as the pineal gland, consciousness is an emergent property of the brain as a whole, a natural consequence of millions of neurons processing information in parallel. It may seem astounding that something so "physical" as electro-biochemical processes within the brain could produce something so intangible as consciousness, but that is what happens. We just don't yet understand how.

What we do know is that consciousness can be associated with particular areas of the brain. In fact, consciousness seems to require several areas of the **cortex** acting together in a broad network – the **frontal lobe** (essential for attention) and the **parietal, occipital** and **temporal lobes** towards the rear and side of the brain. The identification of these "neural correlates of consciousness" (components of the brain that are necessary for consciousness) has reinforced the idea that for an animal to be conscious it needs to possess a highly developed cortex such as our own. This is found only in mammals.

It seems that, in addition to the cortex, deeper, more primitive areas of the brain are also involved, although they are not in themselves sufficient to cause consciousness. Consciousness seems to require a functioning **thalamus** (see p.34), and cooperation between the thalamus and the cortex. We know this because if the **centromedian nucleus** (part of the thalamus) is damaged, a person will lose consciousness (see p.107). Indeed, it is those who have experienced damage to their brain, whether through disease or some form of trauma, who have been instrumental in helping scientists to understand the nature of consciousness and its relation to the functioning of the brain. Below are two examples, which reveal first the importance of proper communication between different brain areas to the emergence of a unified consciousness, and second the relationship between consciousness and unconscious brain processes.

## Fragmented consciousness: the split brain

As we saw in Chapter 4, in the normal human brain sensory information from the right side of the body enters the left hemisphere of the brain, while sensory information from the left side of the body is fed into the right hemisphere. Once inside the brain, all this information is processed and, importantly, shared between the two hemispheres. They are connected by a thick, flat bundle of nerve fibres called the **corpus callosum**. This fibrous structure forms a bridge between the two halves of the brain's cortex, allowing each to quickly communicate and share information with the other.

However, in some cases of severe epilepsy, the corpus callosum is deliberately severed. This drastic surgical procedure prevents the spread of seizures from one hemisphere to the other, greatly improving the patient's quality of life, but renders the two halves of the brain separate, isolated from one another. Such "**split-brain**" patients are able to function quite well in normal situations, as their brains are able to compensate for the lack of communication between the two hemispheres, but some ingenious experiments devised by Roger W. Sperry in the 1960s show that something remarkable is going on all the same. Because when the brain is split in two, so is its consciousness.

The key to Sperry's experiments is the knowledge that the speech centres of the brain (**Broca's** and **Wernicke's areas**; see p.19) are found only in the left hemisphere.

In a typical split-brain experiment, the subject is sat in front of a screen which is set up in such a way that it is able to flash images to either visual field of the eyes (each eye has a right and a left visual field, each reporting to the opposite hemisphere of the brain; see p.41). At the bottom of the screen is a gap allowing the subject's hands to pass beyond the screen, to a table holding an assortment of objects. If a picture of a screwdriver is flashed in the subject's right field of vision, this visual information is processed in the left half of the brain, the same side as speech. When asked what they saw on the screen, they correctly reply "a screwdriver", and when asked to reach their right hand (again controlled by the left hemisphere) beyond the screen to identify the object on the screen by touch, they will pick up the correct tool.

But if an image, say of a fork, is flashed in the subject's left visual field, which reports to the right half of the brain, things are not so simple. The experimenter asks the subject what they saw – a question they would be able to answer easily if the two halves of the brain were connected. In this instance, however, the right half of the brain knows about the fork, but to answer the question they need to use speech, which is controlled by the left hemisphere. Because of the split in their brain, the line of communication between the two halves has been severed. The subject is unable to answer the question except from the perspective of the left half of their brain, and so replies: "I see nothing." Which is true, for the left half of the brain did see nothing as it only receives input from the right visual field.

A similar problem is encountered when the subject is asked to select the object, by touch, from behind the screen. If the experimenter asks them to use their left arm, there's no problem – the right hemisphere of the brain received the fork information and is happy to send that information down to the left hand, enabling it to identify the object by feel. The subject now has a fork in their left hand, hidden behind the screen. Next, the experimenter asks them what they are holding. They can't get out of this situation so easily – they can't reply "nothing" because they know they're holding something with their left hand. Placed in such a cognitive tight spot, the subject relies instead on the logical left hemisphere to do something it's good at – guess. The subject answers – wrongly – that they are holding a spanner.

Some split-brain patients experience the bizarre phenomenon of **alien hand syndrome** (also known as anarchic hand syndrome). In each of our brains, one hemisphere – the left one if you're right-handed – has dominance over the other and is able, to an extent, to dictate its behaviour. The corpus callosum allows the two halves of the brain to communicate freely, such that we never notice this power-play within the brain, only the smooth, coordinated results as the body performs the tasks consciousness directs it to. However, in the split brain, the dominant left hemisphere is unable to exert its influence over the right side of the brain. The two near-separate consciousnesses inhabiting a single skull are free to exert their own influence over the body. This can result in situations where the actions of one hand are beyond conscious control, as if being directed by some external influence. The behaviour of the "rebel" hand often seems to be in direct opposition to what the dominant half of the brain is intending to do. It might remove a cigarette from the person's mouth that the other hand has just inserted, or undo buttons on a shirt that the other hand has just done up. But it's unlikely this half of the brain is declaring war on the other. What's more probable is that the less dominant hemisphere is simply trying to join in the current activity but, in the absence of precise instructions from the dominant half of the brain, acts like a dancer walking in halfway through a performance they have no prior knowledge of – it improvises.

The experiences of split-brain patients suggest the radical idea that, in Sperry's words, each hemisphere of the human brain is "a conscious system in its own right, perceiving, thinking, remembering, reasoning, willing, and emoting, all at a characteristically human level". If the two hemispheres are separated, each is able to produce its own consciousness. But in a normal human they are united via the corpus callosum to produce the experience of a single consciousness.

## Blindsight: unconscious vision

As we have seen in earlier chapters, much of the activity in the human brain takes place below the radar of conscious thought. The autonomic system (see p.58) operates in an entirely unconscious way. And George Sperling's experiments described on p.62 clearly demonstrate that the mind continually perceives far more than we are conscious of. Such things as creativity and intuition don't operate at the conscious level but hover somewhere beneath, just out of reach. Flashes of inspiration are probably the result of minutes or hours of unconscious processing going on in the brain. This might be while we're asleep – we have all had the experience, on waking, of seeing the answer to some problem that was bothering us the night before.

It seems that consciousness really is the tip of a mental iceberg, dealing with the results of a mass of hidden processing. This makes sense: if every input was directed to the conscious mind, if we were aware of every bit of processing going on, our consciousness would be overwhelmed, and unable to do what it does best – direct its attention to whatever is most important and pressing at that moment in time.

The phenomenon of **blindsight** provides some fascinating insights into the relationship between the conscious mind and the unconscious processing going on beyond its reach. This condition is found in some patients who are blind as a result not of eye damage but of brain damage. People with blindsight have received damage to their **primary visual cortex** (known as V1 – the other cortical regions involved in vision being V2–V5). They have no conscious awareness of seeing yet, in some ways, are able to act as if they can see. They are able to track a moving object with their finger, or tell an experimenter the shape of an object in their "blind" field.

The reason this is possible is because visual processing does not occur in just one location within the brain. Certainly, the primary visual cortex is a major player in vision but it is not the only one. Visual information is shunted to other regions of the brain for processing before it reaches V1, such as the more evolutionarily ancient **superior colliculus** and **thalamus** (found at the back and top of the brain stem respectively). Without the higher cortical functions of V1, a person with blindsight has no conscious experience of seeing and feels they are simply guessing the location of a given stimulus. What appears to be happening is that these "lower" processing centres are still capable of detecting and responding to visual cues, transmitting the visual signals to other parts of the visual cortex such as V5, for example. But the destruction of V1 means the visual signals can no longer be sent for further processing within the temporal lobes, suggesting that this pathway, and these lobes, are central to the conscious experience of having seen an object.

# The spectrum of consciousness

The experience of consciousness exists along a continuous spectrum. At one end of the spectrum is high alertness, or **attention**, such as we might experience when engaged in a stimulating conversation or attempting to solve a maths problem. Next comes **inattention**, in which the mind drifts off, perhaps as a result of boredom or mental exhaustion. Below inattention lies **sleep**, in which the brain loses all track of time and space. Deeper still comes **unconsciousness**, in which all higher brain activity ceases, and at the far end of the spectrum is **brain death**, in which the brain is totally devoid of activity. In the remainder of this chapter we will examine these different states of consciousness in more detail. First, we will explore two aspects of the conscious mind, reasoning and emotions. Then we will take a closer look at sleep. Finally, we are going to explore what is going on when we fall unconscious.

# Reasoning and decision-making

In Conan Doyle's *The Hound of the Baskervilles*, Sherlock Holmes, that master of inductive reasoning, characterizes reasoning thus: "We balance probabilities and choose the most likely. It is the scientific use of the imagination." We often think of reasoning – the ability to weigh up situa-

## Meditation

The mind of an average person is like an intelligent, but untrained dog, leaping around from one thought to the next, yapping away as the attention of the prefrontal lobes flits about. In a person practised in **meditation**, the mind becomes much more obedient and still, as the brain's attention is directed to focus on a specific thought, or is trained to eschew thoughts entirely.

Scientists have used scanning equipment to discover what is going on in the brain of a person when they meditate. Imaging studies have revealed that at the height of meditation the **parietal lobes**, responsible for our sense of orientation within space, can become dampened down. This could explain the loss of spatial awareness often experienced during meditation.

Other studies have revealed that the effects of meditation last well beyond the meditation session itself. In experienced meditators it seems the brain becomes persistently more active in the **left prefrontal cortex**, sitting just beneath the skull above the left eye. This brain region is associated with feeling good, and with concentration and planning. Why this increase in activity occurs is not understood, but it fits nicely with what we know about brain functioning – for example, in major depression (see p.159) the left prefrontal cortex is often found to be underactive. Meditation, it seems, truly does make you happy. This heightened prefrontal activity is also what seems to tame the mind, giving a meditator (either during or after a session) the power to deliberately place their attention where they want, so that they can focus more fully on an image, situation or task. And the potential benefits of meditation don't stop there. Some researchers believe meditation gives the reasoning, prefrontal cortex the upper hand over the **amygdala**, which is strongly associated with emotional responses (see p.99), especially fear. By giving reasoning the upper hand over our primitive flight or fight response, the brain is able to reflect upon and react to situations in a more rational manner – hence the unshakeably calm demeanour of a meditating monk.

tions and evidence, to analyse and reach informed decisions on the basis of information storming around the brain – as the quality that ultimately sets us apart from other animals. We are able to reason thanks to at least two critical brain regions: the **anterior cingulate cortex** nestling above the thalamus, deep within the brain, and the **orbitofrontal cortex** sitting right at the front, just above the eyes.

Of course we're all guilty of glitches in our reasoning. Optimists preferentially perceive the good in the world, ignoring factors which might suggest a less favourable future. Even scientists, for all their emphasis on rationality and objectivity, can inadvertently seek out evidence that backs up their own hypotheses whilst ignoring information that doesn't. And we all harbour prejudices and stereotypes which mean we over-generalize the world around us. One thing the brain is particularly bad at is numbers – a fairly recent "invention" in human evolutionary terms. The chance of winning the UK National Lottery is 1 in 13,983,816. The problem is we have no capacity to understand precisely what this probability means; every week millions of people feel their adrenaline rise as those candy-coloured balls bounce around the TV screen. There are numerous websites devoted to telling you how to "improve your chances". They had better be good because a person has considerably more chance of spotting a UFO, dying from a bee sting or being hit by a piece of falling aircraft than they have of winning. But the brain still *feels* it has a good chance.

So we don't always get it right. But, considering the huge number of decisions we are faced with every day – from the choice of breakfast cereal to the split-second decisions we are forced to make while negotiating traffic on the way to work – we do okay, making the correct decisions most of the time. It is in real-life, everyday situations, and our interactions with our fellow human beings, that we excel at decision-making, because this is the environment in which we evolved.

So what is it that enables us to make decision after decision in this way? What is the essential ingredient? It is our **emotions**. This may surprise – we tend to think of reasoning and emotion as in opposition – but without our emotional compass, we would find it impossible to make decisions. Take Elliot, for example…

## The real Mr Spock

"Elliot", a patient of the neurologist and physician António R. Damásio, is a potent example of how important emotions are to the ability to reason successfully. A charming, intelligent and successful businessman in his prime, Elliot started to suffer from severe headaches and lapses in concentration and was diagnosed with a brain tumour. The swiftly growing tumour, located right behind the eye sockets, was pushing Elliot's frontal lobes upwards, placing them under increasing, damaging pressure. The necessary operation was successfully carried out, but by then the tumour had destroyed regions of Elliot's frontal lobes, especially on the right side. After the surgery, Elliot seemed to make an excellent recovery, but something had changed and gradually his life spiralled out of control.

After losing his wife, his family and his job, Elliot embarked upon a series of poor personal decisions and ill-fated business ventures.

Eventually he hit rock bottom, unable to gain employment and in his brother's care. The problem was determining precisely what was wrong with Elliot. He was still charming, wry and knowledgeable, and scored very well on established tests of intelligence (see Chapter 7) and personality. What Elliot no longer demonstrated, however, was emotional ups and downs. He was neutral, calm, flat – a sort of real-life Mr Spock. Elliot was able to generate many solutions to hypothetical social problems that were presented to him but, by his own admission, no longer knew how to choose between them.

## Expert view

*Professor Geraint Rees is the Director of the University College London, Institute of Cognitive Neuroscience and a world leader in the area of consciousness. His research is focused on nothing short of attempting to understand the neural basis of human consciousness, in particular what Geraint refers to as the "contents of consciousness".*

### What is consciousness?

Consciousness is the manifold of subjective experiences we all have on waking from a dreamless sleep and that will continue until we fall asleep tonight. So it's the set of thoughts, feelings and emotions that we have that are private, subjective and internal to ourselves that we experience in our waking moments.

I'm interested in content – we could be tasting a fine wine, eating food, looking at a painting in an art gallery. All these involve different contents of consciousness and those contents have a distinct quality. The contents of our consciousness is a central part of conscious experience.

### With respect to your work, is there any part of the brain you think is most relevant to, for example, dealing with content?

No. When people started thinking seriously about neuroscience they didn't explicitly think there was going to be a single place in the brain, but they certainly thought there were going to be some regions which were more to do with consciousness than others. People are now more aware of networks playing a role. It's more to do with looking at the way different brain areas along a particular pathway interact to show that neuro-correlates of consciousness are a **network phenomenon** rather than the result of any one area.

People have become more aware that processing isn't a linear kind of thing, so if you're standing at one point in the brain, it's not as if the processing is like a train going past you on the station. There are **waves of processing** and people have started thinking about *when* in the process we become aware of the world.

The problem lay in Elliot's capacity to feed his emotional state into his decision-making process, to listen to the nuances of emotion that would normally help the frontal lobes choose amongst the numerous potential choices. The damage had left Elliot in an entirely rational world. To make a decision, he was trying to work his way through all the potential costs and benefits of all the different possible scenarios that might unfold as a consequence of his decision. Processing hell. In the undamaged brain, as the mind moves through a number of possible choices, it is the emotions that give the thumbs up or down, by fleetingly providing an insight into

### What excites you most about the field today?

The field has been transformed, that is by the ability to stick people in a brain scanner, make some inferences about what they're thinking, maybe even decode portions of their thought. That's something which just was not available twenty years ago and opens up new possibilities for observing how the brain works. We've always had theories about consciousness – "oh it's the pineal gland, oh it's this", but they're basically rhetoric without experiments. What we've got now is an experimental basis which is driving the theories to the point where we can now make testable predictions. Also, a lot of complex problems about society are becoming tractable. Questions like, "I wonder what it is that makes politicians brains different" or "I wonder why I have this personality and my best friend doesn't have that personality"... They're to do with real life but they're also to do with human nature.

### What, for you, are the most interesting findings?

Well, actually it turns out that by looking at the pattern of activity that happens in a brain when it's thinking we can actually decode and predict somebody's thoughts with a reasonable degree of accuracy. I think some of those findings are the most interesting, the findings that suggest we can potentially build a decoder of the brain.

### Why are you so fascinated by consciousness?

It's a big question and the most interesting questions tend to be the biggest ones. Why does the universe exist? Why are we here? What is unique about human nature? Why are we conscious? I also think my basic motivation is nosiness. Operating in something like consciousness, it's a big area, which gives you a lot of freedom to nose around; I'm comfortable ranging around in a field where I have a lot of freedom to manoeuvre – one day I'll work on vision and I'll think, why don't I work on self-awareness because that's rather interesting and it gives me the freedom to follow up leads and hunches.

**What are the big hurdles to understanding how consciousness works?**

The problem with consciousness, the so-called "hard problem", is that something like a car is objective; it's stuff other people can observe – but consciousness is seemingly very subjective and extremely personal, that's its nature: it's *my* consciousness not yours. And there is an argument that says the giant hurdle waiting for us is, even if we explain the physical events leading to consciousness, we still have not come up with an account of how those physical events give rise to subjective experience, something that as far as we know might not actually be anywhere else in the universe.

One philosophical position is that the explanatory gap will shrink until we can just step over it on our way to the finish line. Equally, other people say it's going to stay so wide you're just going to be unable to get over. I think getting down that finish track is a long way off but even if we can't get over the final hurdle, there is an awful lot of knowledge to be generated along

how the consequences of a specific choice would make us feel. However much it goes against our conception of ourselves as rational creatures, the role of the emotions in decision-making cannot be overstated. Marketing agencies know this – which is why advertising plays on our emotions constantly. But what exactly are emotions? How do they work?

# Emotion and feelings

First, we need to get technical for a moment and distinguish between emotion and feelings. An **emotion** is the combination of physical changes we experience when we are exposed to an emotional stimulus – pounding heart, sweaty palms and so on. A **feeling** is the conscious experience of this emotional state, produced by the processing of all of these bodily changes at a higher level in the cortex. António Damásio sums the situation up lucidly by describing feelings as the story the brain constructs to explain bodily reactions to the environment.

The key point here, then, is that emotion – those physiological changes in our body – is not caused by our conscious feelings, as we might expect. Rather, it is an automatic, unconscious response to the emotional stimulus that is independent of our conscious awareness of that stimulus. The cascade of physiological changes is triggered by the body's **autonomic** the way that will lead to terribly interesting things, both in terms of insights into disease or insights about how to build a brain computer interface or just how the brain works, the principles of brain organization.

**Where do you see the field going?**

I think in some respects the early swashbuckling era is giving way to something a little bit more boring and mature. People who study synapses don't have followers who sit under pyramids or go into the desert and lick toads, whereas consciousness does and that's a challenge if you want to ensure the field remains credible... but also it's an opportunity because it engages with people and people can understand why it might be important to study it. I think what's happened is that public engagement activities that scientists who study consciousness have got involved with have hopefully communicated a bit better the distinction between science and pseudoscience. I think neuroscience and science more generally is getting better at recognizing the need to communicate to the wider public.

**system** (see p.58), which controls such things as heart rate, pupil dilation and the release of hormones into the bloodstream, things over which our conscious mind has no control. Let's take a closer look at what's going on in the brain.

## The amygdala and the emotional pathway

The key brain structure in our emotional pathway is the almond-shaped **amygdala** (see p.35), part of the limbic system. The amygdala registers emotional stimuli and is responsible for passing this information on to other brain regions, triggering both our emotional response and the conscious feelings associated with it. When exposed to some kind of emotional trigger, like a charging rhino or an emotional movie scene, the amygdala stimulates the **hypothalamus**, which, as we saw on p.59, is the master controller of the autonomic system. The hypothalamus releases hormones into the body which initiate the physiological changes associated with **emotion**, such as increased heart rate and perspiration. Information about these physical changes is then fed back from the body's extremities and organs into the brain and on to two other areas of the cortex, the **frontal cortex** and the **cingulate gyrus**, resulting in the conscious **feelings** of "fear", "sadness" and so on. Messages from this feedback system are reinforced by direct communication between the amygdala and the cortex.

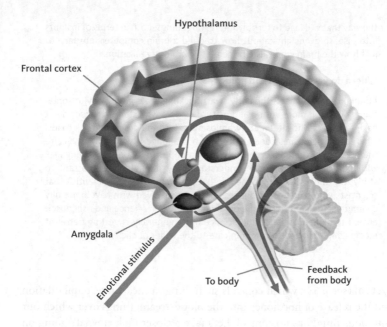

**Frontal cortex**

**Hypothalamus**

**Amygdala**

Emotional stimulus

To body

Feedback from body

**The emotional pathway**

It's worth remembering that the emotional stimulus need not be an outside force. It could be an image or thought dredged up from long-term memory or our imagination. By thinking about an imagined or remembered emotional situation, it is likely you will experience an emotional response – a mild quickening of the pulse, perhaps.

## Emotion as communication

Although our conscious feelings of fear, sadness and so on are internal, our involuntary physical response – our emotions – are visible to all around us. Indeed, "emotion", derived from Latin, literally means an "outwardly directed movement or gesture". As such, emotion is one of the most primitive – and powerful – forms of communication humans have. By wearing emotions externally, both in our facial expressions and in our mannerisms, we are enabling those around us to glimpse our state of mind. We are highly skilled at reading the faces of our fellow humans

# The Duchenne smile

Some important early work on the facial expression of emotion was carried out by French neurologist Guillaume Duchenne (1806–75). In *The Mechanism of Human Facial Expression*, published in 1862, he described his experiments, which used electrical stimulation to determine which muscles were responsible for different facial expressions. His favourite experimental subject was "The Old Man"; afflicted with facial anaesthesia, he was the perfect choice for Duchenne's potentially uncomfortable electrical investigations.

Placing electrodes at different points around the old man's face, Duchenne was able to elicit, and photograph, a wide range of expressions, purely by manipulating muscular contractions. One of his most famous findings was the identification of the key difference between fake and genuine smiles. Rather than simply raising the edges of the mouth by using the zygomaticus major, a muscle stretching from the lips to the cheekbone, the genuine smile (now often referred to as a **"Duchenne smile"**) also involves the orbicularis oculi muscles surrounding the eyes. The thinking goes that the Duchenne smile is caused by a genuine, involuntary emotional response, while the consciously contrived smiles we frequently use to oil the wheels of social interaction involve only the zygomaticus major. The eyes genuinely do have it.

MÉCANISME DE LA PHYSIONOMIE HUMAINE.

FIG. 4

Duchenne (de Boulogne), phot.

**A page from Duchenne's *Mechanism of Human Facial Expression*. Through electric stimulation, Duchenne determined which muscles were responsible for different facial expressions.**

in this way. So good, in fact, that we are able to see emotions where there are none…

:-(          :-)          :-o

Having evolved to be highly social animals, this makes a great deal of sense. Before the evolution of our elaborate system of vocalized language, our primitive human ancestors would have needed other forms of communication to convey their opinions to others within their group, to indicate pleasure or dissatisfaction.

A smile is recognized around the world as an indicator of **happiness**. The same goes for the facial expressions we associate with **anger** and **sadness**, **fear**, **surprise**, **disgust**, **anticipation** and **trust**. This list of the **primary emotions** was put forward by psychologist Robert Plutchik in 1980. So powerful are these archetypes, so deeply ingrained in the brain that, should someone focus on one of them for a few seconds, "happiness" for example, they may find the edges of their mouth start to curl upwards, the body relaxing… They may even experience a lightening of mood. This is one of the key features of emotions – *they work both ways*. Even if you don't actually "feel" especially happy, there's a good chance that if you deliberately wear a smile for a while, you will feel better. And the great thing (when it's a positive expression we wear) is that it spreads to others. Social evolution has turned humans into excellent mimics, so when we enter an environment in which people are smiling, we're more likely to smile too.

**Fear** is the most powerful of our emotions. Imaging studies have revealed the amygdala's preference for fear. If a subject looks at an image of a smiling face, there's hardly a flicker of activity in the amygdala. But if they look at a face showing fear, the amygdala lights up like a firework. As a basic survival adaptation, this makes sense. Seeing fear in the face of someone else in your social group is a good indication of danger, and an advanced warning that you may need to fight or flee to ensure your survival and that of your genes. In the very rare **Urbach-Wiethe disease**, deposits in the brain can destroy certain structures, including the amyg-dala. If the disease hits when young, the afflicted individual can lose the ability to respond to fear in the faces of others. It's in such cases we can glimpse the huge significance of emotions. They're not some frivolous luxury indulged at the expense of reason; they are paramount to our ability to deal with the world – to survive, seek a mate, or avoid conflict and danger.

# Sleep

Until the 1950s, it was believed that when we hit the pillow, we shut down completely, entering a state of profound relaxation which lasted until we woke the next day refreshed. This was a spectacularly wrong assumption. In 1953 University of Chicago professor Nathaniel Kleitman and his student Eugene Aserinsky published ground-breaking work revealing something quite unexpected going on. In one of the world's first "sleep labs", they observed strange, rapid movements of the eyeballs in their subjects around an hour after falling asleep. The movements were sporadic, with the two eyes moving independently of one another. Suddenly the world of sleep was divided into two distinct arenas, one with these **rapid eye movements**, REM sleep, and one without, non-REM sleep. This fundamental breakthrough caused an explosion of interest in the nature of sleep and before too long sleep had been further fractured into several more distinct components.

## The stages of sleep

When wide awake and busy, the brain produces **beta waves**, brain waves of 16–25Hz. As the brain relaxes, the beta waves are replaced by the lower frequency **alpha waves** of around 8–12Hz (see box, p.104). During this phase, lasting several minutes, you are relaxed but alert. As you enter **stage 1** sleep, these waves are replaced by **theta waves** of 4–8Hz. Your muscles relax further but it would still be easy for someone to wake you (though you might deny you were drifting away). You may experience those embarrassing **myoclonic jerks**, otherwise known as nodding off. You will stay in this state for around ten to fifteen minutes before entering the deeper **stage 2** sleep. This second stage is signalled by the onset of two different wave patterns called **sleep spindles** and **K-complexes**. During a spindle there is a short burst (0.5–1.5 seconds) of higher-frequency brain activity, where it shoots back up to between 12 and 14Hz. The ominously entitled K-complex is a big-amplitude spike lasting for about 0.5 seconds that occurs sporadically throughout stage 2. In stage 2, all the muscles have really started to relax and it would be difficult to rouse you. Next comes the imaginatively entitled **stage 3** sleep. Now the brain begins to experience big, slow, rolling **delta waves** of 0.5–4Hz – deep sleep has begun. We only spend a few minutes in stage 3 before moving on to **stage 4** sleep. Here, the brain experiences even more delta waves than in stage 3 and could be said to be dead to the world – this is when it's hardest to wake someone up.

**An example of an EEG trace showing some typical stage 2 sleepy brain waves.**

Collectively, these four stages are known as "non-REM" sleep. After stage 4, the brain does a brief reversal, moving back through stages 3 and 2 before finally entering **REM sleep**.

If you were observing the EEG readings of someone in REM sleep, you'd be forgiven for thinking they were awake. Gone are the slow, rolling delta waves, to be replaced by the wakeful alpha and beta waves. The brain bursts into a heightened state of activity, with some regions, like the occipital cortex at the back of the brain, even more active than when awake. And rapidly moving eyes aren't the only physiological change. Prior

## Measuring zeds

Measuring sleep relies on a piece of technology known as an **electro-encephalograph**, or EEG for short. The brain is awash with electrical activity, minuscule electrical pulses generated by individual neurons. The EEG uses electrodes in contact with the skull to painlessly detect, and massively amplify, these electrical impulses so they can be recorded as a trace over time. These electrical pulses aren't random and disparate, forming a white noise of brain activity. Instead, as the brain performs its many tasks, the pulses of electrical activity tend to form larger peaks of activity, as many of the brain's neurons fire in synchrony – like a heartbeat but faster. The frequency of these peaks of synchronous activity is measured in **hertz** (Hz, after the German physicist Heinrich Rudolph Hertz). A frequency of 8Hz means the brain is firing eight synchronous pulses per second. When scientists refer to the size of the pulse, they generally mean the **amplitude** of the peak; the bigger the peak, the more electrical activity there is.

to REM sleep, the body has been profoundly relaxed – but now it's actively paralysed. Nerves within the central midbrain send blocking signals out via the medulla (involved in relaying information between the brain and the spinal cord) that result in muscles being temporarily switched off. It is a selective paralysis, however; there wouldn't be much of an evolutionary advantage to paralysing the diaphragm that allows breathing to occur. And it's not just the diaphragm that's spared paralysis. During REM sleep, men experience full-blown erections, whilst women experience engorgement and moistening of the clitoris, and nipple erection. In addition, homeostasis, the body's ability to finely regulate itself, becomes dampened and the body starts to drift towards the surrounding ambient temperature. Heart rate, blood pressure, metabolism and even the temperature of the brain itself can all rise during this curious period of sleep.

## Rhythm of light

Take some volunteers and put them in a cave. The cave has everything needed to survive but no possible way of measuring time – no natural light, no clocks, candles or dripping-water devices. The remarkable thing is, they will still naturally adopt a 24-hour cycle (plus an additional eleven minutes, on average). This natural **circadian rhythm** acts as an umbilicus tethering us to the planet's rotation in space. Over millions of years, the body has evolved to closely synchronize its activities – its sleep patterns, the release of hormones, digestion and the **immune system** – with the length of a natural day.

This internal "body clock" is maintained by the **suprachiasmatic nucleus**, a specialized collection of neurons at the front end of the **hypothalamus**, deep inside the brain. Under normal circumstances, the suprachiasmatic nucleus is able to fine-tune the body's circadian rhythm by monitoring light information passed to it by the eyes.

Long-distance flyers routinely interfere with their body clocks by moving between different time zones. The suprachiasmatic nucleus can sense and adapt to changing light cycles, but technological advances now mean a person can travel thousands of miles in a few hours, moving abruptly between different day/night cycles. The **"jet lag"** experienced is literal – it is the time required for the inner clock to adapt to the sudden change in light cues in the new environment.

**Astronauts** on long expeditions travel far beyond the influence of Earth's usual day/night cycle. The effect this has on their bodies is a topic of intense research. However, it seems that by using artificial light to mimic Earth's light/dark cycle and following a regular meal regimen, astronauts are able to keep the body's natural clock happy and maintain health.

Contrary to popular belief, REM sleep is not the only time we dream. **Dreams** can occur at any time during sleep, it's simply that waking during REM sleep means we're much more likely to remember our dreams. Dreams seem to occur in real time, most are in colour, and in true egocentric style, the dreamer often has the starring role. Dreams usually involve details from real life, but often contain events that would be impossible in reality. One difference between dreams in REM and non-REM sleep is that REM dreams tend to be richer, more complex and narrative-driven – they feel like stories. They are often emotional and highly visual.

A phase of REM sleep can last anything from ten minutes to an hour. It is common to wake briefly at the end of REM sleep, before returning to stage 1 and entering a new sleep cycle. Each cycle takes approximately ninety minutes. So, during an average night, a healthy individual will tend to experience four or five full sleep cycles in which around 50 percent of their time is spent in stages 1 and 2, 25 percent is spent in stages 3 and 4, and 25 percent is spent in REM sleep.

## Why sleep?

The perception of sleep in modern, industrialized society has degenerated to the point where it is almost considered a waste of time. Our media-saturated, country-hopping lifestyle leaves less and less time for such seemingly unproductive activities as sleep. Is this a problem?

Most animals sleep. All mammals do, although the amount of sleep they need varies greatly: bats sleep for almost twenty hours, while giraffes need only two. If the behaviour of sleep has evolved in so many species, surely it must serve some important purpose?

Perhaps surprisingly, scientists have struggled to explain why we need to sleep. One instantly appealing explanation for sleep is **energy conservation**. Small animals consume energy faster than large animals and they also sleep more, suggesting a possible connection. That's until you take into account the fact that human energy usage is only about 15 percent less whilst asleep: not that much of a decrease. Perhaps sleep simply evolved as a means of keeping animals inactive when there was no need to be active. Day dwellers do their thing in the sunshine, night dwellers have adapted to do their thing at night. As day-dwelling creatures, we can't see as well in the night, making us more vulnerable to danger. Staying in one place seems like a good evolutionary idea.

That infants sleep much longer than adults – 17 to 18 hours a day compared to 7 to 8 for an adult – suggests that sleep may play an important

## Sleep disorders

Most of us have endured a long night of staring at the ceiling at some point in our lives, perhaps as a result of stress or overexcitement. But this usually forms a mere glitch in an otherwise healthy cycle of rest. For millions around the world, however, this becomes a regular occurrence. **Insomnia**, in which a person has difficulty falling asleep or staying asleep for more than a few hours, leads to chronic **sleep deprivation**. The person may become irritable, may experience blurred vision or memory lapses, and may have difficulty concentrating or become confused. Insomnia can be caused by a number of things, including stress or anxiety, or stimulants such as caffeine. Many insomniacs rely on sleeping tablets and other sedatives to get some rest; however, it is much better to identify and treat the underlying cause of the disorder.

At the other end of the spectrum from insomniacs are those who suffer from **narcolepsy**. For the narcoleptic, sleep becomes a foe, ambushing them during the course of their day, causing them to suddenly, uncontrollably fall asleep. Narcoleptics frequently experience **cataplexy**, a temporary loss of muscle tone resulting in anything from a drooping head to a rag-doll effect. Often triggered by emotional reactions, including laughter, cataplexy can occur irrespective of whether they're standing in a shop or at home sitting on the sofa. One curious aspect of narcolepsy is that the sufferer bypasses the usual, step-by-step process for falling asleep. Rather than proceeding from non-REM to REM sleep, a narcoleptic enters REM sleep immediately.

role in **early development**. What's more, many important physiological changes occur during sleep, including the release of **hormones** (such as growth hormone, which stimulates cellular growth and division) and an overall boosting and replenishment of the cells needed for a healthy **immune system**. Another popular explanation for sleep is to do with **memory**. Some evidence exists to suggest that sleep is when we consolidate our memories, REM sleep dealing with implicit memories and non-REM sleep with explicit memories (see p.67). Why we sleep is likely to remain an eagerly researched subject, but one thing is certain, not sleeping is very bad for us indeed – see box above.

# Unconsciousness

At the far end of the spectrum of consciousness lies unconsciousness. The body can find itself in this realm by a number of routes. One of the most catastrophic ways is to remove or damage the **centromedian nucleus**, a part of the brain that is critical in keeping us conscious. Deep within the brain, forming part of the thalamus, it consists of only around 600,000 neurons and is all that stands between us and nothingness. It is wired into a number of different brain regions, including the cortex, and is directly involved in controlling levels of arousal and attention. It's here that **general anaesthetics** act, gently removing the person temporarily from consciousness and the perception of pain so that surgeons can perform their work.

Despite their routine use, the precise mechanism by which general anaesthetics (actually a cocktail of various drugs) shut down the nervous system is still being unravelled. It seems that the chemicals used interfere with the electrical activity of neurons at the molecular level, strongly depressing their activity.

Destruction of the centromedian nucleus can lead to **coma**, in which the person enters a prolonged period of unconsciousness, resembling a deep sleep. However, most comas are induced by "diffuse pathologies" – widespread, global damage to the brain as a result of conditions such as head trauma, drug overdose, blood glucose anomalies and other metabolic conditions. The brain demands a very consistent internal environment; should core body temperature, amount of oxygen or pressure (due to haemorrhage, for example) drift away from their usual levels, the brain can respond by entering a coma.

In a coma, the patient no longer experiences the usual sleep/wake cycles, they demonstrate no perception of pain and do not exhibit any obvious signs of conscious awareness. Despite the condition superficially resembling sleep, the comatose patient's brain waves tell a different story – the normal patterns of brain activity seen during sleep are absent, and the patient cannot be woken.

The depth of a coma is measured using the **Glasgow Coma Scale** (GCS), devised by neurologists Graham Teasdale and Bryan J. Jennett. Patients are subjected to three tests – eye opening, speech abilities (from reasoned speech to incomprehensible moans) and movement (mostly in response to a pain stimulus) – and given a score between three and fifteen points. Three indicates deep coma or death; fifteen means the person is wide awake. Minor comas score GCS 13 or above, moderate comas GCS 9–12 and severe comas GCS 8 or below.

Most comas last a few days or weeks (usually a month at most), after which the patient may slowly start the journey back to consciousness. They may begin by briefly opening their eyes, and in the first days they may remain awake for only minutes at a time, but gradually they will increase their existence in the conscious world and may eventually make a full recovery. Other patients may make only a basic recovery, requiring therapy to regain independence. For those who don't emerge from a coma in several weeks, it's possible they will die, or enter a **persistent vegetative state** (PVS), potentially lasting months or even years. In this state, the patient has lost higher, cognitive functioning, causing some to call this condition "cortical death". They have no awareness of the environment but the brain holds onto the lower brain functions, such as breathing. Disturbingly, in PVS the patient can exhibit many signs of consciousness: the sleep/wake cycle, eye opening in response to some stimuli, moaning, smiling or crying. However, it's a cruel illusion as they lack any sense of awareness of the outside world. Even from this distant place, however, the brains of some people still manage to make it back, with younger patients having the greatest chance of recovery.

Beyond coma and PVS lies **brain death**. This is defined as the irreversible cessation of all brain activity. There is no electrical activity and no clinical evidence of brain functioning in the form of responsiveness to outside stimuli.

# Reading the mind

## Form and function

In the past few years, scanning technology has allowed scientists to see into the brain with ever-higher resolution, affording them the ability to correlate thoughts, feelings and experiences with patterns of activity occurring within specific neurological structures. While the idea of visualizing the conscious brain may seem a tad mechanistic to some, reducing the mind to nothing more than an organic computer, to others these techniques allow tantalizing insights into how this most complex of organs achieves its innumerable tasks, from mental arithmetic to appreciation of art.

At a purely structural level, scanning techniques, such as **diffusion MRI**, are allowing scientists to build up a far more complete picture of the fine structure of the brain, tracking bundles of **neuronal fibres and tracts** along their length. The data being gathered by such techniques is critical for understanding how each part of the brain is connected to every other part, building a complete three-dimensional map of the brain's circuitry. Such studies lie at the heart of the **Human Connectome Project** (see p.256), a bold attempt to map every single connection, right

**Three-dimensional modelling of white fibre structures in the human brain using diffusion MRI tractography data.**

down to the level of synapses, within the human brain. Such information alone is academically interesting but rather inert, until it's combined with the multitude of functional studies that allow these structures and pathways to take on meaning. Eventually, such work could lead to an unprecedented understanding of how the brain's myriad functions unite to form a coherent, conscious mind.

And there's reason to be optimistic that this research will succeed. Not least because imaging studies performed by Dr Tali Sharot at the Wellcome Trust Centre for Neuroimaging, London, reveal that the human brain is predisposed towards a positive outlook. Perhaps surprisingly, around eighty percent of people have a positive outlook on life, even when the odds appear stacked against them. Incredibly, the human brain is literally wired this way – at a biological level, functional studies reveal that we are far more prone to ignore negative information. For example, during a series of questions, if a person guesses that the rate of cancer in the UK is ten percent and is then told the actual figure is closer to thirty percent, repeat questioning at a later date shows their answer still teetering around the ten percent mark – their brain has not learnt. If, however, a person believes the rate to be forty percent and is given the "good news" that it's only thirty percent, when questioned at a later date they're far more likely to have assimilated the positive information, dropping their response from forty to thirty percent. From an evolutionary perspective, this makes sense. Take two pre-human animals, one who has evolved to possess a positive, highly motivated approach to life, hunting, procreation and survival. Our second pre-human has evolved purely to possess a hard objective take on reality. Reason suggests that our positive pre-human might take more chances, more risks – but, despite the potentially more risky nature of their life, they simply try harder, seeing hope and possibilities where our objective relative may only see barriers. We have evolved to believe we can succeed.

From a medical perspective, imaging is also presenting a fresh wealth of hope and opportunity for patients and doctors alike. In 2011 a scientific paper presented evidence in which brain scans were used to predict the onset of **Alzheimer's disease** (see p.184). By using imaging technology to zero in on what the scientists refer to as **AD-signature regions** – parts of the cortex known to undergo thinning in people who develop Alzheimer's, even before symptoms of dementia appear – the team hoped such scans might reveal this cortical thinning. If so, the hope would be that such scans could act as early warning indicators, targeting patients for early treatment

**MRI scans of the living human brain allow doctors to identify early signs of the onset of degenerative diseases such as Alzheimer's.**

of Alzheimer's disease, such as they emerge, before the disease progresses far enough to incapacitate the patient. Results from their small initial study are encouraging: while none of the test subjects with thicker signature regions developed the disease, of eleven individuals found to have thinner signature regions in their cortex, more than half went on to develop Alzheimer's.

Scanning technology is deeply tied to computing power – better machines naturally mean the ability to handle larger amounts of data, something the living brain is superlatively gifted at producing. But computer brains are evolving too and at the raggedy edge where brain scanning meets artificial intelligence, scientists are teaching machines to interpret human brain scans. Dr Janaina Mourao-Miranda of the Centre for Computational Statistics and Machine Learning, University College London, is one such pioneer (see interview, p.274). The heart of the problem lies in diagnosis – how can we be certain that a person is clinically depressed, schizophrenic or suffering from bipolar disorder? By training computers to interpret patterns of activity in normal and abnormal brains, the hope is that machines will be able to help clinicians make a correct diagnosis and, importantly, analyse brain scans of patients as they are being treated to determine whether or not that treatment is working.

## Deception and the brain

Experts in the field of neuroimaging may, and currently do, shrug off notions of such technology being used to literally delve into another's thoughts and read their mind but that hasn't stopped the legal profession from flirting with the notion of using brain scans in the courtroom. The reason for this heightened legal interest largely revolves around lying. Television dramas, such as *The Mentalist* and *Lie to Me*, revel in the fact that the programme's heroes are able, with near supernatural ability, to detect when a person is lying. But beyond television, most of us would be grateful for something that could level the playing field and remove the advantage a liar has over their victims.

> **"If you tell the truth you don't have to remember anything."**
>
> Mark Twain

Lying, wilful deceit, is not such a straightforward act to pin down. Naturally, at some level it involves avoiding, concealing or misrepresenting the truth. But the shape of a lie can vary as wildly as paint colliding with a canvas. Even if we ignore the fact that lies contain a range of information types (spatial and temporal information, episodic memories, explicit knowledge) there is also the multitude of ways in which a lie can be constructed: one can pretend to know a piece of knowledge, pretend not to know a piece of knowledge, say one was not somewhere one has been, say one was somewhere one has never been, tell partial truths, white lies, exaggerate, hold back certain specific parts of information… In the same way that finger and DNA fingerprinting revolutionized courtrooms with their unshakable, factual presence, perhaps the very complexity of lying is responsible for legal experts turning to hard, factual, scientific data – you may be able to lie verbally, but can you lie neurologically?

The use of **fMRI** to detect lies depends on two simple facts:

## Dr Tali Sharot
*Wellcome Trust Centre for Neuroimaging*

**What is your favourite part of the brain and why?** The amygdala. It is very small – about the size of a cherry tomato – but is responsible for a vital part of our being: emotion. It has been conserved across evolution and modulates activity in most of the rest of the brain, including regions involved in memory, perception and action.

**What scientific breakthrough helped us to understand the brain the most?** fMRI – as it gave us the opportunity to examine the living human brain in a non-invasive manner.

**What's the next big thing in neuroscience?** Understanding how minds interact and influence each other.

when a person lies they must both suppress the truth as known to them and construct an entirely new artificial truth. While this neurological sleight of hand is invisible to an external viewer, it requires the brain to work – to actively suppress truths, to actively create false information – and this can be detected as neurological activity by scanning equipment. Regions of the brain that appear to be specifically correlated with truth and deception include the **prefrontal cortex** (perhaps unsurprisingly, as this is also where humans perform most of their more complex mental tasks, such as reasoning) and **anterior cingulate cortex**, deep within the frontal region of the brain, enveloping the thick bundle of nerves connecting the two halves of the brain, the corpus callosum. While evidence suggests that regions of the prefrontal cortex play a general role in deception (for example, pretending both to know or not to know something), it seems the anterior cingulate region of the cortex only comes into play when we pretend *not to know* something. Numerous studies pinpoint the anterior cingulate cortex as having a role in error, or conflict, detection, for example asking a volunteer to respond "A" whenever a test presents them with the letter "M".

## Misconceptions about the brain

Of all the claims made about the human brain, by far the most popular is that we use a mere 10 percent of our neuronal mass; that somehow, the remaining 90 percent lies unused, wasted. It's a seductive idea, an intellectual American Dream, offering hope to humanity that if we only try a little harder, we will discover deep wells of cerebral potential, make it big, become a genius. This is, unfortunately, just a dream.

**Natural selection** abhors waste – every part of the brain has a very specific function, honed over millions of years of evolution; if facets of the brain were surplus to requirements, they would have been binned by nature. Brain imaging reveals the continuous eddies of activity that wash across and through the brain as we think, relax, watch. And whilst sleeping, there are times when the human brain experiences periods of activity akin to when awake. The brain is always on, 24/7, with numerous regions communicating, processing, consolidating, responding, organizing.

Like many myths, the one grain of truth here may lie in our ability to *attend* to situations. We are flighty creatures, often splitting the brain's attention between multiple activities. By doing so, it's simply not possible to commit 100 percent of the brain's processing equipment to any one goal. If we want to "use more of our brain", performing fewer simultaneous tasks with a higher level of concentration is a good start.

Another popular myth determined to survive is the **Mozart Effect**: that by listening to classical music as a youth (or even foetus), it will raise a child's

While still a relatively new field, companies such as No Lie MRI have not wasted any time in turning such findings into business, allowing corporations to screen employees and the hope that such technology will be accepted by the courts. However, while seductive, the idea of relying on cutting-edge science – particularly such a young science – in determining a person's guilt or innocence, is yet to be embraced by any legal system. Indeed, in 2010, a Tennessee judge (Judge Tu Pham), produced an extensive report that specifically excluded such **fMRI-based lie-detection evidence** from his courtroom until such time as it was able to fully satisfy certain legal criteria, such as reliability. Given the complex nature of how the mind handles information, it is debatable whether such a time will ever be reached to the satisfaction of scientists and lawyers alike. Indeed, Professor Geraint Rees (see interview, p.96), an expert on consciousness and contributor to the Royal Society's Brain Waves project, sums it up by saying:

IQ. The origins of this idea hark back to 1993, when a research paper was published in the prestigious science journal *Nature*. The authors found that, after listening to classical music for 10 minutes (which happened to be Mozart's piano sonata, K.448), test subjects experienced a temporary, improved performance in tests of spatial-temporal reasoning, one small facet of general tests of IQ. Over time, this original and interesting finding snowballed into claims – not by the authors – that classical music can permanently boost overall intelligence. Such claims may make good business but are unscientific. While no one would argue that being raised in a culturally enriched environment is a good thing, no amount of Mozart, Bach or Tchaikovsky can permanently boost the brain.

One explanation for the observed effect is that music simply affects the mood or level of arousal in the brain, making it more receptive to spatial-temporal tasks. Intriguingly, tests performed with rats, not commonly known for their musical sophistication, may support this idea. In this bizarre-sounding experiment, rats were either exposed to Mozart's sonata, a minimalist piece by Philip Glass, white noise or silence, both in utero and for sixty days after birth. Remarkably, rats exposed to the complex music of Mozart performed significantly better in spatial tasks – in this case navigating a maze. A possible explanation is that both listening to complex music and performing spatial-temporal tasks employ similar regions of the brain during processing. By doing so, complex music may temporarily prime the brain for specific mental tasks.

Neuroimaging technologies for lie detection show some promise in being able to explore the neural correlates of deception (a covert mental state), but none currently has anywhere near sufficient sensitivity, specificity and reliability to be deployable in the criminal justice system of England and Wales. Indeed, it remains uncertain whether such technologies will ever be sufficiently robust to be used in such "real world" settings.

A more established technique being employed to visualise the brain's secrets goes by the name of '**brain fingerprinting**'. Once again, the brain's activity is monitored but this time the technique employs electroencephalography (EEG) measurements, the same technology used to monitor brain waves in sleeping individuals, for example (see p.104). Of all the electrical activity the brain produces, this type of fingerprinting seeks something very specific, an electrical response known as the **P300 wave**. The foundation of the technique relies on an entirely involuntary response the brain emits (involving the parietal lobe) between 300 to 600 milliseconds after being presented with a piece of familiar information. Involuntary emotional responses to given stimuli, such as words or images, are irrelevant (the foundation of the polygraph test). And there's no need to ask questions as the method isn't detecting actual lies – the brain either is, or is not, familiar with a piece of information, for example, a murder weapon, person, or terrorist event, and the brain activity seen at P300 is the result. While still controversial, the technique has been used in court, both to convict and exonerate individuals.

# Beyond consciousness

## Nine Long Years

for nine long years I haven't eaten from a plate
for nine long years I haven't drunk from a glass
for nine long years I haven't had a single drop of alcohol pass my lips
for nine long years I haven't smoked at all
for nine long years I haven't made love to any woman
for nine long years I haven't painted a picture or drawn a cartoon
for nine long years I haven't read a book
for nine long years I haven't gambled
for nine long years I haven't sat on a horse
simply for nine long years I haven't existed
for nine long years…

Piotr Kniecicki, *Reduced to Clear,* 2011

This poem was written by Piotr Kniecicki, just one of a multitude of creative works he has written, and published. What distinguishes Piotr from other poets is that he has **locked-in syndrome**, a condition rendering him almost entirely immobile whilst leaving his mind completely untouched. In 2001, Piotr suffered a stroke (see p.145) that destroyed a region of his brain stem, terminating the vast majority of his voluntary movement. Thanks to the herculean efforts and dedicated staff at The Royal Hospital for Neuro-disability in London, Piotr is now able to express his inner self on a daily basis via a customized computer interface. However, cases such as this, where the true extent of consciousness may be ambiguous, can also arouse a basic human fear, or suspicion, that a loved one, categorized as being in a persistent vegetative state, may still have a hidden level of awareness or consciousness (see p.85).

A 23-year-old woman sustained a severe traumatic brain injury as a result of a road traffic accident. Five months later, she remained unresponsive. Using fMRI researchers demonstrated that the patient retained the ability to understand spoken commands and to respond to them through her brain activity, rather than through speech or movement.

In 2010, a remarkable research paper was published, permanently altering the clinical perspective on how such patients are perceived. Led by Adrian Owen and Steven Laureys of the MRC Cognition and Brain Sciences Unit (UK) and the Coma Science Group (Brussels), a research team used fMRI (see p.26) to scan the brains of people classed as minimally conscious or in **vegetative states** – whilst being asked to think specific thoughts.

In a set of "imagery tasks", patients' brains were scanned as they were asked to imagine carrying out one of two actions – hitting a tennis ball back and forth to an imagined instructor, or walking around a familiar location (either local streets or their own home). Of the 54 patients tested, five were able to alter their brain activity at will, showing activity in the **supplementary motor area** (associated with planning movement) of the cortex when "playing tennis", or in the **parahippocampal gyrus** (associated with the storage and retrieval of spatial memories) during the spatial, wandering task.

Having established a simple line of communication with these five people, the team then carried their testing one step further with one of the patients, embarking on a series of six yes/no autobiographical questions (for example, "Is your name Thomas?"). In order to answer, the patient was asked to think of one type of imagery, for example, if the answer is "yes", think about playing tennis, if the answer is "no", imagine walking through your home. Remarkably, one particular patient, who prior to this moment had been classified as being in a vegetative state, was capable of answering the questions to the complete satisfaction of the research team.

The implications of this work clearly resonate on clinical, ethical and powerfully emotional levels. While it's important to remember that of the 54 patients, 49 still showed no measurable response to the scans, this study has clearly paved the way for more work to be done in the precarious area of patient classification in the hope that misdiagnosis can be avoided.

## Gender differences

Time and again, the issue of sex and the brain comes to the fore; we are fascinated by it. But do the physical differences between men and women extend to the brain? And might these differences somehow extend to how the brains function – surely this is the only way to explain the eternal struggle each sex seems to face in the battle for mutual comprehension.

From the moment egg meets sperm, a human's genetic fate is sealed, largely dependent on the lottery of genes and chromosomes it received. An embryo will become male if it received male sex chromosomes – one copy each of the X and Y chromosomes – while it will become female if it receives two copies of the X chromosome. Contained within these long stretches of DNA are the genes necessary to shape the biological development of each sex. Skip ahead to puberty and these young, vaguely androgynous humans now experience a sex-specific hormonal onslaught – akin to a caterpillar metamorphosing into a butterfly, childhood fades as adulthood slams into our unsuspecting youths, effecting a slew of bodily and neurological changes. There are indeed structural differences between the male and female brain – but do these differences make us think differently?

> "God made man stronger but not necessarily more intelligent. He gave women intuition and femininity. And, used properly, that combination easily jumbles the brain of any man I've ever met."
>
> Farrah Fawcett

Aside from the differences in grey and white matter, plus the slightly larger overall brain size in the male (see p.130), the **caudate nucleus** is often found to be larger in females. Nestled astride the thalamus, deep within the brain, the caudate nucleus is linked to memory and language comprehension. The **hippocampus**, centrally located and critical for memory function also appears to grow faster in females. For males, it's the **amygdala** that seems to be different; perhaps surprisingly, this brain region – associated with the formation of memories with emotional dimensions – tends to be larger. Functional imaging reveals that while patterns of activation can differ within the brains of the two sexes during specific tasks, they're able to perform comparably, suggesting that each brain type is able to achieve the same goals via different routes. As ever, there is more than one way to skin a cat.

Mathematical workings
and a figurative drawing
by Albert Einstein.

# CHAPTER 7
# Intelligence

How "brainy" are you?

Perhaps the most prized feature of the human brain is its capacity for intelligence. But what exactly do we mean by intelligence? How do we measure it? And what is it about some brains that lifts their owners into the intellectual stratosphere while others struggle with algebra and French grammar?

## What is intelligence?

What do we mean by intelligence? Is it the ability to learn and remember lots of facts? Is it being able to solve maths puzzles faster than others? Or cryptic crosswords? Is it being able to construct and understand complex arguments? Given the high esteem in which intelligence is held, and the fact that we possess it in varying amounts, it's not surprising that this is a touchy subject. Too-narrow definitions are criticized for promoting academic elitism, while too-broad definitions are accused of muddying the waters by confusing intelligence with other skills and traits.

In 1994 a group of 52 internationally respected scholars formulated a definition summing up the scientific consensus on the subject. Their definition, part of the article "Mainstream Science on Intelligence" published in *The Wall Street Journal*, was as follows:

> Intelligence is a very general mental capability that, among other things, involves the ability to reason, plan, solve problems, think abstractly, com-

prehend complex ideas, learn quickly and learn from experience. It is not merely book learning, a narrow academic skill, or test-taking smarts. Rather, it reflects a broader and deeper capability for comprehending our surroundings – "catching on", "making sense" of things, or "figuring out" what to do.

That sounds eminently reasonable. But how can we measure vague-sounding abilities such as "catching on" or "thinking abstractly"? Over the years experts have attempted to translate such abstract terms into a series of concrete tests that, between them, are intended to cover all aspects of intelligence, literally putting the human intellect through its paces. These tests are categorized under the broad headings **verbal comprehension**, **perceptual organization**, **working memory** and **processing speed**. Below are examples of the kind of tests one might encounter in each of these strands:

## Verbal comprehension

▶ **Vocabulary:** knowledge of the meaning of words: "What is meant by 'belfry'?".

▶ **Comprehension:** questions relating to everyday situations, problems or proverbs: "Why do plants need sunlight?" "What is meant by 'you can't judge a book by its cover'?".

▶ **Similarities:** explaining what two words have in common, for example a car and a bike, or an iPod and a CD player.

▶ **Information:** the general knowledge round – here, your explicit knowledge (see p.67) gets tested: "Who painted the *Mona Lisa*?" "What's the capital of Japan?".

## Perceptual organization

▶ **Picture completion:** you're shown a picture, and must indicate in what way it is incomplete, for example a car with no windscreen wipers.

▶ **Picture arrangement:** presented with a series of seemingly random drawings, you must create a storyboard, putting the pictures in a sequence that suggests a logical story.

▶ **Block design:** you are shown pictures of designs made up of red and white squares and triangles. Your task is to recreate that shape using solid blocks with red and white faces.

A classic matrix reasoning test. The aim is to pick the correct final piece of the matrix from the eight options below. Correct answer overleaf.

▶ **Matrix reasoning:** essentially "What comes next?" You are presented with a series of shapes, shaded in a number of different ways (solid black, striped…) in a matrix (i.e. a grid). After examining the sequence of shape/pattern combinations, you select which shape/pattern comes next from a range of options.

## Working memory (see p.63)

▶ **Arithmetic:** like it says, basic head sums utilizing working memory.

▶ **Digit span:** testing your ability to retain, then recite back, a sequence of numbers. To make things juicier, in later stages of the test you may be asked to recall the numbers in reverse order.

▶ **Letter–number sequencing:** a real brain-ache, this one – after being told a sequence of alternating numbers and letters, the task is to recite the numbers back first, in numerical order, then the letters, alphabetically. For example, B–8–A–3–Z–6 is disentangled to reveal 3–6–8–A–B–Z.

## Processing speed

▶ **Symbol search:** after being shown a pair of abstract symbols, you must quickly search through a larger list of symbols to identify which of your original two shapes is present. You get two minutes to plough through as many as you can

▶ **Digit–symbol coding:** you're presented with a "key" – a table showing, for example, one = $\Omega$, two = $\Delta$, three = >, and so on. Now, against the clock, you're faced with a grid of numbers and must insert the corresponding symbols beside them

These mental tests form the basis of the most rigorous assessments of mental ability out there: the **Wechsler Adult Intelligence Scale Version IV** (replacing its predecessor, **WAIS-III**, in 2008). First published in 1955, it was developed by the rather ominous-sounding Psychological Corporation of the United States and United Kingdom to test the cognitive abilities of adults (16+). The current version has been refined and updated, making it more able to assess working memory and deal with the greater age span (16–90 years) of modern humans, to name two examples. The latest test has also been designed to offer more clinical utility, helping physicians assess different types of cognitive impairment, such as **autistic disorder**. Unlike many over-the-Internet intelligence tests (see box on p.127), this one costs a lot of money, is available only to professionals, and is administered under strict guidelines on a one-to-one basis. This might seem to be taking the whole thing a little too seriously, but it does mean the information gathered about an individual's intelligence is highly reliable. What's more, the accumulated data from the large number of these tests that have been conducted provides a rich source of information about the nature of human intelligence itself. In particular, it reveals something that may surprise…

# The g factor

We tend to think certain people are better at certain tasks. That some people are good with words, and others good with numbers, for instance. What the WAIS-III test scores showed, after the results from thousands of participants were analysed, was that this simply isn't the case. Scores on each of the tests were positively correlated with scores on every other test. In other words, if a person tested well on one of the thirteen tests, they performed well on them all. We are not good at *either* word tests

## Multiple intelligences

There are those who feel that traditional pen-and-paper tests such as WAIS-III define intelligence too narrowly and do not measure the full range of human intelligence.

One of the most famous of these critics is the psychologist Howard Gardner. Gardner argues that the accepted definition of intelligence is too narrow and unfairly weighted towards linguistic and logical-mathematical abilities above others, such as artistic or athletic abilities. In his theory of **"multiple intelligences"**, which he developed in the 1970s, he proposes that there are seven dimensions of intelligence: linguistic, logical-mathematical, spatial, bodily-kinaesthetic, musical, interpersonal and intrapersonal. The last two roughly correspond to what others have termed **"emotional intelligence"** – the ability to perceive and manage the emotions of oneself and others.

Gardner is primarily concerned with education, arguing that teachers should recognize these different kinds of intelligence and tailor the curriculum to suit the strengths of each child. His theory has been espoused by a number of schools and teachers. However, it has attracted criticism among intelligence theorists, who have argued that Gardner's ideas are based on his own intuition rather than on empirical evidence. A more fundamental issue is that Gardner's definition of intelligence is so broad that it bears little relation to the way most people think of the term. He is essentially using "intelligence" as another word for "ability" or "talent". As such, although few would argue with the theory's promotion of a broader curriculum in schools, it may be that its contribution to the intelligence debate is more confusing than informative.

or number tests. If someone is good at verbal tests, they're also good at perceptual, memory and speed tests. Rather than being a jack of all trades, master of none, we can be a master of all.

Scientists have been aware of this correlation for some time. It has led to the idea that there is a dominant, underlying factor determining intelligence, which affects every aspect of intelligence and is more significant than other factors that may influence our abilities in specific areas of intelligence. Scientists call this factor the **general intelligence factor** or, more commonly, simply "**g**". The term was originally coined by the London psychologist Charles Spearman (1863–1945). He had observed that children's grades in unrelated subjects tended to show positive correlation – if they did well in one test, they did well in others too. To account for this he devised a two-layered theory to explain intelligence. On one level, the brain deals with the specific task in hand, for example verbal comprehension or mental arithmetic. But on a higher level, the "g" factor is operating – a property of brain functioning affecting every task we perform. It is as if the brain were the engine of a car and "g" the engine's overall performance – the individual tests might be: how fast the car can accelerate, round corners, brake or do a three-point turn. The car's performance in each of these tests is influenced by factors specific to each test, but in all of them the most important factor is what's under the hood.

## The three stratum model

Today, psychologists favour a refined version of Spearman's model, the **"three stratum model"** first proposed by American psychologist John Carroll in 1993. In a monumental effort of analysis, Carroll used statistical techniques to show that an intermediate layer should be added to the model: intelligence was in fact determined by a three-level hierarchy of factors. While "g" was the most important factor governing mental ability in any given test, there were a series of eight sub-factors which each helped determine ability in a particular group of tests. Below them, at the lowest level in the hierarchy, were factors specific to performance

in each individual test. He called the top level in his hierarchy (i.e. the "g" factor) **Stratum III. Stratum II** contained the eight sub-factors: fluid intelligence, crystallized intelligence, general memory and learning, broad visual perception, broad auditory perception, broad retrieval ability, broad cognitive speediness, and processing speed. **Stratum I** contained 69 specific tests, each belonging to one of the Stratum II groups.

Of the Stratum II groups, the meanings of "fluid" and "crystallized" intelligence aren't immediately obvious. The crystals of **crystallized intelligence** are essentially grains of knowledge – things we have learned over our lifetime. **Fluid intelligence**, on the other hand, is not learned: it is our innate ability to make sense of the world, to solve problems and understand information.

## Testing time

Up for a brain challenge? Give these a try.

**The International High IQ Society** www.highiqsociety.org
Pleasing and straightforward to navigate, this is the site of the International High IQ Society. It offers two free online IQ tests, a standard one and one for those who consider themselves to be of above-average abilities. Those who score at least 124 in either test are invited to become a member of the society.

**IQ Test** www.iqtest.com
This site offers another rigorous online test. A basic score will be provided free of charge, but, should you desire a full Personal Intelligence Profile, you will be asked for your credit card number. The complete profile provides scores for thirteen individual abilities – spatial skills, logic and so on.

**The Classic IQ Test** www.testq.com
If your concentration can withstand the slew of flash advertisements, you could try this site's free test, consisting of 44 questions spanning a range of mental abilities. You will, however, need to provide an email address to receive the results.

**IQ Testing Online** www.iq-testing-online.com
Those with less time on their hands may opt for this more basic site. Designed to be completed within 20 minutes, the test can be finished in the time it takes to have a cup of coffee – however, a small charge is required to access your score.

There are also a number of books out there which offer tests designed to measure your IQ. Here are two of the best:

**IQ and Psychometric Tests: Assess Your Personality, Aptitude and Intelligence** Philip Carter (Kogan Page, 2003)

**IQ Testing: 400 Ways to Evaluate Your Brainpower** Philip Carter, Ken Russell (John Wiley and Sons, 2001)

# Measuring intelligence: IQ

The history of intelligence testing begins in France, with psychologist Alfred Binet and his collaborator Théodore de Simon. Binet was asked by the French government to devise a test which would show how schoolchildren were coping with the curriculum, and in particular identify children who were likely to struggle with formal education and might benefit from extra help. In 1905, they published the first modern intelligence test, the **Binet-Simon Intelligence Scale**, comprising thirty individual tests designed to flex a broad range of mental abilities. As a way of conveying their results, they developed the concept of

## The high-flyers clubs

**Mensa International** is the most famous of the high-IQ societies. Founded in England in 1946 by Dr Lancelot Ware and Roland Berrill, it welcomes anyone who falls in the 98th percentile or above. Members can attend social events, at which they will have the opportunity to mingle with similarly intellectually gifted people. Famous Mensans include actress Geena Davis and hand-drawn Lisa Simpson. But Mensa is only the beginning.

Snubbing those in the 98th percentile, **Intertel** sets the bar a little higher. Prospective members must score at or above the 99th percentile in a standard IQ test. Founded in 1966, Intertel has around 1200 members. Its Hall of Fame highlights the exceptional achievements of its most outstanding members. If you find yourself in the 99.9th percentile, you could consider joining the **Triple Nine Society**, which encourages intellectually stimulating correspondence between members through its journal, *Vidya*. Still further into the intellectual stratosphere, the **Prometheus Society** is open to those who fall in the 99.997th percentile. Established in 1982 by philosopher Ronald K. Hoeflin, it seeks "to promote fellowship among individuals with extremely high intelligence". For those who want to stick a flagpole in the 99.9999th percentile, the **Mega Society**, also founded by Ronald K. Hoeflin, provides a home for those who literally have a one-in-a-million IQ. Last, and most definitely not least, is the **Giga Society**, with as many as 30 members – plus founder Paul Cooijmans, the club's administrator. This society is open to anyone scoring at or above the 99.9999999th percentile, opening its doors to around one person in a billion. Maybe.

**Mensa** www.mensa.org
**Intertel** www.intertel-iq.org
**Triple Nine** www.triplenine.org
**Prometheus Society** www.prometheussociety.org
**Mega Society** www.megasociety.net
**Giga Society** giga.iqsociety.org

**"mental age"**: an individual of any age who scores as well as an average twelve-year-old is said to have a mental age of twelve.

Binet and Simon continued developing their scale, but it wasn't until 1916 (after Binet's death) that the tests really took off. Stanford University's Lewis M. Terman published a new version of their test, incorporating a central idea from the German psychologist William Stern. Stern proposed that rather than simply assigning a child a mental age, it would be more informative to compare a child's mental age with their actual age, to produce an **intelligence quotient** or **IQ**. A quotient is simply the number that results from dividing one number by another; Stern calculated IQ by dividing mental age by actual age and multiplying by 100 to remove the decimal point. For example, if a 10-year-old had a mental age of 10, his IQ would be 100, but if he had a mental age of 12, he'd score 120. Terman called this new, IQ-based method the **Stanford-Binet Intelligence Scale**.

This method works well for children, but doesn't work for adults, because scores on IQ tests tend to level off around the age of 16 to 18. This means that if you have a mental age of 18 at 18, you'll likely have a mental age of 18 at 36 too, but your IQ would have dropped from 100 to 50.

A new method, known as **deviation IQ**, was devised that got around this problem and allowed IQs to be calculated for adults. This method ditched the problematic concept of mental age, comparing a person's performance directly against that of their peers. Instead of being given a raw score based on the number of questions you answered correctly on the test, you would be given a rank based on the proportion of similarly aged people your test score matched or exceeded. This is known as a

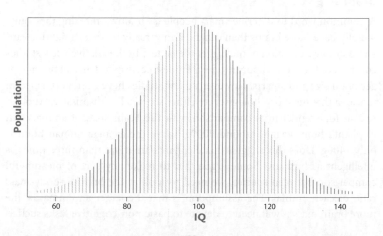

**percentile rank**. So if you scored equal to or better than 90 percent of people taking the test you would fall in the 90th percentile. Your percentile rank is then converted into the standardized IQ score with which we are familiar. The system for translating percentiles into IQs is set up so that a percentile rank of 50 means an IQ of 100 and the distribution of IQs forms a bell-shaped curve or "**normal distribution**". All this means is that, as we might expect, most people fall relatively close to the average IQ of 100, with decreasing numbers above and below this average value.

# What determines intelligence?

Naturally, we're drawn to wonder why some people appear smarter than others – what separates the brilliant from the blockheaded. There are several things to think about in answering this question. Are there structural or other differences in the brain that appear to affect intelligence? Do average IQs for men and women differ, and if so can we find differences between male and female brains to explain this? And what is the relative significance of genes and the environment in determining our intelligence?

## Intelligence and the brain

Scientists have looked at a number of brain factors in an attempt to grasp the elusive key to intelligence. The key areas of investigation have been the brain's size, the quantity of grey matter it contains, and its processing speed.

### Brain size

A common word to describe smart people is "brainy", implying they quite literally have more brains than others. Can it really be this straightforward – is it simply a question of the bigger the better? In the relatively few studies conducted, there does appear to be a modest correspondence between bigger brain size and smarts. However, so few studies have been performed in this area that most psychologists are either sceptical or dismissive. Another reason for scepticism is comparison with the brain sizes of animals. An elephant's brain weighs around 5000g, while the average human brain is only 1400g. Does this suggest that elephants are more than three times as intelligent as humans? Some argue that to make any sort of meaningful comparison between species, we need to look at the brain-to-body-mass ratio of each animal. The assumption is that the larger an animal is, the more brain mass it will need to devote to basic non-cognitive tasks such as

# Einstein's brain

The most famous human brain is arguably Albert Einstein's. On his death in 1955 it was removed from his skull by Thomas Harvey, the doctor who performed the autopsy, apparently without the family's permission. Harvey was very protective of the brain, which he sliced into sections ready for analysis, and it remained hidden for years. It wasn't until 1978 that a reporter, Steven Levy, approached Harvey in Kansas and discovered that he still had the famous brain in his office, stored in two large jars of preservative in a box marked "Costa Cider". Levy's subsequent article caught the public's imagination, but also attracted the attention of scientists. Finally Harvey's ambition was realized: scientists began to examine Einstein's brain In the hope of finding something unusual in it that might account for his extraordinary intel-

ligence. Of course, no serious science can be done with only a single test subject the brains of many "geniuses" would need to be examined before serious conclusions could be drawn. But there have been some interesting findings nonetheless.

Einstein's brain was smaller than average (immediately blowing the size argument into orbit), weighing 1230g rather than the average 1400g. However, Sandra Witelson at McMaster University in Ontario discovered that his **parietal lobes** were unusually large, meaning his brain was 15 percent wider than the other brains studied. Since the parietal lobes are involved in visuo-spatial cognition, mathematical thought and imagery of movement, this could explain Einstein's spatial and mathematical prowess.

Another finding concerned Einstein's **glial cells**, the brain's non-neuronal housekeeper cells that, despite being largely ignored until recently, outnumber neurons by between ten and fifty to one. Marion C. Diamond's team at the University of California, Berkeley, found Einstein's brain had a significantly higher than average number of glial cells in part of the left parietal lobe. What remains unclear is whether this relative glial abundance helped Einstein think spatially, or whether his intense interest in mathematics induced this part of his brain to produce more glial cells.

breathing, controlling movement and so on. If an animal has a very large brain in relation to the size of its body, it might have more brainpower left over from these housekeeping tasks for more complex cognitive tasks. Humans have a much higher brain-to-body-mass ratio than elephants, and indeed nearly all animals. However a spanner is thrown in the works by the humble shrew, which outstrips humans with a brain weighing ten percent of its body weight. Few would argue that humans and mice are intellectual equals. Clearly there is more to braininess than just brains.

## Grey matter

If overall brain size isn't the key, what about the way the brain is constructed? The tissue of the brain can be divided into **white matter** and **grey matter**. These names derive simply from the appearance of these tissues to the naked eye. White matter is tissue containing many long axons. It is white as a result of the myelin insulation surrounding the axons (see p.31). Grey matter consists of the cell bodies of neurons, their dendrites and axon terminals, and glial cells. So white matter is responsible for transporting information from one part of the brain to another, while areas of grey matter are the brain's processing centres. The cortex covering the entire outer brain is grey matter, while the spinal cord, for example, is primarily white matter, carrying information from the body's extremities back to the brain. If grey matter is where the serious processing of information gets done, might intelligence share a correlation with a greater amount of grey matter within the brain?

Recent research suggests this is indeed the case. Richard Haier and colleagues at the University of California, Irvine, together with researchers from the University of New Mexico, used brain imaging to obtain detailed information about the volume of grey matter in 47 adult brains. They then correlated these volumes with the test subjects' scores on a standard IQ test. Significantly, they found that the overall size of a person's brain is less important for IQ scores than the amount of grey matter found in specific regions of the **frontal**, **temporal**, **parietal** and **occipital lobes**.

Intriguingly, these findings imply intelligence is not related to just one brain area, such as the "higher-functioning" frontal lobes, as is often thought. What's more, variations in the distribution of grey matter could explain why some do better at spatial tests and others perform better at verbal comprehension, for example. It's entirely possible that the highly heritable distribution of these grey "hot spots" throughout the brain is what establishes which particular skill-sets we excel at.

In 2011, new research provided some clues as to the biological basis of intelligence – turning the spotlight on the **cerebellum** (p.33). Situated behind the brain stem, in the lower rear regions of the brain, the cerebellum is commonly associated with fine motor control, timing and coordination. In order for us to move with elegance, the cerebellum receives and then combines a range of sensory inputs, whilst communicating with the cortex. The subjects of the 2011 research were 228 adults in their sixties, former participants in the Scottish Mental Survey of 1947, in which their general intelligence was assessed, and the results of which have provided a rich vein to mine for intelligence research (a similar survey was also conducted in 1932, see p.139).

Each of the subjects was again subjected to a test of general intelligence but this time they also had their brain scanned, not to observe flows of neuronal activity but to measure the specific volume of brain structures (a technique known as **voxel-based morphometry**), including the cerebellum along with the quantities of white and grey matter present within their brains. The team, led by Lawrence J. Whalley of the University of Aberdeen, found that the volume of grey matter (cell bodies as opposed to axons) in the cerebellum correlated with general intelligence in the participants. While the correlation between general intelligence and cerebellum volume is stronger for males, suddenly, the cerebellum is front stage in the quest for the roots of intelligence, the implication being that beyond movement, this structure could play a key role in the highest of cognitive abilities. As lead author of the research Michael Hogan puts it:

> This is exciting research, as it suggests that there may be a backdoor route into maintaining higher cortical functions in old age, that is, through the sustained activation of cerebellar networks via novel sensory–motor and cognitive activities, all of which I believe the cerebellum seeks to regulate and automate, working in concert with the cortex.

## Processing speed

We commonly use the word "slow" to describe people who don't seem very bright, and "quick" to refer to those who seem highly intelligent. Is brain speed involved in determining intelligence? A popular test to measure the brain's overall processing speed examines **inspection time**. Subjects are placed in front of a screen on which a simple shape is flashed for varying lengths of time (thousandths of a second). The shape is made of three lines – a horizontal "cap" of constant length, from which descend

*Professor Robert Plomin is Professor of Behavioural Genetics at the Medical Research Council Social, Genetic and Developmental Psychiatry Centre at the Institute of Psychiatry, King's College London. His "whole genome studies" on twins and behaviour continue to generate valuable insights into the relationships between environment, genes and psychological traits, such as intelligence.*

### What is intelligence?

I think it's one of the best documented constructs in the behavioural sciences. It has a history of over a hundred years of research and we generally refer to it as the letter "g", symbolising general cognitive ability – Spearman, in 1904, defined it that way because the word "intelligence" connotes a lot of excess baggage for people. So "general cognitive ability" is what diverse tests of cognitive ability have in common. For example, tests for spatial ability, memory, verbal ability ... You can't come up with a single test of anything that reasonable people would call "cognition".

Most people accept that "g" measures things like abstract reasoning and learning in new situations. "G" seems to help people in every area, especially when they're doing things that they don't know the rules for, like learning a new situation, like problem solving. And then some people talk about information processing, speed and so on.

### What exact aspect of intelligence is it that you work on?

I'm interested in what we call the "generalist genes hypothesis". What we've done is used behavioural, quantitative genetic techniques, like twin and adoption studies, to ask *to what extent is there a genetic overlap among tests?* Using quantitative genetics, you can ask to what extent variance between people is due to genetic and environmental influences. Similarly, the biggest advance in the last twenty years has been **multivariant genetic analysis**, where you ask to what extent is the co-variance between things genetic or environmentally mediated? And genetic correlations here are about 0.8. That means if you found a gene for verbal ability, there's about an 80 percent chance that it's also associated with very different cognitive abilities, like memory or spatial ability. Using these techniques we found the genetic overlap is about 80 percent; so "g" is a good index of what's in common genetically among these diverse tests.

### Are there any particular genes you feel have heightened significance for intelligence?

Fifteen years ago I started using molecular genetics to try and identify some of the genes and what we've found is the same wall that everybody's hitting in everything in the life sciences – you can identify a few genes of very small effect, but the biggest effects are much smaller than anyone ever thought they might be. As a result they're very difficult to find and replicate.

**With respect to the field today, is there anything you find particularly interesting or exciting?**

I think the implication of generalist genes for the brain is pretty interesting. But what we're finding out from the way genes work and how they're expressed in the brain is two rules. One is called **pleiotropy** which is kind of a general rule in genetics that says most genes do lots of different things – most genes have many different effects. There's only about 24,000 genes, most of which are expressed in the brain. I mean everything's expressed everywhere and it's a question of quantity. The other rule is polygenic expression: that each trait is affected by many genes. So the big issue with the brain is that maybe generalist genes, like in the case of "g", can have their effect because there are these independent processes in the brain, many of which affect any one trait.

**What do you kind of feel are the big hurdles for understanding how intelligence works?**

If you accept that there's a strong heritable influence on g, then it does seem to me that you want to try to understand the mechanisms by which that occurs and you could go down to the level of the brain to understand it, but what I wanted to do was to go down to the level of DNA. So at the most basic level, if you could find these genes then you could – even if the genes have very small effects on intelligence – you could begin to treat each of them as kind of a discrete window onto how it works and you could begin to look at gene expression and transcription – **proteomics**. You could kind of work your way up to the brain with these solid toe holes.

We're also finding that another way to find genes with small effect is to look at the extremes. What's interesting about intelligence, unlike the disorders that a lot of other people study in genetics, is that you can study both the high and the low end. With intelligence, it seems reasonable to think that the only way that you can be very, very high-functioning is if you have most of the positive genetic components and few of the negative ones. In pursuit of this we've established a sample of 2000 of the brightest people in the US – these are people with IQs over 160, which is quite a bit higher than the average IQ of Nobel Laureates. We should get a great deal of information out of that study.

There's also the problem of gene interactions, in which case we're screwed – because if you can't detect the effect of a single gene, then trying to understand single interactions between two genes or three genes or fifty genes is going to be nigh on impossible. We've focused a lot on genes, traditional genes that are transcribed and translated into amino acid sequences – but maybe the answer will come from a dark area, **non-coding RNA**, for example. So stay tuned. I really think that there can't be any more fast moving, exciting areas of science.

two vertical lines, one longer than the other. Sometimes the left line will be longer, sometimes the right. The subject simply has to say which side was longer. To prevent iconic memory (see p.62) holding on to the image, as soon as the shape has been flashed up it is replaced by a "mask" of thicker lines (a capping horizontal line with two long vertical lines dropping down either side).

There is reasonable correlation between a person's ability to correctly identify "the long side" of the flashed shape and their performance in intelligence tests. What this suggests is that this test measures more than just the speed of visual processing – it measures some fundamental, widespread property of the brain: its speed at performing simple processing operations. This low-level property of the brain seems to influence its ability to perform higher functions associated with intelligence. This makes sense: the faster you can think, the more options you will have time to consider when faced with a problem, and the more information you will be able to assimilate from the environment to inform your decisions.

## Sex and IQ

Men's and women's average IQs are very similar. However, when psychologists look at the individual tasks making up an IQ test, they do see some differences between the sexes.

On average, females fare better when faced with certain **verbal, linguistic** and **memory tests**. Results from numerous studies show females excel at tests in literature, English composition, reading and spelling. Girls also outperform boys in **maths tests** in the initial years at school, but this advantage swings in the direction of males before puberty, and remains steadfastly in the male corner from that point onwards. Males tend to fare especially well when it comes to **visuo-spatial tasks** and score significantly higher at **spatio-temporal tasks** (tracking a moving object in space – as in most sports).

What causes these differences? Are they solely the result of environmental factors – the social expectations that weigh down on a child from the moment its gender is announced to the world – or are there genuine physiological differences between male and female brains which could account for these differences?

Male brains are, on average, about ten percent heavier than female ones. When standardized against body weight, this difference is almost eliminated. However, as we saw on p.130, the relevance to intelligence of brain size or

## Nutrition and intelligence

Nutrition, or rather a lack of it, does have an effect on intelligence. World War II provided the opportunity to witness the effects of **malnutrition during pregnancy and infancy** on the eventual IQ of the resulting adult. Surprisingly, a human female seems able to withstand several months of famine whilst pregnant without any apparent effect on her child's intelligence. Once free of the womb, however, the picture changes and malnutrition can have a serious impact on intellectual performance. A study in which some children were allowed extra nutrition for a period of years found that they performed better in mental tests than their malnourished peers. But care must be taken when interpreting such results – a lack of proper nutrition also impacts on motivation and energy levels, meaning a person may score badly because they are simply not up to being tested, rather than because they have a low IQ.

Researchers have also found that supplementing normal diets with micronutrients – **vitamins and minerals** – produced significant increases in test scores. This reflects badly on the modern diet: we should be getting these micronutrients naturally.

even brain-to-body-mass ratio is hard to prove. A more promising line of enquiry might be to look at the relative sizes of relevant parts of the brain.

Richard Haier and his team at the University of California, Irvine, followed up their research into grey matter and intelligence (see p.132) with a study of the relative quantities of grey and white matter in male and female brains. They found significant differences: males have more grey matter, responsible for local processing of information, while females have more white matter, responsible for transporting information around the cortex. In fact, men tend to have more than six times as much grey matter as women in the areas of the cortex devoted to intellectual abilities, while women tend to have around ten times as much white matter related to intellectual abilities as men. Given that, overall, men and women perform equally well in tests of intelligence, this implies that different brain arrangements can lead to equivalent outcomes: male brains emphasize discrete, local processing of information (such as in mathematical reasoning), while female brains emphasize connectedness and flow of information between different parts of the cortex (perhaps leading to enhanced linguistic abilities).

Both the functional and structural differences between males and females are partly due to the hormonal differences between the sexes. Puberty is a powerful testament to the effects of hormones on the body. But hormones affect the brain too: females who have been exposed to high levels of the male hormones do better at spatial tasks.

## Genes vs. environment

Identifying the relative significance of genes and the environment in determining our intelligence, or any other characteristic, is extremely difficult. We are the result of a complex interplay between our genes, our surroundings and our experiences that begins even before we are born, in the womb.

Scientists' favourite weapons in the battle to untangle this myriad of influences are **twin studies** and **adoption studies**, what psychologists refer to as experiments of nature and experiments of society respectively. While non-identical twins are produced when two different eggs are fertilized by two different sperm, resulting in two genetically different children, **identical twins** are formed when a single fertilized egg splits in two. The result is genetically identical siblings. The elegance of this situation is that when twins are genetically identical, variations in their IQ can be attributed to environmental effects.

Even if identical twins are raised together, their environment will not be identical. Environment is more than just your surroundings: it is everything that happens to you in the course of your life. Even if a pair of twins both have a passion for sci-fi novels, it's unlikely they'll read the same novels at the same time; these variations become part of a unique perspective.

## Dr Christopher Connolly

*Centre for Neuroscience, Ninewells Medical School, University of Dundee*

**What is your favourite part of the brain and why?** No favourite; why should I have one?

**What scientific breakthrough helped us to understand the brain the most?** Too many breakthroughs, but in terms of the essence of the brain, it has to be Bliss and Lomo on plasticity.

**What's the next big thing in neuroscience?** A genetic model for social interaction that we can interpret (like in hymenoptera).

But if identical twins are raised apart from a very early age, in completely different families, their environments will be much more different, and the influence of environment on intelligence consequently easier to spot. When all they have in common are their genes, what then? If any individual were to take a specific set of mental tests one day, then repeat the same tests a week later, it is likely that their score would be a little different, but it would still tend to hover within around five points of their first score. In comparison, grab two random people off the street and their test scores will vary on average by roughly eighteen IQ points. The astonishing finding is that genetically identical twins, raised apart, produce test scores that resemble the same person being tested on two different days.

These findings are reinforced by the results of studies involving children who have been adopted. Does an adopted child's IQ come to mirror that of their adoptive parents or their genetic parents? Again, it would seem the genes have it, for an adopted child's IQ ultimately correlates more closely with that of their birth mother than of their adopted mother. This swing in favour of our genes becomes more pronounced as a child grows into an adult. It seems that our childhood environment does have an effect on our IQ, but this effect is only temporary: as we grow and move away from that environment to make our own way in life, our IQ gradually reverts to that suggested by our genes.

# Ageing

What happens to intelligence as we age – does the brain start to "rot", or do the collected experiences of a lifetime create a powerhouse of wisdom? The best way to find out would be to perform a whole slew of rigorous mental tests on a large group of children, around eleven years old, then test the same people again when they were in their twilight years. Fortunately for intelligence researchers, there has been just such a study.

In one of the most ambitious studies ever undertaken, in 1932 the Scottish Council for Research in Education decided to take a mental snapshot of the young minds that were to become Scotland's future. On 1 June that year every eleven-year-old attending school – an astounding 87,498 children – simultaneously sat a mental test, similar to that given to English children in the "eleven-plus" examination.

As the years passed, the amassed test data was nearly forgotten. But in 1996 Lawrence Whalley from the University of Aberdeen contacted Ian J. Deary at the University of Edinburgh and the two of them decided to mine this rich vein of intelligence information. They set about the intimidating task of trying to recruit the original participants from the 1932 test, eventually getting 101 of them to come back. The elderly participants sat in the Music Hall in Aberdeen and took exactly the same test, 66 years later, in 1998.

The good news was that, on average, scores were significantly better at age seventy seven than they had been at eleven. But the finding that most interested intelligence researchers was the discovery that an individual's IQ was relatively stable over the decades. There was a strong correlation between a person's test score at age eleven and their score at seventy seven

## Smart animals

When it comes to non-human intelligence, scientists prefer to talk of **animal cognition**: this being an animal's apparent capacity for acquisition of knowledge, thought and understanding. This is hardly surprising, given the difficulties incurred when trying to characterize human intelligence – extending the human definition of intelligence to other animals would simply be misplaced. Instead, researchers look for signs of how well a particular animal appears to have mentally adapted to its specific habitat.

The great apes, such as the gorilla or chimpanzee are certainly up there when it comes to assessing animal cognition. With large brains and a fully developed cortex, these animals are capable of recognizably complex thought. Demonstrating a capacity for language and, particularly in chimpanzees, exceptional working memory, researchers have uncovered hidden depths to these animals' smarts. Naturally, such animals have evolved to inhabit complex social systems, with hierarchies, relationships and complex hunting strategies, all the ingredients one would expect to be associated with higher cognition.

**Chimpanzee memory test video:** www.youtube.com/watch?v=zJAH4ZJBiN8

Crows and ravens, belonging to the corvidae family of birds, are thought to reign supreme in the realm of bird-brains. These birds possess the largest brain-mass-to-body-weight ratios of birds and, as with the great apes (and humans), they live in complex social groups. But how do you measure a

– those who scored above average when they were eleven tended to score above average at seventy seven too. However, by looking at performance on specific tasks, researchers discovered that while **verbal** and **numerical skills** stay reasonably constant throughout life, we tend to experience decreases in **perceptual speed**, **spatial orientation** and **abstract reasoning**. In other words, while crystallized intelligence – what we have learned – remains constant or increases over our lifetime, what changes for the worse is fluid intelligence, our ability to think on the spot when faced with new problems.

## Use it or lose it?

Some individuals are more successful than others at holding on to, or improving, their mental faculties as they age. So what's their secret? Psychologist K. Werner Schaie conducted a large survey of intelligence across the ages and found a few pearls of wisdom for those who want to keep bright in old age:

bird's IQ? Most of the work examining corvid cognition revolves around the animals' ability to innovate in the area of food acquisition, vital for survival. For example, in Japan, local crows took to dropping hard nuts onto busy roads to let passing traffic smash them open, freeing the nutritious interior. Not bad for a bird but that still left the issue of avoiding vehicles. To eliminate this issue, some of the crows took their methodology one small step further, by dropping the nuts at traffic crossings. By doing so, they simply waited for the traffic to be halted by traffic lights before swooping down for their prize.

**Ravens use buoyancy to retrieve food:** www.youtube.com/watch?v=lrYPm6DD44M

When it comes to man's best friend, the Border collie is amongst what are considered to be the brightest of the domestic canines. Leaving the rest of her species trailing, Betsy, an Austrian collie featured in a 2008 edition of *National Geographic* magazine, may be the smartest dog on the planet, with the ability to recognize and respond to more than three hundred words or commands. Thought to have an intellect on a par with a small child, Betsy doesn't just learn fast but is capable of making mental leaps – when shown photographs of objects, not only is she able to recognize the two-dimensional object but she is then able to seek out and locate its three-dimensional counterpart, suggesting an ability to recognize and interpret symbols.

▶ **Have a smart spouse**

▶ **Remain content yet flexible in mid-life**

▶ **Stay healthy**

▶ **Try to keep yourself in an intellectually stimulating environment**

It seems the old saying "use it or lose it" really is the key to an intelligent later life. This is the principle behind Nintendo's computer game *Brain Age*. Produced in collaboration with Japanese neuroscientist Ryuta Kawashima for the handheld "DS" console, *Brain Age* is aimed at those wanting to ward off ailing brainpower. It consists of a series of short mental tasks including verbal and mathematical tasks, logic puzzles and mini-games like sudoku. The aim of the game is to gradually reduce your "brain age" – a figure representing the intellectual performance of your brain.

The Interior of Bedlam (Bethlem Royal Hospital), from *A Rake's Progress* by William Hogarth, revised edition, 1763.

# CHAPTER 8

# Fragile systems

## Brain disorders, illness and ageing

Schizophrenia, epilepsy, attention deficit hyperactivity disorder... Today we have many different names for what used to be labelled madness. We are still far from a complete understanding of mental illness, but we have come a long way, from possession by spirits and witchcraft to modern psychoanalytic and pharmaceutical treatments.

Early asylums, such as London's **Bedlam Hospital**, which opened in 1547, were no better than prisons for the "insane and hysterical". Poorly fed, abused, chained up and dirty, the "patients" were paraded in front of London's public for pennies and tortured by a variety of painful "treatments" to encourage them to *choose* rationality once again.

Only in the eighteenth and nineteenth centuries did the notion of kindness enter into the treatment of such individuals, along with a growing acceptance that these conditions could be attributed, not to demons, but to the workings of the brain, either biological or psychological (the gap between the two is narrowing yearly). Since then, treatments and classifications of conditions have dramatically improved. The American Psychiatric Association's *Diagnostic and Statistical Manual of Mental Disorders* was published in its most recent iteration *(DSM-IV)* in 1994, but the latest update, *DSM-V*, is aiming for release in mid-2013. This book attempts to clarify and categorize the various disorders and illnesses of the human brain, such that they can be treated more effectively. It is used globally by psychiatrists, clinicians and drug companies and has helped create a near-unified approach to describing and treating the enormous range of conditions the human brain can experience.

The systematic and detailed understanding we now have of mental illness is, of course, of great benefit to those suffering from a mental disorder or illness. However, it can also lead to "labelling", where those who are diagnosed become defined solely in terms of their clinical tag (depressed, alcoholic, Parkinson's). This is unwelcome not only because it ignores everything else that makes up a person's identity but also because of the negative stereotypes still associated with mental illness, and the **stigma** arising from them. Although things are improving, such stigma can still be strong, and can prevent people from seeking treatment.

This stigma is, to a large extent, born of ignorance and some fear. However, perhaps there is something else going on too. Like physical health, mental health is a sliding scale, stretching from idealistic mental perfection at one end to complete mental collapse at the other. The presence of a person with a mental illness may remind us of this fact, prompting us to wonder where on it we sit, to ask "How normal am I?"

The following collection of diseases and maladies possesses a rough order, journeying from **brain disorders** to **mental illnesses**. That is, from diseases and disorders of the brain caused by clear structural damage, to illnesses in which the root cause is more complex, less obvious and more subtle.

Brain disorders leave clear, physical signs of damage, whether in the form of burst cerebral blood vessels, as in stroke, or the neuronal death caused by Huntington's disease. In mental illnesses things are less straightforward. The root of these conditions seems to lie more in *how* the brain is functioning at a much more basic level – hence the mountain to climb with respect to understanding. In many mental illnesses, the problem seems to be some sort of **chemical imbalance**. As we'll see in Chapter 9, the brain's ability to coordinate and process the huge amounts of information it deals with is critically dependent on a fine balance of many different chemicals. The transmission of these chemicals, called **neurotransmitters**, from neuron to neuron in controlled quantities along carefully defined pathways is the foundation of brain functioning. Abnormally high or low levels of these neurotransmitters have been implicated in everything from depression to ADHD.

At the far end of the spectrum lies the murky ground of **personality disorders**. Here there are no holes in the brain, no obvious chemical imbalances to remedy. What seems amiss in people with these types of disorder is a persistent, inflexible way of seeing the world, which affects everything they think and do.

The distinction between brain disorder and mental illness is really a reflection of current understanding. The assumption is that some form of brain disorder is at the core of all brain/mind problems – it's simply that the neurological problem in Huntington's disease is more easily characterized than in schizophrenia, for example.

At the end of the chapter we will look at two brain disorders associated with old age, Parkinson's and Alzheimer's disease.

# Brain disorders
## Stroke

Our circulatory system keeps every cell in the body supplied with the nutrients and oxygen it needs to function, whilst carrying away waste. In the vast majority of strokes (around ninety percent), the blood supply to the brain becomes blocked. Suddenly, brain cells are starved of their supplies of food and oxygen. And due to their enormous complexity and the high demands placed on them, they quickly start to die. The blockage is caused by a **clot**, which may have developed within an artery of the brain itself, or may have formed elsewhere in the circulatory system, become dislodged, and travelled to the brain, coming to rest within the mesh of blood vessels supplying the brain.

The part of the brain that dies after a stroke takes with it the function it was responsible for; if it was a region of the motor cortex, for example, the person could lose mobility. Fortunately, the brain's **plasticity** – its ability to rewire and relearn – means that a portion of functionality can often be regained in the months following a stroke. For those for whom brain damage was minimal, physiotherapy or speech therapy, combined with nursing and occupational therapy, may eventually help the patient return to a relatively normal lifestyle. However, if the stroke is big enough, or in a region of the brain vital for existence (controlling breathing, for example), the result can be death.

Stroke is a huge problem, falling short of only cancer and heart disease as the West's third-biggest killer. However, there are simple things we can do, or not do, to help dodge these blood bullets. As usual though, they're the things people rarely want to hear: stop smoking (immediately), exercise (including walking), and eat a decent diet.

In the treatment of stroke, time is the enemy. If someone experiences sudden weakness or numbness, confusion, or loss of vision in one eye, get them to hospital as soon as possible, because the clock is ticking. The

**Head MRI showing deep intracerebral haemorrhage due to bleeding within the cerebellum, approximately thirty hours old, in a 68-year-old male patient with a stroke.**

sudden onset of stroke combined with the limited and time-dependent treatment options (usually a "clot-buster" drug) mean that the quicker the person can be treated – preferably in under three hours – the less damage their brain suffers. They may have suffered a transient attack, serving as a warning, or a full-blown stroke, in which case they need immediate treatment from a professional, as the area of initial brain damage can spread to surrounding brain tissue within hours.

Prevention is far more successful than cure in the case of stroke and several drugs exist – aspirin (see p.212) being chief amongst them – for those at risk to help thin their blood or lower blood pressure, literally preventing a burst blood vessel. There are also an increasing number of surgical options – from miniature metal sieves that are used to physically block clots heading towards the brain, to a highly specialized "corkscrew" that's skilfully manoeuvred through blood vessels until it reaches the blockage, where it literally uncorks the offending blood clot.

In the future, **stem-cell therapies** (modern medicine's great new hope) may become available for stroke patients. Stem cells, the body's ultimate cellular chameleons, are capable of becoming any sort of cell we want, given the right impetus. The hope is that if they can be introduced into a stroke-damaged area of the brain, or the patient can be stimulated to produce their own, these cells will adapt to their environment, replacing dead neurons with healthy cells.

**The Stroke Association** www.stroke.org.uk

# Creutzfeldt-Jakob disease (CJD)

Originally described in the 1920s by Hans Gerhard Creutzfeldt and Alfons Maria Jakob, a couple of German neurologists, CJD is a rare yet devastating neurological disease. It afflicts one in every million people each year, giving it a global prevalence of around 6500. Highly aggressive, the normal form of CJD can obliterate a person of around 50–75 years of age in less than a year: their brain deteriorates rapidly, leading to dementia, memory loss, hallucinations and personality changes. These changes are accompanied by a host of physical problems including jerky movements, a loss of coordination and speech impairment. The vast majority of cases (85 percent) occur spontaneously, while 10–15 percent are inherited, and the final few cases are caused by accidental infection. There's no cure, as yet.

CJD belongs to a family of diseases known as the **spongiform encephalopathies**. They get their name because when the brain of a victim is scrutinized under a microscope, it resembles a sponge, full of tiny holes. The pathogen responsible for this devastating brain disorder, the **prion**, was discovered in 1982 by Stanley B. Prusiner. Years later, in 1997, Prusiner received the Nobel Prize for Physiology and Medicine for his discovery of prions but the scientific community was initially highly sceptical. It's not every day that a form of scientific heresy is committed, but that's exactly what Prusiner did, by suggesting prions can replicate, spreading their infection *without using DNA*. This spat in the face of the central dogma of biology – that the DNA double helix is essential for all reproduction.

The harmless form of the prion (from proteinaceous infectious particle) normally exists within us all – a protein sitting in the outer surface of neurons, known as prion-related protein (PrP). While speculation as to the normal function of this protein continues (suggestions spanning everything from copper ion transport to formation and maintenance of axons), nobody knows precisely what PrP's day-to-day function is, nor is it clear what causes it to malfunction – it may be a mutation, it could be spontaneous, or it could be triggered by some other infectious agent. But when it does, PrP changes its shape, suddenly becoming both incredibly resilient and capable of facilitating the conversion of other normal proteins to the disease-causing form.

In the realm of proteins, shape equals function – in the same way that a hand's shape allows it to grip. In CJD, the protein's normal shape is changed, it stops doing what it should and instead transforms into the

## Kuru, the laughing disease

In the 1950s it became clear something strange was afoot on the eastern tip of Indonesia, Papua New Guinea, when a rapidly increasing number of women and children of the South Fore tribe began dying of a disease known locally as **kuru**.

The name comes from the Fore word for "trembling", and in the preliminary phase, known as the **ambulant** stage, sufferers would experience a general unsteadiness of movement, a slurring of speech and shivering. The severity and range of movement that was impaired strongly suggested this disease was targeting the **cerebellum** (see p.33) of those afflicted. In the second, sedentary stage, the person would all but lose the ability to walk, and experience uncontrolled muscular jerks. They would also begin to slow down mentally, experiencing dramatic swings in mood, from depression to outbursts of laughter (hence the disease's other name, the **"laughing disease"**). Finally, some six to twelve months after the initial signs of illness, the person would reach the terminal stage – by now they would be shaking badly, incontinent and unable to move without help.

At the height of the kuru epidemic in the mid-1950s, there was widespread panic. More than a thousand (of the tribe's eight thousand) people died in less than a decade. Governments spoke of isolating the tribe to prevent the disease's spread while scientists began looking for the cause.

The women of the Fore took part in ritualistic **mortuary cannibalism**. Once a person had died, their female relatives proceeded to prepare the body. The extremities (arms and feet) were removed, and the body stripped of muscle (the relatively short time to death experienced in kuru meant bodies were still reasonably nourished). The chest would be cut open to remove the internal organs and the brain would be removed. These "ingredients" were used as the basis for ritualistic meals, combined with various herbs and vegetables and steamed over a fire before being eaten. The prepared brain, considered a delicacy, was reserved for close relatives. These posthumous feasts were eaten by the women of the tribe, who would share their meal with children – no men were allowed to partake.

The symptoms of kuru were first described by a young German–Lithuanian physician based in the Fore Tribe region of New Guinea, Vincent Zigas. In 1957 he convinced two infected members of the tribe to travel with him to his makeshift hospital for observations. There they were also seen by the scientist Daniel Carleton Gajdusek. Gajdusek and Zigas tirelessly analysed

malicious form of the prion – like a hand adopting a permanent fist. In its new shape, the prion begins to propagate – by an unknown mechanism – changing all the other harmless prions into harmful ones. This chain reaction spreads quickly throughout the nervous system. The only thing this misshapen prion is good at is causing damage. The misfolded proteins blood samples and human tissue for the cause of this perplexing disease. Significantly, Gajdusek discovered that kuru stopped dead at the edge of the Fore's territory – the disease was theirs alone.

Gajdusek began working on the idea that kuru might be the result of some kind of slow-acting virus that, once contracted, would slowly destroy the central nervous tissue of the infected individual. In a breakthrough, he linked the tribe's ritualistic cannibalism with the spread of kuru – an idea which predicted the disease's behaviour perfectly. It explained why it was mostly women and children who became victims (infected men were rare and were thought to have come into contact with infected material through wounds). It also explained the familial path the disease seemed to take. Cannibalism was subsequently banned in the region and kuru died out. In 1976, Gajdusek was awarded the Nobel Prize for Medicine for his work.

As it turns out, there was no virus, but it took more Nobel-Prize-winning research to discover the cause of kuru. Only with the discovery of **prions** in 1982 by Stanley B. Prusiner was the true nature of kuru revealed. Belonging to the family of diseases known as the **spongiform encephalopathies** – including scrapie, BSE and CJD – kuru was being triggered by a rogue protein ingested during ritual meals (prions are extremely hardy, capable of withstanding the heat of cooking), not an alien virus from the region.

New evidence suggests our early human ancestors may have embraced cannibalism more enthusiastically than we might find palatable. As we saw on p.147, the harmless form of the prion exists in all of us. Research led by John Collinge of University College London has revealed the presence of slightly different versions of the gene which makes this prion protein. Looking at representative populations all over the globe (more than two thousand DNA samples), researchers found that everyone possessed two copies of the gene making the prion protein – one "normal" version and either of two altered, mutant versions. This led the researchers to speculate that the mutant versions of the prion gene somehow protect humans from developing a prion disease, possibly because the mutant versions of the prion protein are less easily persuaded to form damaging clumps. It may be that in our cannibalistic prehistory we were far more partial to "family dinners" than we might imagine, causing natural selection to favour those whose mutant genes provided protection against the inherent dangers of eating our own kind.

aggregate together, forming stubborn clumps, disrupting and destroying normal neuronal function – until all that's left is a brain full of holes.

In 1996, a **new variant form of CJD** was reported in the UK, affecting much younger people and thought to be the direct result of humans eating meat from cattle infected with **bovine spongiform encephalopathy**

(**BSE**), or "mad cow disease". In 2006 the Health Protection Agency Centre for Infections reported that there had been 161 cases of vCJD within the UK to date, 156 of whom had died. Incidences of the disease peaked in 2000 and have now declined to a level of one or two people per year.

**UK Health Protection Agency** www.hpa.org.uk/infections/topics_az/cjd/menu.htm

# Huntington's disease (HD)

George Huntington was only 22 years old and just one year from having qualified to practise medicine when in 1872 he published a paper describing in detail the disease that now bears his name. Huntington's disease, or **chorea** as it's sometimes known (from Greek, *dance*), is a rare genetic disorder affecting between five and eight people, male or female, in every 100,000 – a total of over 400,000 people on the planet. Those who inherit the disease tend to develop symptoms between 25 and 55 years of age; from that point, it may take anything from 10 to 25 years for them to finally yield to its relentless progression.

The disease gradually steals a person's intellectual abilities: their memory, their ability to think, speak and maintain emotional composure and attention. In addition, the body is subject to physical jerks and twitches, the origin of the term chorea.

The Venezuelan fishing village **Barranquitas** has the highest incidence of Huntington's disease (HD) on Earth. Almost half the population of around 25,000 carry the gene causing the disease. The prevalence of HD in Barranquitas has been invaluable to scientists trying to identify the gene responsible for the disease. Unfortunately, HD continues to flourish in the remote village as suggestions of sterilization and contraception have met with opposition and inhabitants continue to produce large families, many of whom will die a sad, slow death.

In 1993 the search was over, the gene responsible for HD was identified and the protein the gene makes was named **huntingtin**. The faulty gene was found to have a form of genetic stutter – at a specific point in its genetic code, it repeats itself unnecessarily. The stuttering gene passes this extra, repeated information onto the huntingtin protein it produces, making it too long to function correctly. What the huntingtin protein does in a healthy individual is the topic of vigorous research. However, it seems the normal, shorter protein somehow protects the brain, so that in its absence the brain deteriorates. The result is neuron death – especially in the **frontal lobes** and the **basal ganglia**, responsible for higher functioning (such as reasoning) and movement respectively.

The faulty gene sits on chromosome 4. As you may remember from biology lessons, each of us has 46 chromosomes – vast, single continuous threads of DNA – which come in 23 pairs, each pair containing one chromosome from our mother, and one from our father. Because the gene responsible for Huntington's disease is "dominant", even if only one of your chromosome 4s carries the faulty version of the gene, you will develop HD. What's more, you will have a 50 percent chance of passing the disease on to your children. This genetic Russian roulette is exacerbated by the fact that the late onset of the disease means many

## Dr Daniel Glaser
*Neuroscientist and Head of Special Projects, Wellcome Trust*

**What is your favourite part of the brain and why?** The parietal cortex because it's where we put what we see and what we feel together.

**What scientific breakthrough helped us to understand the brain the most?** Antibiotics so that people can survive after having their brains exposed (whether by accident or design) so we can learn better what bit does what.

**What's the next big thing in neuroscience?** Non-invasive imaging that allows us to see down to single neuron level with millisecond time resolution in the living human brain (or steps in that direction).

of those carrying the gene have had a child before they experience the symptoms of HD – or even before their parent develops symptoms. This means people can suffer the double anxiety of not knowing whether they have the disease themselves and worrying that they may have passed it on to their child. For those who fear they carry the faulty gene, counselling combined with a genetic test for HD is a valuable option.

**Huntington's Disease Association** www.hda.org.uk

## Multiple sclerosis (MS)

In multiple sclerosis, the nerve cells' white insulating layer, known as the **myelin sheath** (see p.31), is attacked and gradually stripped away – by the victim's own body. The irony is that they become the victim of a system that has defended us from external attack for millions of years, the **immune system**. The immune system wrongly identifies the myelin sheath as a foreign body and sets out to destroy it. In a battle against itself, the body attempts to repair the damage it's doing to itself, covering the

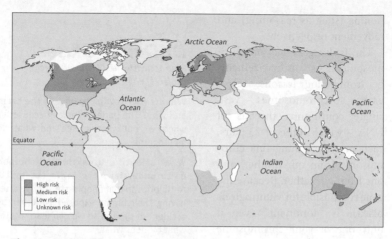

**The geographical distribution of multiple sclerosis.**

damaged areas with new myelin. This leaves toughened regions (sclerosis comes from the Greek *skleros*, hard) on the nerves, called **plaques**.

MS is the most common disabling neurological disease amongst the young, usually presenting itself between the ages of twenty and forty. The pattern of the disease varies from person to person, with attacks often being followed by periods of calm or remission. The attacks can take many different forms, including painful eye movements or visual problems, tremors, weakness and unsteadiness, depression and emotionally inappropriate behaviour – crying whilst hearing good news, for example.

MS affects around 2.5 million people worldwide. Unfortunately, no one yet knows what causes it. One clue might lie in the disease's **geographical spread**. Almost nonexistent within equatorial environments, the prevalence of MS steadily increases as you move towards the poles, with regions above 40 degrees latitude experiencing a distinct increase in the condition. Even then, it is not randomly distributed, with Europe, North America and Australasia experiencing a higher incidence than Eastern Asia, for example. Could these regional variations be due to **climate**, with temperature and light levels in temperate climes facilitating disease onset? Researchers have found that MS onset and relapses occur more frequently in springtime, and less often in the darker winter months. Given the strength of the body's connection to light levels generally and the relationship between the day/night cycle and the immune system (see p.105), this hypothesis seems plausible.

Alternatively, what about an invisible enemy – a virus, for example – some type of MS-triggering **pathogen**, rare in equatorial regions but vigorous in temperate regions? Research in this area is attempting to find a link between earlier infection from some such pathogen, and the human immune response. The idea is that once the body is infected, the immune system searches out the invading enemy in order to destroy it. But the invader is disguised to look a little like its surroundings, so when the body mounts an attack it begins to destroy both the invader and itself.

Even **diet** is being analysed for possible triggers, with studies revealing a possible causative link with high consumption of red meat and dairy products and a protective link with high consumption of fish, which is rich in omega-3 oils and vitamin $D_3$.

As yet, there are no clear answers but it seems likely that a combination of genetic factors heightening susceptibility to the disease combined with, as yet, unknown environmental triggers is responsible. But despite MS's elusive origins, hope still exists as research into myelin repair continues to make significant leaps. In 2011, a team led by David H. Rowitch (Departments of Pediatrics and Neurosurgery, Eli and Edythe Broad Institute for Stem Cell Research and Regeneration Medicine and Howard Hughes Medical Institute, University of California, San Francisco) identified a protein called **Axin2** as being critical for the conversion of stem cells within the brain into **oligodendrocytes** – cells responsible for creating new myelin. While the head of the UK's MS Society acknowledges "myelin regeneration treatments" are probably still some ten to fifteen years down the road, there is a new sense of optimism in the scientific, medical and patient communities.

**US National MS Society** www.nationalmssociety.org

# Epilepsy

> You have no idea what joy that joy is which we epileptics experience the second before a seizure … I do not know whether this joy lasts for seconds or hours or months, but believe me, I would not exchange it for all the delights of this world.
>
> Fyodor Dostoevsky (1821–81)

Dostoevsky was talking about his personal **aura**, sensations he would feel whilst succumbing to a seizure. Although not all epileptics experience an aura, he is not alone in finding it a powerful experience. An aura may take many forms. If the seizure occurs in a part of the brain dealing with

## Ellen Gould White: a prophetic epileptic?

Born in Maine in 1827, Ellen Gould White was a smart, well-behaved child, part of a large, religiously devout family. Unfortunately, a ferocious attack altered Ellen's perceptions permanently.

At nine years old, Ellen received a blunt projectile to the head (a stone in her face from an older, female assailant), causing her to lose consciousness for three weeks – anything longer than 24 hours is considered severe. In a head injury like this, damage to the brain can occur in several ways. The shock to the head – resulting from the projectile's impact causing rapid acceleration/deceleration – probably sheared the brain away from its supporting membranes, flinging the soft, delicate tissue from one side of the skull's interior to the other, damaging its surface. It is also quite likely that Ellen experienced bleeding on the surface of her brain, due to these shearing forces.

Once awake, Ellen was found to be suffering from retrograde amnesia (see p.79), being unable to remember her attack or the events leading up to it. She also experienced headaches, dizziness and weakness. In the years following, it became clear her formal education was over, much to her disappointment. This, combined with her disfigurement and her continued physical suffering, brought on a period of intense depression.

When she was twelve years old, Ellen and her family became involved with the Millerite movement, an Adventist organization with a strong belief that Christ's return was just around the corner (they even predicted it to be 22 October 1844, resulting in the "Great Disappointment"). In her depressed state, Ellen felt unworthy, a sinner rejected by God. Her despair continued to deepen – and that's when her first vision occurred.

The visions Ellen experienced turned her life around. They were deeply religious, filled with images of heaven, Jesus or angels, with whom she was able to

perception, it can take the form of sounds, images, smells, or a feeling of numbness or tingling in part of the body. If the seizure begins in the motor cortex, the first warning could be a tremor in the body part under the control of that brain region. And if the seizure begins in the temporal lobe, dream-like or ecstatic feelings may overwhelm the person. Some auras can be unpleasant, including nausea or feelings of anxiety, but they can still be useful in acting as a warning of the approaching seizure.

Those with a regular susceptibility to seizures are said to have epilepsy, from the Greek word meaning a taking hold of, or seizing. Epilepsy has been recognized at least since the time of Hippocrates, the "father of modern medicine", around 400 BC. In those days, however, the condition communicate. Sometimes they would occur as in dreams, at other times they would occur while awake, during times of prayer. She quickly gained a reputation as a conduit between God and the devout on Earth, eventually co-founding the Seventh-day Adventists. But, given the serious nature of Ellen's head trauma and her ensuing mental condition, the question of whether her visions were the result of **temporal lobe epilepsy** has doggedly remained associated with her name. Experiencing strong emotions, such as fear, is common in TLE, as are hallucinations involving many of the senses. Could her powerful beliefs have predisposed Ellen to experience a more directed form of hallucination than someone less devout? For more on studies of religious visions and temporal lobe epilepsy, see p.237.

**Ellen White, with husband James.**

was regarded with a degree of fear and suspicion, and associated with possession by spirits.

Real progress towards an understanding of what was happening during seizures began in the 1860s with John Hughlings Jackson, one of the early pioneers of neurology. Jackson made many observations of the various types of seizures, cataloguing their complex patterns and symptoms. A particular type of motor seizure is even said to have a "Jacksonian march", the term describing a gradually spreading and intensifying movement which begins at an extremity – often the fingers – and spreads up the limb, before eventually overwhelming the entire body, possibly resulting in a loss of consciousness.

Epilepsy may be caused by a number of things, including head trauma, fever, a brain tumour, stroke or a genetic condition, but many may never know precisely what has caused their condition. But whatever the underlying cause, damage at a specific region of the brain results in it becoming susceptible to a kind of hyperactivity, like a small electrical storm. Triggers for these storms can be tiredness, stress, alcohol, illness or flashing lights – things we expose ourselves to every day. In a seizure, the mini electrical storm can overwhelm the surrounding nerve cells, allowing it to spread quickly from one brain region to another, until the entire brain is in the grip of this electrical overload. If you encounter someone having a seizure, don't put anything in their mouth – a common mistake. Place them on their side with their head on something soft – don't restrain them – and gently reassure them until the seizure is over (usually just a few minutes).

One estimate suggests that as many as three percent of those living to the age of 80 in the United States will be diagnosed with epilepsy. Fortunately, thanks to our increasing understanding of the condition, there are many lifestyle changes someone with the condition can make to improve their quality of life. Combined with other treatments, both natural and drug-based, they mean that many live a happy, normal life.

**Epilepsy Action** www.epilepsy.org.uk

# Cerebral palsy (CP)

In 1860 surgeon William John Little (1810–94) provided the first detailed description of the various conditions we now know as cerebral palsy. Due to the unchanging nature of cerebral palsy, neither improving nor deteriorating over time, it's thought of as a *condition* rather than an illness or a disease. At some point in the brain's development, whether in the womb or during infancy, something goes wrong, leaving the young brain damaged or unable to mature correctly. Little believed cerebral palsy was caused by the foetus being deprived of oxygen during birth. However, the young Sigmund Freud contested this idea, suggesting that a difficult birth was a symptom of CP, not the cause. We now know that the vast majority of CP cases are not the result of oxygen deprivation. Other causes include head trauma, infection during pregnancy, premature birth, complications during birth and genetic susceptibility.

The global, non-specific nature of the damage to the brain means that the effects of cerebral palsy are seen throughout the body. About seventy percent of cases involve severe tightening of the person's muscles, causing restricted movement and interfering with posture and coordination. In addition, CP can sometimes be accompanied by other neurological problems, including disorders of sight or speech or learning difficulties. Problems with controlling facial expressions or speech can lead to the incorrect assumption that someone with CP will inevitably have learning difficulties. However, most people with CP have perfectly normal mental faculties.

Around one in every five hundred babies will develop cerebral palsy. The amount of support they will need depends on the severity of their disability; however, as long as they receive proper care, a person with the condition can live to a good age.

**Scope** www.scope.org.uk

# Self-inflicted brain disorder #1: ecstasy abuse

Ecstasy is the street name for a drug called **MDMA**, or 3,4-methylenedioxymethamphetamine. Like many drugs, MDMA was originally intended for medical, rather than recreational, use. Ignorant of its effects on the brain, its creators intended it as a mere chemical intermediate to be used in the synthesis of a drug to stem bleeding, and a patent was filed on Christmas Eve 1912. However, in 1960s America, some psychoanalysts began to use MDMA as part of their treatment, finding that the self-awareness, introspection and empathy the drug induced helped certain clients, such as Vietnam veterans suffering from post-traumatic stress disorder (see p.167). A few decades later, MDMA found a new home in the rave scene. Illegal MDMA sales soared in the 1990s as dancers found the sense of euphoria and energy it produced enhanced the clubbing experience.

Ecstasy abuse can kill, usually via acute dehydration and overheating. In addition, ecstasy pills are often mixed with impurities or other drugs (such as aspirin or paracetamol), which increase the dangers. However, the drug also has longer-term effects on the brain. MDMA causes the brain to experience unnaturally high levels of the neurotransmitters **serotonin**, **dopamine** and **noradrenaline**. These elevated neurotransmitters work together to alter the user's perceptions and emotional state. The problem is that repeated exposure to such unnatural levels of these mood-altering chemicals upsets the brain's chemical balance. Over a prolonged period of ecstasy use, the brain attempts to compensate for the huge levels of neurotransmitters being thrown at it. One of the ways it does this is by reducing the number of routes through which these neurotransmitters can enter its nerve cells – additionally, it's possible that the nerves producing the neurotransmitters can simply die. This means that, when not taking an MDMA-containing drug, the brain experiences a chronic lack of the very neurotransmitters it has been drowning in. Now, without even the natural levels of neurotransmitters to form the vital communication links between nerve cells, a person can experience a number of negative side effects, including **depression**, **confusion** and **reduced concentration**. And the global nature of these neurotransmitters, functioning in many brain areas, means that the effects on the cortex can be even more widespread: research has revealed that additional mental qualities such as the **visual, spatial and working memories** can also be affected.

**US National Institute on Drug Abuse** www.nida.nih.gov

## Self-inflicted brain disorder #2: Wernicke-Korsakoff syndrome

Alcohol contains almost twice as many calories as carbohydrates or protein, making overindulgence an effective way to gain weight. As far as the body is concerned, one calorie is much like any other when it comes to energy creation, so is it possible to live on a diet of beer and wine? In cases of **alcohol dependency**, an alcoholic can drift from irregular or poor eating habits to barely eating at all. The problem with using alcoholic drinks as fuel is that they contain almost no nutritional value whatsoever. Spirits, for example, contain no protein for muscle, no carbohydrates for energy, no fat, and no vitamins or minerals.

In severe alcohol dependency, the body becomes seriously malnourished. In particular, long-term, severe deficiency in vitamin $B_1$ (thiamine) leads to **Wernicke-Korsakoff syndrome** – named after medical practitioners Carl Wernicke and Sergei Korsakoff. In the first "half" of the disorder, **Wernicke's encephalopathy**, progressive brain damage results in signs such as involuntary eye movements, partial or total paralysis of the eyes, unsteadiness and short-term memory loss. **Korsakoff's syndrome**, as we saw on p.79, results in both amnesia and confabulation, as sufferers invent a new world to fill the void left by their memory loss.

The syndrome is the result of widespread damage to the brain, caused by the thiamine deficiency. Many neurons and glial cells (see p.21) will have died. In particular, the brain's **mammillary bodies**, two small spherical structures deep within the brain, will have been damaged. Since they are connected to the hippocampus, a central player in the formation of new memories, it is clear why serious damage to them would result in memory problems.

**US National Institute on Alcohol Abuse and Alcoholism** www.niaaa.nih.gov

# Mental illnesses

## Depression

The term "sad" is rarely used today, with people often opting to describe themselves as "depressed" without fully understanding what true depression is. It is as if society has bought into the notion that healthy, natural sadness and depression are one and the same. But while it is quite normal to experience feelings of helplessness, pessimism, sadness and a general lack of energy and zeal at some point in our lives, particularly following a trauma such as divorce or sudden redundancy, severe **clinical depression** or "major depression" goes way further than this. To be diagnosed as clinically depressed, *DSM-IV* says a person must have continuously experienced a number of specific symptoms for at least two weeks, including recurrent thoughts of their death, feelings of general worthlessness, sleep disturbance, poor concentration and a slowing of mental activity including difficulty making decisions. In major depression, it's clear that the mind is struggling to hold itself together.

Our contemporary notion of depression derives from the older idea of **melancholy**, itself arising from the Greek for "black bile", *melancholia*. Hippocrates believed the body contained four humours – black and yellow bile, blood and phlegm – with imbalances in these humours influencing both personality and health. Today, black bile has been replaced by chemical imbalances in the brain, but the central idea remains unchanged.

Several decades ago, it was discovered (by accident) that certain drugs seemed to improve mood, and the pharmaceutical industry blossomed. These original drugs were found to increase levels of the neurotransmitters **serotonin, dopamine** and **noradrenaline**. Nowadays, these accidental discoveries have been replaced with designer drugs such as **selective serotonin reuptake inhibitors** (SSRIs), a class of antidepressants that keep the brain's natural serotonin hanging around for longer, so it can have more impact on the nerves around it (see p.204).

But it was never going to be so straightforward – we would have been fortunate indeed to wipe out depression with a simple serotonin boost. For a start, serotonin does not have a single function in the brain – it's not simply a "happy" neurotransmitter, switching on a single neural pathway determining how good a person feels. It is involved in mood more generally – that is, the brain's entire state of mind, as well as its appetite, both sexual and nutritional. As such, the long-term pharmaceutical boosting of serotonin has far-reaching and incompletely understood effects on the

## The modern phenomenon of depression

Depression, as we know it, has only existed since the publication of *DSM-IV* in 1994. It defines the criteria for "major depressive disorder" as follows. A person must experience five or more of the following symptoms at the same time for a period of at least two weeks (note that bereavement is excluded as a cause):

▶ **Depressed mood** most of the day, nearly every day

▶ **Markedly diminished interest or pleasure** in all, or almost all, activities most of the day, nearly every day

▶ **Significant weight loss** when not dieting or weight gain, or decrease or increase in appetite nearly every day

▶ **Disturbed sleep** – too little or too much nearly every day

▶ **Restlessness or sluggishness**

▶ **Fatigue** or loss of energy nearly every day

▶ **Feelings of worthlessness** or excessive or inappropriate guilt nearly every day

▶ **Diminished ability to think** or concentrate, or indecisiveness, nearly every day

brain. And mood is a complex beast – the sum of thoughts, feelings and memories, combined with feelings of motivation and self-worth. A drug's intervention is just one facet of this, and as such it is not surprising that it will affect different people in different ways.

Antidepressants are not the only treatment for depression, however. Psychological therapies such as **counselling** can be very useful in helping the sufferer to understand and resolve underlying problems that may be causing their depression. **Cognitive behavioural therapy** can challenge negative, depressive thought patterns and help sufferers develop more positive thinking habits. It can also help patients develop coping behaviours and skills. Often psychotherapy is used in conjunction with medication, as research has indicated that combining them gives the most effective treatment.

Intriguingly, brain-imaging studies have shed a little light on why those with severe depression might find decision-making and concentration so difficult. Scientists have observed reduced activity in the **left prefrontal cortex** of some people suffering from depression – precisely the area involved in higher functioning, such as reasoning and judgement. Each of these breakthroughs brings us a little closer to understanding the neurophysiology of depression.

**NIMH Depression Guide** www.nimh.nih.gov/publicat/depression.cfm

▶ **Recurrent thoughts of death** (not just fear of dying), recurrent suicidal ideation without a specific plan, or a suicide attempt or a specific plan for committing suicide

To experience at least five of these simultaneously over a period of time is a fairly tall order – and highly disruptive to normal functioning – so why has the diagnosis and medical treatment of depression exploded? Each decade, higher numbers of people are being diagnosed with major depression, and now, in the twenty-first century, the expectation is that nearly twenty percent of people will suffer from major depression at some point in their life.

Depression is highly lucrative for the global **pharmaceutical industry**. The first antidepressants were discovered in the 1950s and, curiously, the numbers of those diagnosed as "depressed" has dramatically increased ever since. But **lifestyles** have also changed in recent decades, with increasing isolation replacing the feeling of belonging and support that earlier, smaller communities provided. And modern life is increasingly complex, so that there are more and more situations – career-related stress or unhappiness, poverty, living far from family or breaking up with a partner, for example – that could send the human brain spiralling towards depression. Could this dark trend be a growing warning about contemporary living habits?

# Bipolar disorder (manic depression)

Major depression, described above, is also known as **unipolar depression**. In **bipolar disorder**, sufferers experience periods of major depression, but are also catapulted to the other end of the spectrum, where **mania** resides.

According to *DSM-IV*, to be recognized as bipolar, or manic depressive, a person with severe depression must have experienced at least one manic episode lasting for at least one week. During this week, thoughts of hopelessness and worthlessness are cast aside in favour of a sense of intense **euphoria**. The person may speak or write furiously and will probably sleep very little, their mind constantly buzzing with ideas. They will become much more extrovert, and possess terrific self-esteem. This mountain-like self-belief can, however, tip over into **delusion**, and feelings of infinite power and importance.

These episodes can also be characterized by intense productivity and **creativity**, and indeed bipolar disorder is disproportionately common in highly creative or talented people. Many famous artists, musicians and authors, including Stephen Fry, Spike Milligan, Kurt Cobain, Stuart

## Talking therapies

In the last few decades many drugs have been developed with the purpose of redressing chemical imbalances in the brain. Such drugs have proved effective in the treatment of, for example, depression and generalized anxiety disorder.

However, pharmaceuticals are not the only way to treat mental illness. Some of the most successful treatments rely less on chemical intervention and more on **talking therapies**. Counselling, social support and cognitive behaviour therapies demonstrate how much more there still is to learn about the mind – by literally talking someone back to good mental health.

One of the therapies reaping the greatest rewards in recent years is **cognitive behavioural therapy**. This therapy helps a person change both how they think (cognitive) and what they do (behaviour). Rather than delving into a person's past to resolve underlying issues, CBT focuses on the present, attempting to help a person deal more effectively, and rationally, with their day-to-day routines and perceived problems. CBT may take a situation a person finds completely overwhelming, and break it down into smaller, more manageable parts: a specific situation, plus the associated thoughts, feelings, physical sensations and actions taken. A trained therapist can then guide a client through their patterns of thinking, suggesting more positive alternatives – for example, an acquaintance walking past without acknowledging you could be a sign of preoccupation, rather than an indication of their disregard. By slowly changing their patterns of thoughts and emotional responses to situations, the client can regain a far more balanced perspective on life.

Goddard (aka Adam Ant), Jackson Pollock, Edvard Munch and Lord Byron, are believed to have been affected by bipolar disorder.

Both unipolar and bipolar depression possess a clear genetic component, but it's considerably stronger in bipolar disorder. The struggle to identify the genes responsible is still ongoing, but some progress has been made. A mutation in one gene, known as **GRK3**, has been implicated in a possible ten percent of cases (the protein made by GRK3 forms part of the vast communication network between neurons). It's a good start, but chances are the complex pattern of brain activity seen in the disorder is the result of numerous genes, somehow conspiring together to produce bipolar behaviour. Indeed, the genetic scale of the problem has given rise to the Bipolar Disease Research Network (BDRN), the largest study of bipolar disorder in the world. Supported by the Wellcome Trust and Stanley Medical Research Institute and led by Professor Nicholas Craddock at the Cardiff University School of Medicine, the BDRN con-

**Few pictures convey a sense of desperation as powerfully as *The Scream* by Edvard Munch, who is believed to have suffered from bipolar disorder.**

tinues to study the DNA of thousands of volunteers, searching for genetic clues as to the condition's origins.

It has been suggested that the same neurotransmitters associated with major depression are involved in triggering manic episodes, but researchers haven't yet been able to dissect the multi-layered consequences of these chemicals acting on their various brain pathways. The most effective treatments for bipolar disorder are **lithium-based salts**, also known as **mood stabilizers**. Chemically quite similar to sodium, pure lithium is a soft, shiny metal you could cut with a knife, but to stabilize moods it's combined with another chemical (most commonly carbonic acid) to form a soluble powder. Lithium's effect on mood was discovered by Australian psychiatrist John F. J. Cade (1912–80). But as with most drugs discovered by accident rather than through "rational drug design", lithium salts lack specificity, having multiple effects on the brain. Precisely how they influence mood is still being resolved, in part because of their very broad range of effects. One major effect of lithium is to block the action of a specific enzyme involved in signal transduction – a molecular relay-race in which one enzyme's product triggers another enzyme to become active. The cause of the intense mood extremes experienced in bipolar disorder is thought to be swings and imbalances in levels of neurotransmitters. When this crucial enzyme, inositol monophosphatase (IMPase), is blocked, its downstream cascade of activity is reduced, leading to a stabilizing in levels of neurotransmitters and, therefore, mood.

Brain-imaging techniques reveal telling patterns of activity in some bipolar cases. When depressed, the same patterns of activity are seen as in major depression, that is, decreased activity in the **left prefrontal cortex**. However, during a manic episode, it is the **right prefrontal cortex** (involved in higher functions, such as working memory and attention) that experiences a drop in activity, perhaps contributing to impaired planning and judgement. In addition, certain structural anomalies are seen in the **right temporal lobe**, involved in processing non-verbal memories and visuo-spatial information. Researchers are still getting to grips with what such findings mean, but "bipolar" seems like an appropriate name, after all.

**NIMH Bipolar Disorder Guide** www.nimh.nih.gov/publicat/bipolar.cfm

**The Bipolar Blues** www.youtube.com/watch?v=pAIJGX3RICA (in this short film, Professor Craddock of the BDRN discusses bipolar disorder and his ongoing work to unravel its genetic cause)

# Attention deficit hyperactivity disorder (ADHD)

ADHD has had a meteoric rise since 1980, when the term **attention deficit disorder** was first introduced. It is now one of the most common mental disorders diagnosed in children, with between three and seven percent of children being diagnosed with the condition. There is an unresolved controversy surrounding this situation, even suggestions of conspiracy. Are we now able to recognize and treat the disorder in an increasing number of children, or is over-prescription of ADHD treatment a convenient and profitable way to take the boisterousness out of boys?

Affecting around three times as many boys as girls, often under eight years old, ADHD can be a nightmare for parents, teachers and the children themselves. Constantly agitated, unable to concentrate and bad-tempered, the child will disrupt a classroom, acting totally "out of control", ignoring the lesson, pestering other children, and generally being an all-round pain in the neck. The child inevitably becomes a source of profound irritation to his classmates, leaving him with few friends. And of course home life is put under serious strain too.

The observation that ADHD often runs in families has caused a flurry of scientists to search for the underlying genetic cause of the disorder. In 2010, Professor Anita Thapar and Dr Nigel Williams at Cardiff University's School of Medicine discovered the first direct genetic evidence of alterations within the DNA of a proportion of children with ADHD. It's still early days but the hope is that such findings will help pave the way for both greater understanding of such neurological conditions and, in turn, potential treatments. As with most mental disorders, there is no single genetic factor responsible for the condition; instead, it is the result of a number of different genetic changes occurring in the same individual. Of the genes associated with ADHD, a number are involved in making proteins responsible for **dopamine** "reuptake". Neurons are tidy, functioning best in the absence of mess. When a neuron releases dopamine into the gap between it and another neuron, the **synapse**, it rapidly vacuums up any dopamine left nearby. By doing this, it keeps its signal clean and precise, allowing dopamine to reach the target neuron on the other side of the synapse, but not to slosh around and affect other neurons. In ADHD, these dopamine transporter proteins may be abnormal, either in function or in quantity, leaving the brain with less dopamine than it needs to work correctly.

Attention, directing the brain's sensory and cognitive apparatus, requires conscious effort, a function reserved for the **frontal lobes**. Normally, dopamine, amongst other functions, is involved in modulating the flow of information to the frontal lobes from other parts of the brain. If dopamine levels become impoverished, this can have a direct impact on higher functions, such as problem-solving and attention.

The rising star of ADHD treatment is methylphenidate, better known by its trade name, **Ritalin**. Originally prescribed as an adult antidepressant, Ritalin is a stimulant from the amphetamine family of drugs (see p.196). But, paradoxically, this stimulant has proved highly effective in combating the behavioural problems found in ADHD. It seems to work by blocking the errant dopamine transporters, and so preventing the reuptake of dopamine back into the releasing neuron, leaving more dopamine to do its thing on surrounding neurons.

As for the brain's overall structure and functioning in ADHD cases, there is a growing body of evidence from brain-imaging experiments revealing increased activity in regions such as the frontal lobe and basal ganglia. These regions, specifically the **prefrontal cortex** and two parts of the striatum associated with it – the **caudate nucleus** and **anterior putamen** – are involved in voluntary movement and motor learning respectively. It has been suggested that this increase in activity reflects increased effort on the part of the brain, as if it is working harder to control attention and the desire to move. Size could also be significant: studies have suggested that in ADHD certain regions of the brain tend to be smaller than normal. These regions include the prefrontal cortex and basal ganglia, as well as the corpus callosum and cerebellum, a structure which plays a central role in movement.

**NIMH ADHD Guide** www.nimh.nih.gov/publicat/adhd.cfm

**First evidence of genetic changes linked to ADHD** www.youtube.com/watch?v=3NlaekvCZ48 (In this short video, Anita Thapar and Nigel Williams explain their genetic findings and their relevance to ADHD and other mental disorders)

## Schizophrenia

What if, one day, you were able to see associations between words, people and thoughts that no one else could? If, suddenly, you believed people were transmitting thoughts directly into your brain, telling you how to behave? In schizophrenia, the brain can lose the ability to tell what is real from what is not; its interpretation of the outside world becomes unreliable, a condition known as **psychosis**. One of the most stigmatized mental disorders, schizophrenia usually hits a person in their prime, during the late teens or early twenties. The affected person may have periods of normal perception, but episodes of psychosis – which can last for months – will start to intrude. During these times, they can experience "positive" symptoms, such as **delusions** – powerful, persistent ideas that are either highly unlikely or downright impossible – or "negative" ones, such as **apathy** or a general lack of emotions.

Psychiatrist Thomas Szasz said: "If you talk to God, you are praying. If God talks to you, you have schizophrenia." Therein lies one of the most disconcerting aspects of schizophrenia. We all do or believe things that others might consider odd. Some might say praying is delusional, considering the notion of speaking to a god sheer fantasy. However, millions do it, and we accept it as normal. The difference is that in schizophrenia the delusions are harmful to the person experiencing them. They're also much more powerful and extreme, and are not, like praying, considered normal for the culture in which the person lives. Someone with schizo-

## Stress and mental illness

Much research into mental illness focuses on searching for an underlying genetic factor responsible for the disease. However, it is clear that genetics does not hold all the answers. There is still a great deal of uncertainty about the causes of mental illness, but many in the field believe it to be the result of a combination of genetic and environmental factors.

The environmental factor might be an infection such as a virus (influenza has been tentatively associated with schizophrenia), but it could also be a major life event or traumatic experience. Such experiences can be **contributory causes** to the development of a mental illness: alone, they would be unable to directly cause mental illness but, combined with a genetic predisposition, they can help tip a person over the edge.

Stress is associated with a number of mental illnesses. In cases of **schizophrenia**, psychiatrists have noted that, in the months prior to the illness becoming apparent, patients have frequently experienced a steep rise in stress levels. **Post-traumatic stress disorder** is an extreme case in which those exposed to terrifying, often life-threatening, experiences can suffer for months or years after the event. But not everyone exposed to such events will experience the nightmares, depression and flashbacks of the disorder. Exposure to experiences such as plane crashes, rape, torture, violence or war are common triggers for PTSD. But it seems to be the underlying personality that determines precisely how someone will react. During war, around thirty percent of civilians from the war zone will experience PTSD, clearly implying PTSD is not an inevitable outcome, as seventy percent don't develop it.

phrenia might truly believe (and see, and smell and feel) that they are melting from within, that their thoughts are being transmitted into space (in which case they may try to stop thinking completely), that the government is controlling their every action (resulting in fear and paranoia), or that casual glances from passers-by contain telepathic signals (that they hear as voices inside their mind).

In addition to these delusions, a person with schizophrenia may be subject to powerful **auditory and visual hallucinations**. They may hear voices barking instructions (possibly to harm themselves), or see the faces of people they love twist into savage grimaces, full of malice. And because people with schizophrenia can become disorganized in their behaviour and appearance (poor hygiene or shouting in public, for example), they can cause others to be fearful of them.

Schizophrenia affects about one percent of the population. There's pretty strong evidence that, at the very least, the risk of developing

**Identical twins David (left) and Steven (right) Elmore in front of brain scans revealing that Steven, who has schizophrenia, has slightly larger ventricles (the dark areas) than his brother.**

schizophrenia is heritable, but no single culprit gene has been identified. As with many complex disorders, several genes, combined with environmental and social factors, are likely to be responsible. Brain imaging has found some brains of those with schizophrenia to have less activity in the **frontal lobe**, or larger **ventricles** – fluid-filled "spaces" within the brain – suggestive of a loss of grey matter. But there does not seem to be a single, primary cause for the symptoms we see. Given the disorganization and confused associations experienced, some scientists believe that the very wiring of the brain itself is wrong – that somewhere in the brain's development, neurons lost the ability to make sense of perceptions.

In adolescence, the brain goes through a process known as **pruning**. As in gardening, this is a form of tidying up, removing redundant associations between neurons throughout the cortex. In schizophrenia, it is possible that the brain experiences overzealous pruning during this time, destroying useful associations that the brain had made. There are several ideas as to why this might occur.

One curious association is between schizophrenia and **the seasons**: children born in winter or early spring are more likely to develop schizophrenia. And it has been tentatively suggested that **influenza** (or some other type of infection) experienced by the mother – especially in her second trimester – may trigger this neurological time bomb, possibly by affecting the developing immune system or by altering the behaviour of genes involved in foetal brain development. It could be that such an infection in a person who is genetically susceptible might combine with environmental and emotional factors to trigger the disorder.

**SANE Schizophrenia Guide** www.sane.org.uk/uploads/schizophrenia.pdf

# Generalized anxiety disorder (GAD)

Worrying is not a uniquely modern phenomenon, but as societies have expanded, so have the number of stressful situations we encounter in our everyday lives. Dealing with colleagues, family, health and finances frequently results in feelings of worry and stress. But most of us are able to look at the source of the worry, analyse the cause, and find a rational approach to eliminating it. For those diagnosed with generalized anxiety disorder, it's a different story. Whether awake or asleep, the mind worries incessantly, focusing obsessively on possible future threats, and ruminating over past decisions and possible negative consequences arising from them. The sufferer is unable to control this worry, and it is completely out of proportion to any perceived source of concern: your son will break his neck at the fairground, you can't go to dinner because the bedroom is a mess, you're a day late paying the electricity bill and are terrified of being cut off... It simply never stops. The result of this constant internal onslaught is disturbed sleep, poor concentration and irritability – all of which feeds into more worry.

A significant part of the problem is the "free-floating" nature of the worry. The mind jumps from one perceived problem to the next, spending just enough time on it to maintain feelings of anxiety but never long enough to let the brain deal with the source of anxiety in a rational manner. The sufferer will invent reasons why it's beneficial to worry – for example, by worrying about this, it stops me thinking about other things that make me feel worse.

As we saw in Chapter 6, consciousness, emotions and reasoning are strongly interlinked. One theory which attempts to account for the symptoms of GAD is that the various structures in the brain responsible for emotions and our response to them (including the **amygdala** and

**hypothalamus**) may suffer from a lack of the neurotransmitter **GABA** (gamma-aminobutyrate). GABA's primary function is to calm nerves down, decreasing the chance of them firing impulses, and so slow the brain.

The pharmaceutical industry has developed drugs such as the **benzodiazepines** Valium and Xanax (see p.201), chemicals that try to replicate the effect of GABA. But we shouldn't be too quick to leap into the hands of the drug industry – drugs such as these can reduce the sensation of anxiety but do nothing to remove the underlying reasons behind it. Like many mental illnesses, GAD is a complex and poorly understood condition, a disorder of perception and reasoning that may benefit more from talking therapies. **Cognitive behavioural therapy** (see box on p.162) is rapidly gaining in popularity as a treatment for GAD, as it becomes increasingly recognized as one of the most effective ways of treating anxiety disorders such as this. It doesn't provide overnight success, but over time it can help sufferers develop a more objective and constructive and less stressful way of seeing the world.

**Anxiety Disorders Association of America** www.adaa.org

# Phobias

As we saw on p.102, our fear response is a natural and vital function, prompting us to avoid danger. The problem with someone who suffers from a phobia is that the focus of their phobia, often something quite harmless, creates a dominating and disproportionately large fear response.

It may seem easy to mock someone's terror of spiders or flying, but such phobias, known as **specific phobias**, are very common, possibly affecting as many as one in ten people. The terror associated with being exposed to the phobic focus can be debilitating – for example, someone who has a phobia of enclosed spaces (claustrophobia) will avoid lifts, air travel or trains, placing limitations on both their work and everyday life. Their entire life can be taken over by the need to avoid the trigger.

What causes someone to experience such an excessive fear response to a particular trigger? It appears that we are not born with our fear responses set in stone; instead we learn to fear by observing those around us. Monkeys raised in captivity show no fear in the presence of a snake. However, if these monkeys observe a wild monkey's fear response to a snake for just a few minutes, the next time they see a snake they react with the traditional fight or flight response. The incredible thing is that the wild monkey doesn't even need to be in the same room: even watching it on a video monitor is enough to trigger the fear response in the lab monkeys.

This makes good evolutionary sense. Clearly, it's better to learn fear by observation of one's peers than by actually being bitten (and possibly killed) by a snake. It should come as little surprise that humans also show this sort of learned fear response. A study conducted by New York University professor of psychology Elizabeth Phelps and graduate student Andreas Olsson took a closer look at this phenomenon, using three groups of volunteers. The first group received a mild shock paired with the image of a face. The second group watched the emotional expression of another person receiving a mild shock paired with the face. The third group was told an image of a face was anticipating a mild shock. Despite only the first group receiving a shock, every group experienced physiological changes consistent with fear, demonstrating that merely witnessing a traumatic event, or anticipating such an event, can produce a similar fear response to directly experiencing it. The implications for the media we expose ourselves to every day are profound.

These studies suggest that a person who suffers from a phobia might at some point in their life – perhaps during childhood – have experienced or witnessed a traumatic event involving the feared object which has triggered their disproportionate fear response. It is not yet fully understood why some will brush off such an experience and forget it, while for others it will be the trigger for an intense conditioned fear response, or phobia.

Treatment for phobias is fairly straightforward, with one of the most successful treatments being **behaviour therapy**. In this system, the client is gently and gradually exposed to stimuli related to their phobia. For example, if the fear is of beautiful women (venustraphobia), one might begin by talking about certain beautiful women, then move on to looking at pictures of beautiful women, and ultimately talk face to face with a beautiful woman.

**Phobics Awareness** www.phobics-awareness.org

# Obsessive–compulsive disorder (OCD)

In any hundred people, the probability is that two or three will have obsessive–compulsive disorder (OCD), but it's unlikely you'll ever know who they are. OCD is one of the crueller anxiety-based disorders; in many disorders, the person can be oblivious to the irrationality of their fear and/or behaviour, but in OCD, the person (often of above-average intelligence) is fully aware of how irrational their beliefs and patterns of behaviour are. They simply feel powerless to resist their lure.

It is perfectly natural to experience moments of self-doubt, checking several times to make sure the windows are closed before leaving the house, for example. But the obsessions in OCD are highly intrusive and persistent. Some are more understandable than others. A person might fear contamination or dirt, dread confessing to nonexistent crimes, or be obsessed with symmetry and order. These thoughts penetrate everyday existence, causing tension and anxiety to mount. To diffuse this anxiety, the person experiences a powerful compulsion to perform some kind of ritualistic behaviour. This ritual, usually related in some way to the obsession, causes the tension to decrease. So, obsession with contamination can lead to excessive hand-washing (sometimes to the point of bleeding), and a fear of confession might lead to a constant checking to make sure they haven't left any written confessions lying around the house. This behaviour can, infuriatingly, occupy more than an hour of a person's day – time which they are well aware has been wasted.

As with many complex mental conditions, there is scant evidence of any major structural changes in the brain of OCD sufferers, but looking at brain activity in those with OCD does seem to reveal differences. Activity in regions such as the frontal cortex, involved in reasoning, and the limbic system, involved in emotional responses, can be altered in a way that allows emotions to "outrank" reason (see p.98).

The mild heritability of OCD has allowed scientists to track down a mutation in a specific gene, hSERT, or human serotonin transporter gene. This gene contains the information to make a protein responsible for removing the "emotional" neurotransmitter **serotonin** from synapses. The overall effect of this mutation seems to be reduced availability of serotonin in the brain. This discovery sits well with the knowledge that drugs affecting serotonin levels (SSRIs; see p.204) show some limited success in cases of OCD. The problem is, once the person stops taking the drugs, the rate of relapse is high.

The best way to treat OCD in the long term is not with drugs but a form of cognitive behavioural therapy called **exposure and ritual prevention**. The patient is exposed to increasing amounts of the thing or situation they fear but prevented from acting out the associated ritual. Given time, their brain eventually recognizes that the anxiety created by the obsession passes of its own accord, and the ritual's importance dwindles. This form of therapy is successful in more than half the people treated.

**OCD-UK** www.ocduk.org

## Anorexia nervosa

**Anorexia nervosa** is one of the most difficult mental disorders to treat. It is also the most deadly. In Western society, roughly one young woman in a hundred will enter into a routine of voluntary starvation and excessive activity. And of those who do, as many as twenty percent may perish. Without nutrition, the sufferer's bones weaken, her heart begins to struggle, and her brain's ability to reason and support its vast array of functions diminishes.

For a person with anorexia, there's no such thing as the perfect weight; all talk of body mass index is wasted. She (more than ninety percent of cases are female) believes she is fat and is terrified of gaining weight. This belief comes to dominate her entire existence, and she will frequently display obsessive-compulsive symptoms, with her life revolving around controlling both her food intake and her body's treatment of that food (by taking laxatives, for example).

One of the central problems in anorexia is the discordance between actual and perceived body image. The sufferer's higher thinking has become so distorted that she can no longer see "the truth" in the mirror – that she's wasting away. The eyes see, the hands feel, but the brain misinterprets these perceptions, telling her she is fat.

Research led by Dr Henrik Ehrsson and colleagues at University College London has suggested one possible explanation for this distorted body image. Somewhere within each of our brains, every ounce of flesh, and its location within space, is being monitored in order to create an internal representation of our body. In Ehrsson's experiments, test subjects had their brains scanned whilst experiencing the "Pinocchio illusion". By applying vibrations to the skin above the wrist joints, nerves within the underlying tendon become excited, sending signals back to the sensory and motor cortices. These signals create the vivid sensation that the joint is in motion and, if the hands are resting on the waist, fool the brain into feeling that the waist is shrinking beneath their touch. The seventeen volunteers, eyes closed, all felt this peculiar sensation of a shrinking waistline and brain scans revealed parts of the **parietal lobe** to be the brain regions saying "Huh?" The stronger the experience, the more brain activity there was, as if the brain were rapidly attempting to "recalibrate" its body image. This research suggests a possible link between an over- or underactive parietal cortex and conditions affecting body image, such as anorexia nervosa.

Anorexia sufferers are often fairly reserved and quiet, with a love of routine and a strong perfectionist streak. Their family may also show certain patterns, perhaps being preoccupied with appearance and rules, but poor at managing conflicts and tension. Add an emotional trauma to the mix and all the ingredients are there. The final key to understanding anorexia may lie in the neurotransmitter **serotonin** – involved in affecting our moods, appetite and levels of anxiety. Research is slowly revealing a possible connection between serotonin, its various receptor proteins, and altered activity within different lobes of the brain – frontal, temporal, parietal and cingulate gyrus.

Treating such distortions of perception is very difficult and time-consuming, not least because the anorexic sees nothing wrong with herself, frequently viewing her disorder as nothing more than a "lifestyle choice". The findings surrounding serotonin should eventually lead to effective drug treatments, but currently the best route forward involves a combination of psychotherapy and cognitive behavioural therapy. These therapies attempt to help the sufferer understand why her thinking is so deeply flawed and, perhaps, understand the forces triggering the disorder in the first place.

**National Centre for Eating Disorders** www.eating-disorders.org.uk

**NEDA** www.edap.org

# Bulimia nervosa

It is well known that Elvis Presley experienced periods of uncontrolled **binge eating**. One estimate places his daily calorific intake during a binge at one hundred thousand – enough to feed a normal appetite for a whole month. Consuming abnormally large quantities of food in a single sitting, until food can no longer be squeezed into the stomach, is one of the defining characteristics of someone with **bulimia nervosa**. This binging goes way beyond the need to satisfy basic hunger; it's an irresistible urge accompanied by an overwhelming sense of being out of control.

Sharing many of the characteristics of anorexia nervosa, a person with bulimia is terrified of gaining weight. To prevent this happening, they may take one of several routes: fasting, excessive exercise, or drugs (metabolic boosters and laxatives), perhaps accompanied by vomiting (**purging**). Not all people with bulimia vomit, but those who do are usually more psychologically disturbed and face the additional concerns of dietary deficiencies and tooth erosion from stomach acid repeatedly, unnaturally, spending time in their mouth. Regardless of whether they vomit, a bulimia sufferer is in danger of sustaining serious damage in the form of stomach ulcers or even splitting their stomach open.

One major difference between someone with anorexia and someone with bulimia is the way they feel about their condition. Those with anorexia are frequently oblivious to the harm they're doing to themselves, while a person with bulimia is often consumed with feelings of guilt and shame, spending an inordinate amount of time obsessing over the growing impulse to start another binge, waiting for the near inevitable loss of control.

Bulimia shares many of the same neurological features as anorexia, in particular the brain's altered relationship with **serotonin**. But with reliable pharmacological treatments still in the future, the most successful treatment for bulimia is currently **cognitive behavioural therapy**. A sufferer will be helped to recognize, and then defeat, their "all or nothing" mentality with respect to food. At the same time, a behaviour-modifying system, perhaps involving an "eating diary", will focus on getting their eating pattern back to normal – smaller amounts in more frequent instalments.

**National Centre for Eating Disorders** www.eating-disorders.org.uk

**NEDA** www.edap.org

# Autism

Autism is a disorder caused by abnormalities in the way the brain develops and functions. Those affected show symptoms involving **socialization** (how they interact with others), **communication** and **behaviour**. But autism isn't really a single, "pigeon-holeable" disorder – in fact, there are some who argue against it even being classified as a mental disorder. There is much variation in the patterns of symptoms found in an autistic child (signs are usually evident before three years of age), making it one of the most difficult conditions to understand and, if desired, treat.

Parents can find raising an autistic child highly emotionally challenging, principally because the child is unresponsive to their presence. An autistic child won't seek comfort, make eye contact or play. Almost "doll-like", they can appear oblivious to their surroundings, as if no sensory information is getting into their brain. But it seems that the external senses are working perfectly well; it is the way that this information is processed in the child's brain that is altered, creating an entirely different perception of the world. This can result in the child responding unpredictably to different stimuli – perhaps seeming oblivious to raised voices but being oversensitive to touch. They may also enter periods of "self-stimulation" – rocking, spinning, or even engaging in some sort of self-harming activity for up to an hour at a time.

The child's perception of those around them is also altered. One great human quality is the ability to empathize, to recognize the mind of another human being and understand their needs and feelings. In autism, this ability is severely restricted, apparently leaving the child strangely lacking the need for companionship. As a result, it is likely their speech and social development will suffer or manifest itself in a different way. Rather than "playing", using imagination to manipulate objects and create scenarios, they will tend to become fixated on specific objects (keys, for example) and routines (mealtimes, baths, going to school), and can become desperately upset if these aspects of their environment change. And rather than talk, they may express themselves in different ways, perhaps using symbols or repeating over and over an expression or word they have heard (known as **echolalia**).

Due to the very heterogeneous nature of autism, affecting a range of brain systems, little is known about its causes, but the thinking is that the disorder may have a complex genetic root – that is, several genes working together to trigger the changes in the brain's development and function. Curiously, in a study of a group of autistic children aged twelve years or over, around half were found to have larger brain volumes than their non-autistic counterparts, possibly suggesting some of the genes involved may relate to brain growth. And once again, **serotonin** is implicated in the condition, with higher than normal levels occurring in around a third of cases.

How do you "treat" what seems to amount to an altered state of consciousness? In a condition as complex and so poorly understood as this, treatments focus on forms of behaviour therapy, rather than drugs. These therapies attempt to encourage and support the development of more conventional speech and interactions with others, allowing the autistic child to reach back out to those who care for him.

**NIMH Autism Guide** www.nimh.nih.gov/publicat/autism.cfm

**The National Autistic Society** www.autism.org.uk

# Personality disorders

Increasingly, news reports are referring to people as having some kind of "personality disorder". This heightened media awareness is, in part, due to the increasing realization that many people have this type of mental illness. In 2004, a large study published in the *Journal of Clinical Psychiatry* revealed just how pervasive personality disorders are, arriving at the astonishing figure of just under fifteen percent of the American adult population – more than forty million people.

There are a number of different types of personality disorder. What they have in common are long-lasting, rigid patterns of thought and behaviour that deviate markedly from the expectations of the culture in which the person lives. Someone with **paranoid personality disorder**, for example, will consistently distrust the people around them, even in the absence of any evidence on which to base their suspicions. A person with **borderline personality disorder** (so termed because historically a person with this disorder was thought to be on the "borderline" between psychosis and neurosis; the term does not imply that the person has only a "touch" of disorder) may be prone to extreme mood fluctuations and a persistent confusion regarding their sense of identity and self-worth. These persistent, consuming patterns of thinking can be highly disruptive both to those with the disorder and to those who come into contact with them.

A psychiatrist might describe personality as the sum of a person's ways of interacting with the world: their traits, coping styles, thoughts and emotions. For someone with one of these disorders, their personality development has taken a wrong turn. At an early point in their growth, what should have been a healthy, rounded take on life has become maladaptive and inflexible, leaving them with a persistent, skewed way of perceiving and relating to society. As adults, these people can often "get by", but are not wholesome, fully formed members of society. Most likely, we deal with people who fit into one of the categories of personality disorder on a fairly frequent basis. Depending on the severity and type of their disorder, they may appear a little odd or eccentric, emotional or erratic, or plain unethical or aggressive.

The profound complexity of precisely how a brain "builds a personality" makes this type of mental illness a sort of final frontier. Only when we fully understand how the brain's many components develop and unite to function as a whole can we approach a satisfying biological explanation for these varied disorders.

## Psychopathology and serial killers

A disturbingly normal-looking Ted Bundy (centre) confers with his defence attorneys on the opening day of his trial in Miami, Florida, June 1979.

The terms psychopath and serial killer are often used interchangeably in the media, but while a serial killer is frequently a psychopath, a psychopath is rarely a serial killer. While many psychopaths live out a fairly rudimentary, antisocial existence with sporadic outbursts of violence, serial killers are driven by powerful, murderous fantasy lives they feel compelled to act out. Their intelligence, manipulative abilities and absence of appropriate emotional responses to their actions, namely guilt and remorse, make them modern-day bogeymen.

Theodore Robert "Ted" Bundy was a powerful example of such a person. Charming, intelligent and handsome, this brutal psychopath eventually confessed to killing nearly thirty women during a four-year period between 1974 and 1978, although it's believed he killed more. The abductions and murders were often meticulously planned and executed. Exemplifying the manipulative aspect of psychopathic behaviour, Bundy thought nothing of impersonating a police officer to project an image of authority or feigning some form of injury to attract help from women nearby. Even when in the hands of the US judicial system, he was able to escape several times – once by climbing through a window in a Colorado courthouse library in 1977. While on the run, Bundy continued to kill and, once caught, conducted his own legal defence with alarming clarity in a Miami court. Still, the case against him was strong enough to convict and he was eventually executed in 1989.

There is much to learn from the minds of people like Bundy; the more society is able to understand the machinations of such dysfunctional brains, the more able we are to predict and defend ourselves against them.

One extreme example of a personality disorder which made the national papers in the UK in 2005 was that of the teenager Brian Blackwell, who murdered his parents before using their credit card for an extended holiday and spending spree. Once caught, Brian was diagnosed as having **narcissistic personality disorder** (after the Greek hero Narcissus, who became besotted with his own reflection). From a distance, people with this disorder may simply seem to have an inflated sense of their own importance, but their delusional self-belief permeates far deeper. They may fantasize about obtaining unlimited wealth, power and success. Their self-belief may manifest itself in constant bragging and allusions to their undeniable importance and extraordinary abilities. And, while requiring their admiration, they perceive those around them as being fairly dumb and insignificant. As with other personality disorders, treatment is an extremely difficult process. Assuming the person comes to the attention of mental-health professionals (and many don't), there is no clear way of treating someone's core beliefs, even if they are dysfunctional. As a narcissist, they would believe themselves to be perfect, not in need of treatment, and most likely the intellectual superior of the psychiatrist attempting to get them to readjust their thinking.

Another personality disorder currently attracting media attention is **psychopathic personality disorder**. People with this disorder are unable to empathize with other people, and show a complete disregard for the rules of society. They will lie and manipulate in order to get what they want, and often have a history of impulsive and aggressive behaviour. It is not that these people do not know right from wrong. A psychopath could probably provide a good definition of morals – but, to him (the vast majority are male), they're merely words with no deeper meaning.

Often charming and intelligent, psychopaths may be able to fit into modern society quite well, occupying positions of power and manipulation ranging from con men and drug pushers to politicians and businessmen. However, most people eventually see through the charming façade of the psychopath. Psychopathic individuals tend to be poor at holding down jobs and long-term relationships, moving from one situation to the next, indifferent to the emotional damage they can inflict on the unwary. It's a one-way street, though, because they do not experience emotions in the way most of us do, and are unable to love.

Oddly, for reasons poorly understood, many psychopathic personalities seem to partly peter out once the person hits forty years old. This is fortunate because treating this disorder, assuming it ever comes to light, is problematic to say the least. The best time to start is during childhood, when personality is still developing, and telltale signs of potential future problems such as persistent antisocial behaviour in and out of the classroom can be addressed.

**National Personality Disorder Website** personalitydisorder.org.uk

# Fade to grey: the ageing brain

A person born in the United States in 1900 could expect to live to around fifty years of age. That figure has now risen to around seventy-eight years – a more than fifty percent increase in life expectancy in a single century. And Professor Tom Kirkwood, Director of the Institute for Ageing and Health, Newcastle University, tells us that the human lifespan is continuing to increase at the astonishing rate of two hours per day. This is good news, of course. However, there is one significant problem: we have proved better at extending our lifespan than at curing the diseases that

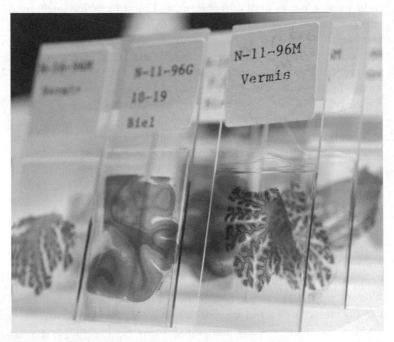

Brain tissue from a long-term ageing study at the University of Kentucky, which is throwing light on diseases such as Alzheimer's.

come with increasing age, with the result that for many, those extra years will be years of increasing ill health.

With advancing age, the body gets to a point where it has simply run its course. We can exercise body and mind as sensible preventative measures, but inevitably time wins. Two of the principal brain disorders destined to become far more prevalent as our lifespan increases are **Parkinson's** (PD) and **Alzheimer's disease** (AD). It's not without reason people talk of a looming "global epidemic" of Alzheimer's disease. In 2011, estimates suggested nearly half a million people in the UK and almost 5.5 million people in the US had the disease. While globally, given current trends, a publication from Johns Hopkins University predicts that, by 2050, one person in eighty-five will succumb (around a fourfold increase). If current estimates surrounding the global human population are accurate, this suggests that by 2050, more than a hundred million humans could have this form of dementia. See pp.111–12, for how brain scans are being used to predict susceptibility to AD.

The sociological and economic burden of these and other diseases is going to present a hugely significant problem, one that will be exacerbated by the fact that the increase in our longevity has been accompanied by a decrease in birth rates, so that there are fewer and fewer young people around to care for the elderly. A census held in the UK in 2001 revealed that, for the first time, sixty-year-olds outnumbered sixteen-year-olds. This trend heightens the urgency to find treatments which will cure or at least relieve the symptoms of these diseases. Fortunately, some progress has already been made, and further breakthroughs may not be far off.

# Parkinson's disease (PD)

Parkinson's disease is characterized by a slowness or absence of voluntary movement, an expressionless or "masked" face, repetitive tremors, general muscle stiffness and affected balance. These symptoms were first described by the British physician James Parkinson (1755–1824) in his "Essay on the Shaking Palsy" in 1817. One of the most common disorders of movement, Parkinson's disease affects roughly two percent of the population.

The history of our understanding of Parkinson's disease is intimately connected with drug abuse. In 1973 a 23-year-old chemistry graduate in Maryland, Barry Kidston, developed serious PD symptoms several days after trying a new batch of his homemade drug, the opioid **MPPP** (1-methyl 4-phenyl 4-propionoxypiperidine). Several years later, in

1982, more surprisingly young severe Parkinson's patients turned up in California, where they came under the gaze of neurologist J. William Langston. They had also been experimenting with homemade drugs, attempting to make synthetic heroin (China White). Langston realized that in both cases the chemical **MPTP** (1-methyl 4-phenyl 1,2,3,6-tetrahydropyridine) had been accidentally made instead of the intended drug. He identified MPTP exposure as the cause of their Parkinson's symptoms, and the modern study of PD began, with experiments in rodents and primates soon confirming MPTP as the cause.

By studying the reaction of animals to the drug, scientists were able to determine that once inside specific neurons, MPTP was modified to a closely related chemical that was highly destructive in a part of the basal ganglia called the **substantia nigra** (literally "black substance", referring to its dark pigmentation). By the time a person develops symptoms of PD (usually in their late fifties), around eighty percent of the neurons in the substantia nigra will have already died.

As the neurons in the substantia nigra normally produce the neurotransmitter **dopamine**, this means that other parts of the basal ganglia, such as the striatum, the brain structure that helps us plan and refine the body's movements, don't receive their usual supply of dopamine. This has a dual effect, stimulating a brain pathway involved in stopping movement and simultaneously deactivating a pathway that usually stimulates movement – the net result being that it's much harder to initiate and control the body's motion. The dopamine-producing neurons seem to die because, for reasons unknown, they form abnormal clumps of protein, called **Lewy bodies** after their discovery in 1912 by neurologist Frederic Lewy (1885–1950). Lewy bodies are composed of several different proteins, including alpha-synuclein – the gene for which is associated with one of the rare, inherited forms of PD (5 percent of cases). Over time, these Lewy bodies may interfere with normal neuron functioning or even trigger a form of controlled cell suicide.

Currently, the most common mutation associated with Parkinson's – both familial and sporadic – belongs to a protein known as **LRRK2** (leucine-rich repeat kinase 2, pronounced "lark 2"). The mutation causes the protein to become overactive and this hyperactivity leads, in turn, to the creation of the protein clumps that ultimately kill the dopaminergic neurons. What's so exciting about discoveries of this nature is that scientists now have a very specific target to home in on – if they can find a way to quench LRRK2's overzealous activity, the implication is that the very cause of cell death could be slowed or stopped. In 2010, a research paper in *Nature Medicine* demonstrated just such a process when scientists, led by Valina L. Dawson and Ted M. Dawson (Johns Hopkins University School of Medicine), used LRRK2 inhibitors to enhance neuron survival in a rat model of Parkinson's disease.

Early treatments of PD revolved around the use of drugs such as L-dopa. Dopamine itself cannot cross the highly selective blood–brain barrier (see p.188), but L-dopa can, and once it is inside, the brain automatically converts it into dopamine. Unfortunately, there can be unpleasant side effects, such as hallucinations or nausea and, while effective in the short term, this treatment doesn't prevent further neurons in the substantia nigra from dying. Rather than introducing new dopamine into the brain, a range of drugs have been developed to increase the levels of existing dopamine, such as the dopamine agonists and monoamine oxidase inhibitors (MAO-B inhibitors). Dopamine agonists act by binding to, and stimulating, dopamine's target receptors – in essence they're molecular mimics, fooling the receptor into "believing" dopamine has bound to it. MAO-B inhibitors boost dopamine via an altogether different route. Under normal circumstances, dopamine would be degraded and removed by an enzyme, monoamine oxidase B; by blocking this natural clear-up mechanism, the dopamine produced within the brain is afforded more time to act on receptors in its environment.

Deep-brain stimulation is a surgical treatment which is proving successful in patients with extreme tremors. A fine electrode is usually implanted into the patient's **thalamus**, the brain region responsible for processing all sorts of sensory input, including movement. A wire travels from the electrode to a battery-powered implant under the skin. A calibration is then performed by the physician, who makes the implant send a specific frequency of electrical impulses into the thalamus. This "neural pacemaker" interferes with the faulty nerve signals causing the Parkinsonian tremors, leading to their cessation.

In the future it is hoped that treatment for PD may include the use of **genetic therapies**, in which specific therapeutic genes are introduced into the brain by a number of possible routes. This may be by way of specially engineered viruses carrying therapeutic genes, designed to be implanted into the brain and persist without harm to the recipient. Some of these genes may provide extra dopamine whilst others may concentrate on trying to keep the remaining dopamine-producing neurons of the substantia nigra alive. Alternatively, **stem cells** (cells capable of developing into any other cell type, given the correct environment) might one day be surgically implanted into the brains of PD patients, and then triggered to develop into dopamine-producing neurons. Research into this area has produced encouraging preliminary results using a rat model of Parkinson's disease.

**Parkinson's Disease Society** www.parkinsons.org.uk

## Alzheimer's disease

In Frankfurt in 1901 a 51-year-old woman called Auguste D. was admitted to the state asylum suffering from a range of problems including delusions, paranoia and memory deficits. She came to the attention of neuropsychiatrist Alois Alzheimer, who studied her while alive and, after her death, dissected and examined her brain, revealing the now characteristic pathology of the disease that bears his name.

When the brain wears out quicker than might be expected from normal ageing, we call it **senile dementia** (from Latin, *senex*, old, and *demens*, senseless). Of the diseases that cause senile dementia, Alzheimer's is the most common. Roughly three percent of those over sixty-five years old and as many as forty percent of those over eighty will succumb to the disease.

The progression of Alzheimer's is slow, insidious and remorseless. Barely noticeably at first, a sufferer's behaviour may start to change; they may become less alert, more withdrawn, more child-like and forgetful. These changes are easily put down to the normal ravages of time. However, as the disease progresses, memory for recent events becomes much worse and the sufferer becomes increasingly agitated and confused, wandering without aim and talking in "empty" sentences. Curiously, certain personality traits from the sufferer's earlier life can become amplified as the disease progresses: someone who was sensitive before the disease took hold could become paranoid and suspicious. Eventually, the sufferer will enter a vegetative state and die an average of ten years after the onset of the disease.

It is really only after death that a diagnosis of Alzheimer's can be positively made, by direct examination of the post-mortem brain. The brain of someone with the disease has very characteristic signs of damage in numerous regions, with little left untouched. The hippocampus, cortex and amygdala are just some of the major brain regions that degenerate, taking with them memory, higher functioning and the emotions. Under the microscope, the brain is seen to possess strange, unwelcome structures. **Senile plaques** are dense clumps, formed from a protein called beta-amyloid, that accumulate between neurons. **Tangles** and **filaments** form inside the neuron's cell body, predominantly from a structural protein called tau. The axon of a neuron is like a motorway with protein

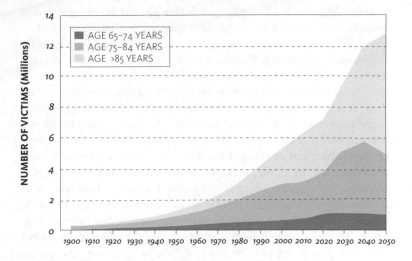

The rise of Alzheimer's disease observed over the twentieth century is predicted to accelerate during the first half of the twenty-first.

traffic moving back and forth between the synapse at one end and the cell body at the other. Normally, tau forms part of this motorway structure, but in Alzheimer's disease it just sits around, forms clumps and clogs up the cell, preventing other proteins from moving up and down the axon. Unable to function, the neuron eventually dies.

Existing drugs for the treatment of Alzheimer's disease currently target the diminished cognitive functioning of the brain, such as loss of memory, predominantly through modifying either the levels or activity of existing neurotransmitters. For example, **cholinesterase inhibitors** (such as donepezil, trade name Aricept) block the action of cholinesterase enzymes, leading to an increase of acetylcholine within the brain. By artificially enhancing levels of this chemical within the brain, nerve cell communication is boosted, slowing the degradation of such higher cognitive functions.

Slowing the progression and symptoms of Alzheimer's is a significant progress but the real challenge lies in developing treatments or drugs that can stop the nerve cells dying in the first place – to completely halt the march of the disease at a histological level. To do so, scientists are turning their attention to the molecular root causes of the disease: **beta-amyloid** and **tau**. If scientists can develop strategies to stop these proteins forming their respective plaques and tangles, it might be possible to prevent neuronal death.

Recent advances in stem cell research have also produced a glimmer of hope. In 2011, researchers in Chicago succeeded in using human embryonic stem cells to create the same neurons that are rapidly lost in the early stages of the disease (basal forebrain cholinergic neurons). Initially, it's hoped a steady supply of such cells will accelerate a new swathe of drug treatments but it's also been mooted that a time may arrive when these cells could be introduced into the brains of Alzheimer's sufferers to replenish their stocks of healthy neurons. To date, much of the genetic research into Alzheimer's disease has focused on the rare, familial form of the disease, and scientists have discovered several genes that seem to be involved, including presenilin-1, presenilin-2 and APP (amyloid precursor protein from which beta-amyloid is formed). However, by far the majority of Alzheimer's cases are sporadic, not inherited. Even for the sporadic form, however, scientists have discovered a clue as to whether one is likely to succumb to the disease in later life. **Apolipoprotein E** (APOE) is one of the proteins our body uses to transport fats, such as cholesterol, around the body. It comes in three different versions, which perform the same task but have tiny structural alterations. Which type you have depends on which version, or allele, of the APOE gene you have. Those in possession of APOE 2 or 3 seem to be in the clear, but those who possess one or two copies of APOE 4 have an increased risk of developing Alzheimer's disease. The benefit of such information is that as physicians' knowledge of the disease improves, those who know they're susceptible can take advantage of new, preventative treatments as they arrive.

**Alzheimer's Association** www.alz.org

# CHAPTER 9

# Chemical control

## How legal and illegal drugs affect the brain

We generally associate the word "drug" with substances such as heroin or cocaine. However, the technical definition of a drug is much broader than that. A drug is any natural or artificial substance that, when introduced into the body (whether orally, intravenously or topically through the skin), temporarily alters its normal functioning. This includes medicinal drugs, but also substances common in everyday life, such as alcohol, caffeine and the nicotine in cigarettes.

Until the second half of the twentieth century, drug use involved little more than alcohol, tobacco and opium. However, in recent times the rise of the pharmaceutical industry has led to a huge proliferation in the number of drugs available. In the 1950s, chemists churned out thousands of new chemical structures that were then tested for some kind of biological effect – a form of chemical lottery. Later, "rational drug design" allowed drugs to be designed and synthesized to specifically target a particular problem. The impact of this drugs revolution on the lives of those suffering from physical or mental illness has been phenomenal. However, our blossoming chemical knowledge has also led to a refinement of recreational drug taking, with whole new families of chemicals emerging whose sole purpose is to help the consumer experience an unnaturally altered state of mind.

In this chapter we will look at the main types of **psychoactive drugs** – that is, drugs that act primarily on the central nervous system and brain, temporarily altering perception, consciousness and behaviour. This includes both medicinal drugs and recreational drugs. But first we need to understand a little more about how drugs get into the brain, and what they do once they get there.

## The blood–brain barrier

Irrespective of a drug's entry route into the body, for it to affect the brain it must cross the **blood–brain barrier** (**BBB**). The existence of this powerful barrier was revealed by a combination of the work of the German scientist Paul Ehrlich (1854–1915) and his student, Edwin E. Goldmann. In the late 1800s, Ehrlich noted that the organic dyes he was injecting into animals (a technique used to reveal fine structures which were otherwise invisible) seemed to leave the brain almost entirely untouched. Ehrlich assumed the brain was simply not able to take up the dye. However, years later in 1913, Goldmann did the opposite of his mentor and injected dye directly into the spinal cord – only to discover that the brain and spinal cord stained perfectly well. But this time, nothing else did – a microscopic barrier was preventing the dye's spread.

**German chemist and bacteriologist, Paul Ehrlich, at work in his laboratory.**

The existence of the blood–brain barrier makes good evolutionary sense. The brain's central biological importance and vulnerability means it is advantageous for it to be sealed off from the many dangerous substances that can find their way into the bloodstream.

The smallest blood vessels, the capillaries, are the point at which the bloodstream and the body's tissues interact. Water, oxygen and other substances can pass through the capillary cell walls into the tissues, and waste products such as carbon dioxide can pass back into the bloodstream

## The pharmaceutical money-go-round

Barely existing until the turn of the 1950s, the drugs industry is now seriously big business, producing a plethora of new drugs designed to treat physical and mental diseases. Globally, more than $300 billion is spent every year on these pills.

Do we really need this endless supply of new drugs? Clearly pharmaceuticals have brought great benefits to many, providing a cure for illnesses which would once have been a death sentence, helping manage chronic pain, and offering an effective treatment for many mental illnesses. But one notable paradox surrounding the drug industry is the discrepancy between how much is spent on developing new drugs and what is spent on marketing existing ones – on average, roughly twice as much is spent on marketing. The top pharmaceutical company, Pfizer, had sales worth more than $67 billion in 2010, resulting in a profit of over $8 billion, largely thanks to the vast sums of money being spent on television, e-marketing and campaigns to encourage people to buy drugs such as the cholesterol-reducing Lipitor and the erection enhancing Viagra. The first edition of the *Diagnostic and Statistical Manual of Mental Disorders* (*DSM-I*, 1952), a primary source of maladies pharmaceutical companies turn to for curative inspiration, contained a mere 106 mental disorders. Around sixty years later, *DSM-IV* contains around three hundred mental disorders and, with the promise of *DSM-V* just around the corner, shows no signs of curtailing its impressive growth. With every new "disorder" comes the demand for some new treatment, a call-to-arms the large pharmas are only too happy to answer – at a cost. But beyond the financial costs of such drugs, there is the lurking concern: as we increasingly medicate the various states of consciousness giving rise to the range and variety that is human existence, could we be diluting the very essence of what makes us human?

to be carried away. This is possible because the capillary walls are made up of only a single layer of cells, **endothelial cells**. However, the capillaries of the brain and spinal cord are different from those throughout the rest of the body, with the endothelial cells being meshed together much more tightly. This tight network allows small molecules such as water (with a molecular weight of 18 daltons), oxygen (32 daltons) and carbon dioxide (44 daltons) to move freely to and fro. But anything with a molecular weight greater than 500 daltons simply will not get through unless "invited" by specialized transport systems. Glucose, for example, is able to cross the barrier via a large "glucose transporter" protein whose bulk spans the entire width of the capillary wall. Forming a cylindrical passage across the BBB, it specifically recognizes and binds glucose molecules as they pass by and allows them to move along its length into the brain.

Most of the time this is an excellent setup, preventing large bacteria, viruses and toxins from entering the sensitive environment of the brain. However, the BBB is so tight that it even refuses passage to the body's own immune system, with large, defensive **immunoglobulin proteins** being unable to pass through and attack any offending invader – this is why diseases such as meningitis can be so dangerous. Unfortunately, most drugs, around 98 percent of them, exceed the size limit for entry into the brain, making the discovery of new ways to deliver drugs into the central nervous system one of the central challenges of our time. Current approaches range from the subtle "duping" of the BBB, by hijacking the natural transport systems that exist and using them to carry chemicals across the barrier, to slightly more heavy-handed methods involving the temporary physical disruption of the epithelial cell lining. However, recent advances in nanotechnology appear to hold great promise. Tiny **nanoparticles** – usually less than 200 nanometres in at least one dimension (around the size of the smallest bacteria) – are attached to the desired drug, circumventing many of the problems inherent in bypassing the BBB. While the precise mechanism underlying how nanoparticles pass through the BBB is still being figured out, this area of "nanoneuroscience" is growing fast. Recent studies with one type of specially coated nanoparticle seem to hint that the diminutive particles take advantage of the natural processes governing a cell's membrane. Rather than simply forming a static barrier between one cell and the next, a cell's membrane is highly dynamic – both engulfing portions of its exterior environment and excreting miniscule volumes of the cell's contents (endocytosis/ macropinocytosis and exocytosis, respectively). By seamlessly becoming part of this natural, cellular ebb and flow, it seems nanoparticles are able to move through and between cells.

## The reward pathway

Eating is vital to survival, and the brain has evolved to make sure that we do eat. We take pleasure in the taste of food, and once we have eaten enough, hunger pangs are replaced by a pleasant feeling of satiety. Similarly, we take pleasure in drinking, having sex and nurturing children – all activities which promote our survival, and the transmission of our genes into the next generation. These pleasurable feelings are caused by

## Love and the brain

Of all the desires and emotions the brain controls, few can be as strong as lust and love. But what actually happens, neurologically speaking, when we feel attracted or attached to another person? According to one expert – anthropologist Helen Fisher – the brain has different modes for lust, romantic love and long-term commitment.

Initial attraction, it seems, is driven primarily by the release of hormones such as testosterone and oestrogen. Passionate or romantic love, by contrast, can be linked to changing levels of various chemicals, including the "pleasure neurotransmitters" dopamine and serotonin. Curiously, while dopamine levels shoot up in the brain of a person in love, serotonin levels fall. The pattern of serotonin reduction is reminiscent of what happens in the brain of a person with obsessive–compulsive disorder – a fact that might explain why someone who is deeply in love can find it very difficult to focus on anything other than the object of their infatuation.

Of course, passion and romance rarely last forever, and dopamine and serotonin levels eventually return to normal. Yet many couples stay together after this happens. This kind of calmer, longer-term bond seems to rely on the brain producing other chemicals, especially the hormones oxytocin and vasopressin. Studies have shown how animals that are usually monogamous can cease to be attached to their partner if the production of these hormones is suppressed.

Of course, sex plays a role in all this. Aside from anything else, sexual activity, and especially orgasm, can kick-start the chemical changes associated with both love and long-term commitment. This suggests that partners may be more likely to fall in love or embark on a long-term relationship once they've slept together.

So why did the brain evolve to handle romance and commitment in this way? The evolutionary role of sexual attraction is clear, but what about love and long-term commitment? One answer could be that romantic love or infatuation increases the chances of a couple staying together long enough to make reproduction actually happen. As for long-term coupling, this would have helped increase the survival chances of the resulting offspring.

**See Helen Fisher's TED talk about loving and cheating here:** www.ted.com/talks/helen_fisher_tells_us_why_we_love_cheat.html.

the brain's **reward pathway** – a neurological network whose role is to reinforce beneficial behaviours by making us feel good when we do them.

The reward pathway, or **mesolimbic pathway**, connects a region of the central midbrain, the **ventral tegmental area** (VTA), to part of the **nucleus accumbens**, within the limbic system (see p.36), and the

**prefrontal cortex**. The VTA, considered to be one of the first specialized brain regions to evolve, is responsible for promoting actions which will aid our survival and evolutionary success. When a body's needs are being fully satisfied, signals from other brain areas inform the VTA, which responds by producing dopamine. This dopamine travels along the mesolimbic pathway to the nucleus accumbens, involved in reward and the sensation of pleasure. In the final stage of the process, the nucleus accumbens communicates with the prefrontal cortex, which is responsible for reasoning and planning. The prefrontal cortex weaves these pleasurable feelings into memories, reinforcing the behaviour by motivating the person to perform it again.

The existence of the reward pathway was established in 1954 by James Olds and Peter Milner, who inserted electrodes into the nucleus accumbens of a group of rats, and trained them to press a lever that activated the electrode. They found that the rats seemed to enjoy the sensation, and continued to press the lever until exhausted.

# Addiction

Many of the drugs humans have discovered and synthesized affect our natural reward pathway by interfering with the levels of dopamine flowing along it. Some, such as the antipsychotics (see p.206), can decrease motivation and our ability to experience pleasure by reducing dopamine activity. Every drug with the ability to cause **addiction** does so by elevating the levels of dopamine in the nucleus accumbens.

The bursts of euphoria felt when in the grip of an addictive drug are the consequence of this increased amount of dopamine flooding through the reward pathway. Were the brain's structure set in stone, addiction probably wouldn't occur, but the brain's plasticity means that over time it responds to these regular, massive bursts of dopamine in an entirely logical manner. Unable to control the amount of drug coming into the body, the brain attempts to re-establish some form of equilibrium by decreasing its responsiveness to the dopamine sloshing around in it. It does so by reducing the number of dopamine receptors in neurons so that the neurons become less excitable. As a consequence, the person becomes tolerant to the drug, requiring more and more to induce the same effect. They will likely enter into a pattern of habitual behaviour controlled entirely by the desire to seek out more of the drug. If they can't get hold of it, they will suffer symptoms of **withdrawal**. They may enter a state known as **anhedonia**, the inability to feel pleasure in situations where others normally would. And they will experience intense **cravings** for the drug, causing them to behave both erratically and irrationally. The symptoms of withdrawal will diminish with time, however, as the brain gradually resets its dopamine equilibrium back to a more normal level.

# Major drug categories

What follows is a catalogue of the major types of psychoactive drugs. Some of the drugs included here are consumed in everyday life, such as caffeine and nicotine, many are used to treat disease and mental illness, while others are swallowed in purely recreational contexts. They are grouped not according to their use, however, but according to their effects on the brain. Thus we begin with stimulants and depressants, move on to antidepressants and antipsychotics, and conclude with hallucinogens and analgesics.

## Stimulants

These are the "uppers" or "pick-me-ups" of the drug world. Hitting the central nervous system from a number of angles, they affect both the brain and the autonomic nervous system (see p.58).

### Caffeine

The most commonly used stimulant – and indeed the most popular of all psychoactive substances – is caffeine (trimethylxanthine). Global annual consumption is an estimated 120,000 tons. Most caffeine comes from the leaves and beans of the coffee plant, but it is also found in tea, the berries of the guarana bush, native to Brazil, and a number of other plants. A typical cup of coffee will contain around 100mg of caffeine, a cup of tea about half as much. Caffeine is also often found in soft drinks such as cola (between 10 and 50mg), and in energy drinks such as Red Bull (as much as 80mg).

Before the rise of the coffee house, coffee beans had another enemy – insects. In the war between plants and bugs, caffeine

Caffeine

was the coffee plant's evolutionary answer, a natural neurotoxin and insecticide capable of reducing a hungry insect to a gibbering, vulnerable wreck. It takes more caffeine to disable a human, but we do respond to this addictive drug with increased feelings of mental and physical alertness.

Caffeine exerts its effects by subverting the natural working of the nervous system – it is a stealth chemical. Once in the bloodstream, it binds to specific receptor proteins on nerve cells. Normally, these receptors await their natural binding partner, the chemical **adenosine**, which, once bound to its receptor, slows nerves down, reducing their activity. Structurally, caffeine looks a bit like adenosine, so much so that it is able to usurp adenosine, binding to the waiting receptor. But that's all it does – it simply sits inertly on the receptor like a doorman blocking an entrance. Because the dampening effect of adenosine is blocked, the affected neurons shift up a gear, firing faster than they should. The body responds to this rapid neuronal firing by acting as if it were experiencing an emergency. The autonomic nervous system kicks in, flooding the bloodstream with noradrenaline. Suddenly, respiration and heart rate increase, pupils dilate, and you feel ready to fight or, more commonly, fly to work.

Caffeine also increases levels of dopamine activity in the brain, which may well account for its addictive properties. Death from caffeine overdose is rare, but overuse can lead to unpleasant side effects, including insomnia, irritability, nervousness and heart palpitations. A sudden cessation of caffeine intake can cause problems, too. Over time, the neurons will have become adapted to the smaller amounts of adenosine getting through to them. This means that, in the absence of caffeine, the neurons are supersensitive to adenosine, slowing down the brain too much and leading to a decrease in blood pressure, which can result in fatigue and headaches. Weaning yourself off caffeine is easy, though: by decreasing intake by one or two cups a day, these withdrawal symptoms can be limited.

## Nicotine

Nicotine is isolated from the plant *Nicotiana tabacum*, which takes its name from French diplomat and scholar Jean Nicot (1530–1600). Like caffeine, nicotine is the result of biological warfare, a natural insecticide and highly potent neurotoxin produced by the tobacco plant to destroy unwelcome guests on its foliage. The Italian explorer Christopher Columbus (1451–1506) discovered the tobacco plant in the Americas in 1492. But the local inhabitants had already been smoking, chewing and drinking extract from its leaves for centuries – mostly for medicinal and ceremonial purposes.

Nowadays, cigarettes are the most common nicotine delivery system. According to the World Health Organization, tobacco killed around six million people in 2011 – six hundred thousand of whom were passive victims, never having touched a cigarette. By 2030, the WHO predicts this figure will rise to eight million premature, cigarette-fuelled deaths, in what it refers to as the global tobacco pandemic. So, despite a now widespread understanding of the health risks implicit in smoking, the highly addictive nature of nicotine means thousands more will die until cigarettes are banned completely.

When smoke from a cigarette is inhaled, it enters the lungs, where nicotine and the many other toxic chemicals it contains cross the delicate biological barrier between the outer and inner world, via the alveoli. Once in the bloodstream, nicotine is rapidly transported to the brain. The entire journey takes less than ten seconds. The actual amounts of nicotine entering the bloodstream when a person smokes a cigarette are tiny, relative to what's present – most of it is destroyed by the burning process or simply not absorbed by the body – but it is so potent that even a small amount is enough to cause significant changes in brain chemistry.

Once nicotine is in the brain, it binds to neuronal receptor proteins called **nicotinic acetylcholine receptors**. Under normal circumstances, these receptors detect and bind to the neurotransmitter acetylcholine. Like many neurotransmitters, acetylcholine performs several functions, depending upon which pathway the target neuron is involved in. By fooling the brain into thinking acetylcholine has been released, nicotine is able to interfere with all these different functions, through excessive, unregulated stimulation of neurons in various parts of the brain. If the neuron is in contact with muscles, contraction results; if it is in contact with the autonomic nervous system, there is an explosion of activity, causing increased levels of stimulating noradrenaline. Attention and memory improve, appetite diminishes, and heart rate and blood pressure soar as the natural fight or flight response is activated. Nicotine also stimulates the release of dopamine – hence the addictive nature of cigarettes.

Ironically, the only major therapeutic use of nicotine is helping people get through the several weeks of nicotine withdrawal experienced when trying to quit smoking. Having become used to regular bursts of artificial stimulation caused by nicotine, the brain adapts by becoming less easy to stimulate – which is why the longer a person smokes, the more nicotine is required to cause the desired effect. By decreasing and then stopping nicotine intake, the natural balance of the brain eventually returns.

## Military use of drugs

With all the expensive, high-tech equipment involved in modern warfare, the human component might often seem like the weakest link. It is, then, perhaps not surprising that the military regularly uses drugs to increase the perform-ance of its soldiers. Pilots, sent on long missions (lasting up to twenty hours), in which they are in charge of extraordinarily expensive and sophisticated equip-ment, use **Dexedrine** to stay vigilant and sharp-eyed. Upon returning from such a mission, they may be given "no-go pills", a sedative such as **temazepam**, to ensure a smooth return to a regular sleep cycle. Like other amphetamines, Dexedrine is not without its side effects – it can be addictive and have effects on memory and vision. As such, its use is carefully monitored.

The properties of **Modafinil**, an anti-narcoleptic drug produced by the pharma-ceutical company Cephalon, have also been exploited for military use. The drug targets **adrenergic receptors** (the sites of noradrenaline binding) in the hypoth-alamus and brain stem, circumventing the normal controls regulating wakeful-ness and alertness. Remarkably, its use in those unaffected by narcolepsy has led to startling increases in their wakefulness, with studies suggesting that as little as eight hours' sleep is needed to keep soldiers alert for stints of up to eighty hours. Free of the side effects associated with amphetamines, this drug may become the pill of choice for soldiers preparing for long, demanding missions.

The systematic use of such drugs in this way may seem unnerving, but it is nothing in comparison to what the US military once had in mind. **MK-ULTRA** was a project truly terrifying in its absence of ethics, a vast programme of covert mind-control experiments carried out by the CIA and the US Army Chemical and Biological Weapons division. Under the guise of counter-brain-washing and torture research, thousands of experiments were conducted in the 1950s on predominantly ignorant test-subjects. One study involved soldiers and civilian participants (or, more accurately, victims) being secretly monitored while under the influence of mind-altering drugs, including the hallucino-gen **LSD**. This "research" was brought to public attention by the US Senate Church Committee in 1975. A year later, on the committee's recommendation, President Gerald Ford issued an order stipulating an absolute requirement for witnessed, written, informed consent for any activities involving drugs.

## Amphetamine ("speed")

Unlike caffeine and nicotine, amphetamine is produced not within plants but in a laboratory. It is an entirely synthetic drug, first created in 1887 by the German chemist Lazar Edeleano. In its early days, amphetamine was studied for its appetite-suppressing properties and it is still used now – albeit less frequently – as an outdated means of helping people to lose weight. Today, amphetamine is used clinically to treat a range of conditions, such as ADHD (see p.164) and narcolepsy (see p.107). It is also used by the military: a derivative of amphetamine called Dexedrine ("go pills") is used by the US Air Force – under strictly monitored conditions – to keep pilots alert and focused during long airborne missions. Amphetamine and its

L-amphetamine

derivatives (including ecstasy; see p.157) are also abused recreationally to take advantage of these stimulating effects.

Amphetamine-based drugs encourage neurons to release their stores of the neurotransmitters noradrenaline (which activates the autonomic nervous system), dopamine (which stimulates the pleasure pathway) and serotonin (which affects mood). They also block neurons' ability to clear up the increased levels of noradrenaline and dopamine from synapses, resulting in wholly unnatural levels of these neurotransmitters saturating the brain. The result? Alertness, euphoria, hyperactivity, decreased appetite, and increased stamina and energy – perfect for nightclubs or warfare. Prolonged abuse, however, can lead to insomnia, aggressiveness and even paranoid psychosis, mimicking some of the symptoms of certain forms of schizophrenia.

## Cocaine

The coca plant, *Erythroxylon coca*, is a native of South America, where it grows in abundance. For millennia, indigenous populations have chewed its leaves, reaping nutritional benefits including valuable vitamins, proteins – and cocaine. Cocaine is present only in tiny amounts in the plant's

**A press advertisement from the late nineteenth century, before cocaine became illegal in the US.**

leaves, but scientists became curious about what was responsible for the marvellous pain-killing and uplifting properties of this plant, and isolated pure cocaine for the first time in 1855.

The history of cocaine is a wonderful example of how wrong things can go when we remove something from the wilderness and attempt to integrate it into our culture. Soon after its discovery, cocaine was being hailed as a miracle drug, and by the 1880s – on the recommendation of Sigmund Freud, among others – it was being prescribed for everything from depression and exhaustion to morphine addiction. It also became popular as a local anaesthetic, and was sold over the counter in the form of tonics and toothache cures. It was also the key ingredient in the original Coca-Cola drink, launched in 1886. Only in the twentieth century did people begin to grasp how powerfully addictive cocaine is. But by then it was already a common recreational drug, and it has increased in popularity over the years, so that it is now the second most popular drug in the US (after cannabis), with the highest street value of any drug.

As with the other stimulants, cocaine targets noradrenaline, dopamine and serotonin. By blocking the transporter proteins involved in vacuuming up these neurotransmitters after their release (normally this prevents the neurotransmitter from over-activating the target neurons), cocaine floods the brain with these stimulating and pleasure-producing molecules. The intense euphoria experienced quickly becomes addictive (hence the high street value), while many of the physical effects associated with other stimulants, such as the milder nicotine, are also seen. But due to the intense burst in blood pressure and heart rate, the risk of heart attack in the hour following cocaine use jumps by a staggering twenty four times. Should a user survive this Russian roulette, continued excessive use will eventually lead to paranoid delusions and hallucinations.

## Depressants

If stimulants are the brain's accelerators, depressants are the brakes. As we saw on p.155, the main excitatory and inhibitory neurotransmitters are glutamate and GABA respectively. **Glutamate** binds to the receptor protein NMDA, revving neurons up and making them more likely to fire an action potential. **GABA** does the opposite – reducing the probability of a neuron firing an action potential by binding to the $GABA_A$ receptor. The normal harmony that exists between these opposing forces is disrupted by depressants.

## Ethanol

You might think the ubiquity of ethanol, the "active ingredient" in all alcoholic beverages, would mean scientists had long figured out how this substance causes the symptoms of intoxication, with which anyone who indulges will be familiar. Ethanol's effects on the brain are complex and relatively poorly understood. In part, this is due to its structure – ethanol is a small molecule, easily absorbed into the blood, happy to drift both between neurons and within them, disrupting their overall functioning. Unlike modern drugs, which have a principal "target" protein

## Alcohol dependence

The human relationship with alcohol is no recent phenomenon. For more than five thousand years we have been producing alcohol from plant life, and using it to deliberately interfere with the extremely well-balanced and complex chemistry of the brain. Most cultures recognize the positive aspects of alcohol, acting as a catalyst for relationships, celebrations, negotiations or battle. However, as medical knowledge has grown, it has become clear that this "gift from the gods" may not be as good for us as we had thought. In particular, its potential for addiction can destroy the lives of those affected. In Britain in the early 1830s, a temperance movement emerged claiming complete abstinence from alcohol was the only way to reduce the illness and disruption this drug was causing. In the first half of the twentieth century a number of countries, including the US and Finland, went even further, introducing Prohibition.

An **alcoholic** is a person whose brain has become physically dependent on alcohol. They may drink heavily every day, only binge at weekends, or go for long periods without alcohol only to collapse into a period of days or weeks of continuous heavy drinking. The brain and body of an alcohol-dependent person is under siege. Over years, major organs, including the stomach and liver, struggle to deal with the toxin coursing through them. The brain finds itself unable to successfully perform even rudimentary tasks: movement, vision, speaking and all of the higher cognitive functions, such as memory and judgement, fall by the wayside.

Recovering from years of heavy alcohol consumption is tough. Within hours of not drinking, an alcoholic can become shaky, jittery and sweaty, possibly experiencing mild hallucinations. By the following day or so, the second phase of alcohol withdrawal can bring convulsions. The worst is left for last and, fortunately, relatively few drink heavily enough to experience the temporary horror of alcohol withdrawal delirium (or **delirium tremens**, DTs). In this last phase, around ten percent die. The rest will experience powerful, often terrifying delusions until the brain eventually recovers.

## Dr Cathy Price
*Wellcome Trust Centre for Neuroimaging*

**What is your favourite part of the brain and why?** My favourite part of the brain is the white matter that connects the cortical, subcortical and cerebellar parts. The white matter integrates the activity in each region to that in many other regions. It therefore supports highly sophisticated human functions that emerge from patterns of activity across regions rather than localized activity within one region.

**What scientific breakthrough helped us to understand the brain the most?** The greatest scientific breakthrough is the combined inspiration, interest and commitment of teams of researchers worldwide.

**What's the next big thing in neuroscience?** I would like the next big thing in neuroscience to be an imaging technique that allows us to measure cellular functions non-invasively in the human brain. This would allow us to test the similarities and differences in the individual cells that contribute to the function of the same region. For example, are there cells that are selectively responsive to different letter shapes, or do the same cells respond during reading and object recognition?

that they dock onto, ethanol has a global influence. It somehow decreases the activity of NMDA receptors, whilst increasing the efficiency of GABA. The overall effect of this double whammy is a general slowing down of the central nervous system, which is why alcohol eventually makes us slur our words, stumble about and generally act stupidly. The pleasurable feelings associated with alcohol arise from its ability to increase levels of dopamine and endorphins (see p.214) in the brain. The release of these feel-good chemicals reinforces alcohol-seeking behaviour, overriding logical judgement – how many times have you heard the expression "Never again"?

## Barbiturates

The first barbiturate, **barbituric acid** (from which all others are derived), was synthesized by the German chemist Adolf von Bayer in 1864. According to legend, von Bayer named his new chemical after the patron saint of artillerymen, Saint Barbara, after strolling into a pub celebrating her day. But a more romantic explanation suggests von Bayer named his drug after a woman with whom he was enamoured.

Testing revealed small doses of barbiturates had a calming effect on the nervous system, similar in appearance to alcohol intoxication. Higher amounts, however, were capable of removing consciousness completely. Barbiturates seem primarily to target $GABA_A$ receptors (see p.198), boosting the duration of their activity and therefore decreasing the likelihood of neurons firing. But these drugs also have a more general impact on the nervous system, blocking sodium channels for example. This reduces the flow of sodium across neuronal membranes, resulting in a further dampening down of neuronal activity.

Barbiturates were a popular depressant in the first half of the twentieth century, and were also used as an anaesthetic, and as an anticonvulsant to help epileptics control seizures. They are rarely used today, however. Their reputation as a sedative was marred as their dangers and side effects became increasingly apparent. The small difference between the amount of the drug which will induce sedation and the amount which will lead to coma made it difficult to prescribe the correct dose. The risk of accidental overdose was made notorious by the deaths of two popular icons, Marilyn Monroe and Jimi Hendrix. Users also became tolerant to the drug over time, requiring increasing amounts to achieve the desired effect, and experienced both physical and psychological dependence. Consequently, alternatives were sought and by the 1960s barbiturates were being phased out in favour of benzodiazepines.

## Benzodiazepines

Benzodiazepines, such as **Valium** and **Xanax**, are the new depressants. As with many great discoveries, their ancestor was found through a combination of luck and good judgement. In 1954, the Austrian scientist Leo Sternbach studied a group of chemicals, the benzheptoxdiazines, only to set them aside and forget about them. But during a clear-out in 1957, a lab assistant came across these chemicals and Sternbach decided to send them for further evaluation and testing. One of these chemicals, Ro-5-0690, turned out to be the mother of all subsequent benzodiazepines and was given the catchier name **Librium**.

> **"Cricket is basically baseball on Valium."**
>
> Robin Williams

By slowing the brain down, benzodiazepines can help treat insomnia and anxiety, and prevent seizures. But there are negative side effects, such as drowsiness, diminished judgement and the possibility of addiction. More specific than the earlier barbiturates, these drugs interact with the brain's $GABA_A$ receptors, enhancing GABA's effect on them and decreasing the probability of their neurons firing action potentials. The potentially addictive nature of these drugs means a person should be weaned off them gradually, as sudden cessation can lead to a "bounce back" phenomenon, with unpleasant consequences such as insomnia, anxiety and delusions.

# Antidepressants

In an ideal world, a person suffering from major depression (see p.159) would receive some form of psychotherapy or counselling. In contemporary society, however, there aren't the time and resources to help every person diagnosed with depression in this way. Antidepressant medication provides doctors with a relatively cheap, quick and self-managed alternative. According to the UK's Royal College of Psychiatrists, of those with depression who take an antidepressant for more than three months, between 50 and 65 percent will be much improved. They also point out, however, that under the same circumstances 25–30 percent of people improve even when given a placebo. Results such as this serve to remind us how complex the human brain is, and that there is far more at work than mere chemistry. Knowing within yourself that you're seeking to improve your mental health with the support of a good doctor clearly has powerful merit in its own right.

Antidepressants are also used to treat anxiety disorders and chronic pain. Despite various side-effects, one thing they have going for them, when compared to the depressants, is that they are far less addictive. The body doesn't become tolerant to antidepressants, and, if the medication is stopped, you're unlikely to experience a craving for the drug. But there can be certain withdrawal symptoms as the brain regains its neurochemical harmony, which is why some of the more modern antidepressants require a "weaning" stage in which a person's dosage is gradually reduced to zero.

## Tricyclics

Like many drugs, antidepressants were discovered by chance. In 1957, a series of lucky breaks brought us both MAOIs and the tricyclics. So named after their three-wheeled molecular structure, the highly potent tricyclics are rarely used today, not because they are any less effective than modern varieties but because it is relatively easy to take an overdose – not desirable when treating someone in the depths of major depression.

The drug seems to have a two-pronged effect on the central nervous system. Almost immediately, it increases levels of **serotonin** and **noradrenaline** in the brain by blocking the neurons' reuptake systems for these neurotransmitters. But it takes several weeks for the person's mood to noticeably improve, so the drug must also instigate some more gradual change within the brain. It is now thought that tricyclics may cause this longer-term change in the brain's cortex and hippocampus (involved in

# The placebo effect

A placebo is a pharmaceutically inert substance given to a person as if it were capable of providing some health benefit. As odd as this seems, placebos are a major component of drug trials – only when a manufactured drug has a significantly greater impact on human health than a placebo is it said to possess any medical value. Which is where it gets even more odd, because placebos work. The **placebo effect** is the name given to a perceived or measurable improvement in health in response to a course of treatment with a placebo.

In a typical trial situation, a person is asked to subjectively report to a doctor whether or not they have experienced any improvement in a particular condition in response to their treatment. The placebo effect arises because, although the drug the patient receives may be a fake, both their expectations of that drug and their relationship with the doctor are very real. A good relationship with a doctor, and a consequent wish to please them, or positive expectations of the trial and a desire to become better may be all that is needed to improve one's health in a number of conditions, such as chronic pain or depression. This is known as the **expectancy effect**. Alternatively, the placebo effect may be the result of a **conditioned response** to treatment from a health professional and the taking of medication, an unconscious association between the consumption of a pill and feeling better.

In 2002 studies published by Andrew Leuchter and colleagues at UCLA's Neuropsychiatric Institute threw some light on this controversial and mysterious effect. Leuchter decided to examine the relationship between the placebo effect and major depression – the successful treatment of which has been attributed by some to more than fifty percent placebo effect. In their study, 51 people with major depression were given either an antidepressant or a placebo for a period of nine weeks. In accordance with standard procedure, this was a double-blind study – neither the scientists nor the test subjects knew whether they were receiving the antidepressant or the placebo.

Leuchter and his colleagues found that 52 percent of those receiving antidepressants and a very significant 38 percent of placebo controls responded positively to their treatment. Brain scans revealed that both groups showed measurable differences in their brain activity, but *not in the same way*. The placebo group showed an increase in activity in their prefrontal cortex within two weeks, while those responding to the drug showed a decrease in activity in the same region after just a couple of days. This clearly demonstrated that the placebo effect is able to alter brain functioning. What's more, since both responding groups felt improved as a result of their new patterns of brain activity, it suggested that the brain is able to regain happiness through more than one route.

higher functioning and emotions) by altering the sensitivity of certain neurotransmitter receptor proteins, the overall effect being boosted levels of noradrenaline.

Tricyclics are considered "dirty" chemicals, as they also affect a range of other biological pathways in the body. This leads to a number of unwanted side effects, including drowsiness, constipation, bladder problems, blurred vision and increased heart rate. However, they still have their uses, both as an alternative to modern antidepressants when they prove ineffective and as a treatment for chronic pain caused by damage to the nervous system.

## MAOIs (monoamine oxidase inhibitors)

Monoamine is the general term used to describe the chemical class to which neurotransmitters such as serotonin, dopamine and noradrenaline belong. When neurons release neurotransmitters, a number of mechanisms kick in to remove them from the synapse as quickly as possible – this helps keep nerve signalling clean and precise. One way of achieving this is via neurotransmitter reuptake, in which the neuron releasing the neurotransmitter vacuums it up again, as long as it is near enough. Another way is via proteins whose sole purpose is to seek and destroy stray neurotransmitters. One such protein is **monoamine oxidase A** (MAO-A), which destroys any serotonin, noradrenaline and dopamine in its path. By using MAOIs to block the action of MAO-A, levels of these neurotransmitters are raised within the brain, boosting mood.

MAOIs have their share of complications, however. Diet must be closely monitored, as eating food containing either of the natural chemicals tyramine or tryptophan can have serious consequences. Tyramine is found in almost anything delicious, it seems, including chocolate, mature cheese and wine. The combination of MAOIs and tyramine is a potent one, leading to extreme hypertension and the increased chance of stroke. Tryptophan is also found in many foods, including red meat, dairy products, turkey and peanuts. The combination of tryptophan and MAOIs can lead to dangerously elevated levels of serotonin in the brain, a condition known as hyperserotonemia.

## SSRIs (selective serotonin reuptake inhibitors)

As indicated by their name, these drugs are more selective than earlier antidepressants, influencing levels of serotonin only. Since their release and vociferous uptake in the late 1980s and early 1990s, a number have become household names. **Prozac** (fluoxetine) and **Seroxat** (paroxetine)

Not just for humans: a vet checks up on Phoenix, a cockatiel who suffers from stress and was prescribed Prozac.

in particular have made the headlines for both good and bad reasons. There have been concerns that doctors have been over-prescribing SSRIs to children and adolescents. The Committee on Safety in Medicines believes that forty thousand children in the UK alone are using these drugs for depression and anxiety related conditions. Partly in light of this, organizations such as the UK's National Institute for Clinical Excellence have called for antidepressant drugs to be the last line of defence in the treatment of depression, with counselling, increased exercise and diet assessment being tried in the first instance.

Fluoxetine

Additionally, studies have indicated that with all of the SSRIs except fluoxetine there is an increased risk of suicidal thoughts and actions in under-18-year-olds. This prompted the prescription to under-18s of all but fluoxetine to be banned in the UK in 2003 and, in the US, the Food and Drug Administration now requires SSRI packaging to contain a "black box" warning (reserved for drugs known to have serious side effects) informing parents of the increased risk to their child.

Despite their great success, it is still not precisely understood how these drugs improve mood. As the name suggests, SSRIs block the reuptake of serotonin back into the releasing neuron, increasing the concentration of the neurotransmitter within the synapse and so making more available to stimulate the next neuron in line. But the means by which they achieve this is still debated. Just as it is very difficult to predict the effect of introducing a single new species to an ecosystem because of the complex web of interactions involved, it is difficult to model the knock-on effects of introducing a chemical such as an SSRI to the brain. When an SSRI enters the brain it sets in motion a series of changes, some in the neuron's cell body, some at its terminal, and some in the neuron's receptor proteins. Ultimately, after several weeks, the brain adapts and, in many cases, the person responds by showing improved mood.

Sexual dysfunction is one of the most common side effects of SSRIs, occurring in about half of those taking the drugs. Unfortunately, the inability to achieve or maintain an erection, or reach orgasm, stifles an important element of psychological recovery. Withdrawal symptoms including headaches, diarrhoea and, on occasion, aggressive behaviour mean reducing SSRI medication must be done gradually and strictly under the guidance of a doctor.

## Antipsychotics (neuroleptics)

As we saw on p.166, the term **psychosis** is used to describe a condition in which a person's perception of reality becomes severely affected, as in schizophrenia or delusional disorders, for example. The purpose of antipsychotic drugs is, as the name suggests, to somehow counteract the psychosis, reeling the mind back into more normal patterns of thinking, perceiving and reasoning – no small task.

The first of these drugs, and still the most commonly used throughout the US, is **chlorpromazine**, better known by one of its trade names, Thorazine. One of chlorpromazine's original uses in the early 1950s was as an antihistamine, helping to reduce the body's allergic response. A Parisian surgeon, Henri Laborit, began exploiting this property of the drug to reduce the anaesthesia-induced shock (a sharp decrease in blood pressure) being experienced by his patients. As with many scientific discoveries, what he found was entirely unexpected – this antihistamine somehow reduced the patients' anxiety levels, making them unconcerned about their imminent journey under the knife. This allowed Laborit to decrease the amount of anaesthetic he was using, reducing the chances of shock and helping his patients to recover more quickly.

At the time, the main treatments for psychiatric illnesses were psychotherapy, shock (using electricity or insulin) or the immensely popular frontal lobotomy (see p.22) – drugs for these conditions simply didn't exist. Thanks to Laborit's persistence, word got around and, in 1953, the drug was used for the first time in a purely psychiatric context, by Pierre Deniker and Jean Delay. The results were remarkable, bringing a new equilibrium to those who had been either violent or uncommunicative. Psychiatrists were now able to help a far greater number of those suffering from schizophrenia and other psychotic illnesses control their condition and lead a relatively normal life.

Presently, there are many types of antipsychotic drugs, divided into the original "typical" type, like chlorpromazine, and the later "atypical" forms, such as olanzapine (trade name Zyprexa).

All antipsychotics block the $D_2$ receptors in the dopamine pathways of the brain, reducing the normal effects of dopamine release. Dopamine is a key neurotransmitter in four pathways within the brain – the tuberoinfundibular pathway (involved in the control of hormones), the nigro-striatal pathway (which regulates movement), the mesocortical pathway (involved in emotions and motivation) and the mesolimbic pathway (the reward pathway; see p.190). It is the blocking of $D_2$ receptors in the mesolimbic pathway that is thought to produce the antipsychotic effect of these drugs, by counteracting an excess of dopamine in these regions of the brain. However, "typical" antipsychotics also block $D_2$ receptors in the other three pathways. This seems to account for a number of the side effects associated with the drugs. Interference with the nigrostriatal pathway is thought to be responsible for Parkinsonian symptoms including tremors and rigidity (see p.181), while disruption of dopamine in the tuberoinfundibular pathway can lead to abnormally high levels of pro-lactin in the blood, associated with infertility and loss of libido. "Atypical" antipsychotics seem to be more selective, having less of an effect on these unintended pathways and also at least partially blocking serotonin receptors. This combination of effects seems to account for their greater efficacy and reduced number of side effects.

# Hallucinogens

The broad grouping of drugs known as the hallucinogens result in an altered state of consciousness, altered perception of sensory inputs and hallucinations. They are divided into three categories: **psychedelics**, **dissociatives** and **deliriants**. These three types of drugs have similar effects on consciousness, but do so through quite different means.

## Drug Classification

How are drugs classified? Who decides what we can and can't use without threat of legal prosecution? In the UK, citizens must answer to an Act of Parliament known as the Misuse of Drugs Act 1971. Often controversial, any drug finding itself covered under this fluid arrangement is regarded as a controlled substance, such that possession, producing, supplying, importing or exporting the controlled substance will result in the weight of the law. Based on their perceived harmfulness to individuals and society, controlled substances are categorized by the Home Office into Class A, B, or C drugs, from the most to the least harmful. Possessing Class A drugs, such as ecstasy, LSD, crack or heroin can result in seven years of jail time while dealing such substances shunts the potential punishment up to life imprisonment. Irrespective of a drug's class or whether one is found to be in possession or dealing, the law has the power to throw an unlimited fine at the accused.

Class B drugs are perceived as less of an overall threat but their categorization can be a little murky, with cannabis in particular having yo-yoed back and forth between Class B and Class C in the last few years. In 2009, Professor David Nutt, then the UK government's chief drug adviser was famously sacked (prompting a wave of further scientific advisers to resign) when he spoke out against the government's reclassification of cannabis from Class C to B. Nutt stated that the reclassification was counter to the scientific evidence whilst also stating that the drug was less harmful than either alcohol or nicotine, two drugs conspicuous by their absence from the classification system.

Currently, cannabis is a Class B drug, finding itself in the company of substances such as mephedrone, amphetamines, certain opioids and, perhaps surprisingly, methylphenidate (Ritalin). Here, the potential jail sentence rises to a maximum of five years for possession and fourteen years for deal-

## Psychedelics

Psychedelics have the capacity to temporarily remove filters the mind places between our senses and the conscious brain, leading to **sensory overload**. The result is as if being wakened for the first time – the world takes on a new vibrancy, with colours, sounds, shapes, thoughts, memories and emotions adopting an intensity we are usually spared. With good reason – if our ancestors had become entranced by the colours of every piece of food they came across, they'd have either starved or been eaten.

In the 1960s these drugs were advocated by countercultural icons such as Dr Timothy Leary for their "mind-expanding" properties. Leary famously encouraged his followers to "turn on, tune in and drop out".

ing. In the Class C category of illegal substances, we find drugs such as the benzodiazepine-based tranquilizers (for example, Valium or Xanax), gamma hydroxybutyrate (GHB) and ketamine. As with Class B drugs, dealing any of these substances can result in a fourteen year jail sentence while possession carries the lighter threat of a maximum of two years.

In the United States, drugs have been categorized into five schedules, rather than classes. These schedules came into being with the Controlled Substances Act of 1970 and, today, it's the combined efforts of the US Food and Drug Administration and the Drug Enforcement Administration that determine precisely which drugs go where. The schedules themselves are organized as a series of five relativistic definitions, so for example, in Schedule I the criteria are:

a. The drug or other substance has a high potential for abuse.

b. The drug or other substance has no currently accepted medical use in treatment in the United States.

c. There is a lack of accepted safety for use of the drug or other substance under medical supervision.

Throughout the remaining four schedules, the drug's potential for abuse drops, it moves from none to some form of accepted medical use and a diminishing degree of concern about the potential for physical or psychological dependence. On the whole, both nations appear in broad agreement but there are differences highlighting alternate cultural perceptions, such as with GHB (notorious for its use as a "date rape" drug), a high level Schedule I drug in the US, versus its Class 3 status in the UK, while in the US, cannabis currently remains in Schedule I, despite its growing acceptance in specific medical contexts.

Aldous Huxley was another famous exponent. Psychedelics have inspired movements in art, literature and music, characterized by colourful, abstract and intense imagery or sounds.

The best-known psychedelic drug is **LSD** (d-lysergic acid diethylamide). One of the most powerful drugs known, if you had an amount of LSD weighing the same as a male African elephant, you would have enough to alter the consciousness of every human being on the planet. LSD was first created in 1938 by Dr Albert Hofmann of the Swiss pharmaceutical company Sandoz Laboratories. Derived from a chemical found in ergot, a fungus which grows on rye (and has been responsible for several mass poisonings over the years), LSD was originally developed as a stimulant of the respiratory and circulatory systems. It was initially deemed unin-

**Albert Hofmann in 1970, thirty years after he accidentally discovered the hallucinogenic drug LSD: he maintained that the drug had extraordinary value when used in psychoanalysis and psychotherapy, but when used recreationally it was like putting an "atom bomb" in the hands of amateurs.**

teresting and gathered dust for five years. But Hofmann couldn't shake the feeling that this drug had more up its sleeve and set about making a new batch.

It was then that the effects kicked in. Probably due to accidental skin contact, Hofmann started feeling peculiar and abandoned his work for the day, went home and became the first person to experience the mental effects of pure LSD. Embracing the spirit of scientific discovery, Hofmann proceeded to experiment on himself with various doses of the drug, experiencing the highs but also the profound lows such drugs can induce – in one terrifying experience believing himself possessed by a demon.

The range of positive and negative experiences the drug can produce results from the fact that LSD doesn't so much induce true hallucinations as amplify or distort what is already there; this makes it unusual in that the user's experience is far more dependent on their mental state and surroundings than with, say, cocaine.

It is believed that the psychedelic effects of LSD are caused by its interference with the flow of serotonin in the brain. LSD's similar chemical structure to serotonin allows it to bind to that neurotransmitter's receptors, exciting the neurons on which they sit. This could possibly create the psychedelic experience by increasing excitation in the cortex. In particular, it may increase input from the thalamus – a major relay for transmitting sensory information to the cortex.

An LSD "trip" lasts a long time – ten hours on average – but there's no guarantee the effects will stop there. Affecting the workings of the mind at

such a basic level inevitably carries risks, and users have reported
experiencing **flashbacks** months
or even years after the drug has
been consumed.

## Dissociatives

In contrast to psychedelics, dissociatives reduce signals from other
parts of the body to the brain,
resulting in **sensory deprivation**. This artificial severing of
the mind–body connection has
led to their use as anaesthetics
and, recreationally, as a means
of facilitating inner exploration,
hallucinations and out-of-body experiences.

LSD

**Laughing gas** (nitrous oxide) is a well-known dissociative used for its
anaesthetic and analgesic effects. Another is **ketamine**, first synthesized
in 1962 as an alternative to phenylcyclidine (PCP or Angel Dust).
Phenylcyclidine had been used as a surgical anaesthetic by the military,
but unpleasant side effects prompted scientists to seek an alternative –
ketamine was the result. Ketamine was widely used by the US military
during the Vietnam War, but its use has since been curtailed because
of concerns about its potential to cause out-of-body experiences. It is,
however, widely used in veterinary medicine as an anaesthetic for cats
and other small animals.

Ketamine works by simultaneously blocking glutamate's NMDA receptors (so reducing the chance of a neuron firing an action potential) and
stimulating opioid receptors (see p.214). The result can be an hour of
hallucinogenic experiences but up to a day's worth of impaired neurological functioning. Unlike many drugs, the user can end up in a state of
complete helplessness (hence its notoriety as a "date rape" drug), oblivious
to pain, their surroundings, or even their own existence.

## Deliriants

Of the three subclasses of hallucinogens, the deliriants are truly the most
hallucinogenic, leaving the user fully mobile but in a state resembling
a lucid dream or waking psychosis – potentially a highly dangerous
situation. The deliriant **atropine** is an anticholinergic drug derived

from the belladonna (deadly nightshade) plant. Anticholinergic drugs compete with the neurotransmitter acetylcholine (see p.195), binding to its receptor and hindering its point of access. Because the brain is chock-full of acetylcholine receptors, anticholinergics affect many pathways of communication, resulting in a large number of side effects which have made them unpopular as a recreational drug. They do have medical applications, however: atropine is used for anaesthesia (where it dampens the parasympathetic nervous system) and eye examinations (in which it blocks pupil contraction, allowing detailed eye examinations). It is also used to increase heart rate when it falls dangerously low (bradycardia), by shutting down the vagus nerve involved in lowering heart rate.

# Analgesics

Pain has protected us throughout evolutionary history, helping us avoid dangerous situations, alerting us to inner problems, or encouraging us to treat damaged body parts gently while they heal. But pain is, of course, an unpleasant sensation. Over the centuries humans have used everything from herbs to opium to alleviate pain. In recent decades a range of medicines have been developed with this aim.

As we saw on p.40, pain signals are relayed from nociceptors in the body up to the brain. For an analgesic to be worth anything, it must somehow interfere with this process, either by preventing the transmission of pain signals, or by affecting our ability to perceive pain once it has reached the brain.

## Aspirin and NSAIDs (non-steroidal anti-inflammatory drugs)

The powdery extract of willow bark has been known to have medicinal properties since the time of Hippocrates in the fifth century BC, easing fevers, aches and pains. The specific pain-relieving substance, **salicin**, was first identified in 1828 by the French pharmacist Henri Leroux, who named it after the willow from which it was isolated, *Salix alba*. In 1897 the German chemist Felix Hoffmann created the version of the drug we use today, acetylsalicylic acid. A novel derivative of salicin, it had all the analgesic benefits but fewer of the nasty gastrointestinal side effects. Hoffmann gave some of his new chemical to his father, who was suffering from arthritic pain. Luckily, it worked and the newly named **aspirin** was patented in 1899. Since then, it has become an undisputed wonder drug, bringing affordable, quick pain relief to millions.

But even in this form, aspirin wasn't without its side effects, and the risk of peptic ulcers and dyspepsia prompted scientists to create something new and improved. In 1961, after developing and testing hundreds of chemicals, the chemists of Boots Pure Drug Company came up with a safer alternative, 2-(4-isobutylphenyl)propionic acid, or **ibuprofen**. Ibuprofen was initially launched in 1969 as a treatment for rheumatoid arthritis. Now, it is ubiquitous, found in treatments that get rid of headaches, swelling, inflammation and fever.

Both aspirin and ibuprofen are **NSAIDs**, achieving analgesia by shutting pain perception down at its source. These types of drugs selectively block the activity of a family of enzymes whose function is to create, amongst other chemicals, **prostaglandins**. Prostaglandins are the chemicals responsible for triggering the sensation of pain. In the presence of a painful stimulus, they are released from surrounding tissue, resulting in the sensitizing and stimulation of nearby nociceptors. By blocking these enzymes, called cyclooxygenases, NSAIDs prevent prostaglandins from being made, meaning nociceptors aren't stimulated, and we are left free of pain.

## Paracetamol

Paracetamol is another immensely successful over-the-counter treatment for pain and fever. Originally discovered in the nineteenth century in the urine of people testing a different drug, phenacetin, it was largely ignored until 1948 when two scientists, Bernard Brodie and Julius Axelrod, finally grasped the significance of this breakdown product. In 1955, paracetamol became available in the US under the name Tylenol and a year later it was launched in the UK as Panadol.

Precisely how para-acetyl-amino-phenol reduces the brain's capacity to perceive pain is still being worked out. It's not yet considered "fact", but one compelling explanation is that paracetamol blocks the activity of COX-2, a member of the cyclooxygenase family of enzymes which, as we have seen, generate the prostaglandins that trigger feelings of pain. This newly identified cyclooxygenase is found in the brain and spinal cord rather than the body's extremities (explaining its lack of anti-inflammatory action). It seems that by preventing this cyclooxygenase from making prostaglandins, paracetamol severs a vital link in the chain of pain signalling, diminishing the brain's perception of pain.

## Opiates

Opium, derived from the opium poppy, *Papaver somniferum*, has been used for thousands of years as a painkiller. Its modern derivatives, includ-

## Natural painkillers?

**Endorphins** (short for endogenous morphines, literally "morphine produced naturally in the body") are natural opioid peptides (small proteins) produced in the pituitary gland and hypothalamus. Of the three best-known endorphins, alpha, beta and gamma, the beta-endorphins are thought to potentially act as a natural analgesic, diminishing the perception of pain. They achieve this by binding to precisely the same neuronal receptor as morphine (the mu1 opioid receptor). Once bound, the endorphin has the ultimate effect of causing increased dopamine within the brain, making us feel good.

Pain, laughter and strenuous aerobic exercise can stimulate the release of endorphins, causing some to experience a sense of euphoria, as in the "**runner's high**". And indeed, following a regular exercise programme does have a positive impact on depression and anxiety, according to one recent meta-analysis. However, it may be too simple an explanation to conclude that this effect is the result of boosting endorphins. Some research does imply an involvement of endorphin levels in conditions such as depression, but findings vary. And exercise has many other possible benefits that might lead to an improved outlook: increased blood flow, raised self-esteem and distraction from perceived problems.

ing **codeine** and **morphine**, are the most powerful branch of analgesics. However, their capacity for tolerance and addiction means their use is closely monitored.

Morphine, the active ingredient in opium, was first isolated in 1804 by the German pharmacist Friedrich Sertürner. His discovery revolutionized the treatment of pain, and morphine soon became immensely popular with doctors on and off the battlefield, who used it to treat opium and alcohol addiction, and as a surgical anaesthetic and painkiller.

Opiates work in an entirely different way to the NSAIDs and paracetamol – they bind to special **opioid receptors** located throughout the body, spinal cord and deep inside the brain. The principal neurons involved in the brain's pain pathways possess these opioid receptors at their synaptic terminal, near the site of neurotransmitter release. Normally, opioid receptors receive natural signals in the form of endorphins, dynorphins and enkephalins from other accessory neurons nearby (known as interneurons) – these signals put the brakes on the main neuron's ability to release its cargo of neurotransmitters. Morphine binds to these same opioid receptors, shutting down the pain pathway and reducing the brain's ability to perceive pain.

# Cannabis

The final drug in our catalogue is cannabis. Containing many different chemicals and having a consequent variety of different effects on the brain, it does not fall neatly into any one of the above categories. It is also by far the most popular illicit drug in the world – consumed in one form or another by around 150 million people every day – which might in itself merit its having its own entry. Human use of cannabis has a long and broad history. It has been in ritual and religious use for thousands of years, and its first documented use in a medicinal capacity is by Shen Nung, one of the fathers of Chinese medicine, in the twenty-eighth century BC.

Cannabis is produced from the flowers, trichomes and resin of the *Cannabis sativa* plant. When the resin is mixed with leafy fragments, the drug is commonly known as **marijuana**. Alternatively, the resin-rich trichomes can be processed to produce highly concentrated, dark blocks of resin called **hashish**.

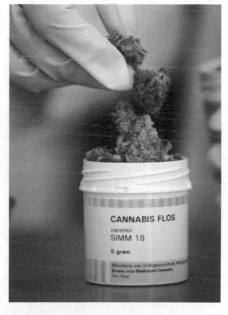

The chemical that is primarily responsible for cannabis's mind-altering effects is tetrahydrocannabinol, or **THC**. Once THC gets into the brain, it is able to dock onto and activate a specific receptor protein, cannabinoid receptor-1 (CB1). This triggers a cascade of events inside the neuron, interfering with its normal flow of activity. Because these receptors are found throughout the central nervous system, THC wreaks havoc on almost every important neurological system. CB1 receptors are abundant in brain regions such as the basal ganglia and cerebellum, which is how THC manages to affect coordination and movement. They are present

**Cannabis is measured into a container at a pharmacy in the Netherlands, which in 2003 became the first country to make cannabis available as a prescription drug. It's available for sufferers of cancer, HIV and multiple sclerosis.**

## Food additives

In the pursuit of longer-lasting, tastier, moister, sweeter and more colourful food, the food industry has developed hundreds of chemical additives. In an attempt to regulate their use, the Codex Alimentarius committee (set up in 1963 by the Food and Agriculture Organization of the United Nations and the World Health Organization) created the International Numbering System, or INS. This is the source of the three- or four-digit numbers we see on almost every food packaging we buy, in Europe prefixed by the letter E. We consume these chemicals daily, relatively ignorant of their existence, purpose or potential dangers.

**Tartrazine**, E102, is a synthetic yellow dye found in a huge number of foodstuffs, from drinks to cakes, soups to curry. Tartrazine can affect a number of physiological systems, not least the brain. Particularly among those with asthma or aspirin intolerance, there are reports of altered perception, agitation, migraine, confusion and blurred vision – a hefty potential price to pay for more vibrantly coloured food.

**Erythrosine**, E127, is an intense, cherry-red dye found in such items as tinned cherries, salmon paste and dental plaque disclosure tablets. Banned in Norway, erythrosine has been implicated in altered thyroid activity and hypersensitivity to light. Research from the 1980s also suggests it is capable of blocking the actions of certain neurotransmitters, including dopamine. Results such as these, although not widely accepted, support a possible connection between this additive and conditions such as **ADHD** (see p.164).

**Monosodium glutamate**, E621, is a widely used flavour enhancer. It is believed to work by stimulating the recently discovered fifth taste bud, sensitive to umami, or "savouriness". By introducing this simple chemical into foodstuffs, manufacturers can replace quality ingredients (ie actual food) with bulking agents with little or no nutritional value – making the production process cheaper while keeping the consumer happy. There have been concerns about its use, however, with studies implicating it in everything from migraines to the death of brain cells. Once ingested, MSG releases **glutamate** – the major excitatory **neurotransmitter**. The blood–brain barrier (see p.188) ought normally to keep glutamate out. But this barrier does have

in the hypothalamus, which controls primal urges such as hunger (hence the munchies), in the hippocampus, an essential component of memory-formation pathways, and in the cortex, the large brain region responsible for all higher thinking and reasoning.

In normal circumstances, the CB1 receptor binds to the neurotransmitter **anandamide**. Quite what role anandamide plays in the brain remains undetermined, but it seems to be involved in mood, memory, pain, move-its weak points – is it possible that glutamate from MSG consumption might leak into the brain to damaging effect? The controversy surrounding the use of this chemical led the Federation of American Societies for Experimental Biology (FASEB) to produce an independent review in 1995 to allay public fears. They found that a percentage of the population might react to MSG, developing "MSG symptom complex", a condition whose symptoms may include a burning or numbness in the back of the neck, arms or body, facial tingling or tightness, chest pain, headaches, nausea, rapid heartbeat or drowsiness. However, there was no evidence connecting MSG consumption to neurodegenerative diseases or nerve-cell damage.

**Aspartame**, E951, is an artificial sweetener, two hundred times sweeter than sugar. In Europe alone, around two thousand tons of the stuff is consumed every year, as an ingredient in drinks and food, or as a sweetener added to hot drinks – it's a highly profitable chemical. It was discovered by accident (after he licked his finger to pick up a piece of paper) in 1965 by James M. Schlatter, whilst developing anti-ulcer drugs. Today, there is a great deal of controversy surrounding the safety of this simple chemical. An early study claimed tumours formed in the brains of rats fed aspartame. However, the rats were fed relatively huge amounts of the chemical, at least 1000 mg per kg of body weight per day. Several follow-up studies were performed to ascertain how significant these results were and, overall, the findings don't currently support aspartame's role as an inducer of brain tumours. The daily recommended maximum for aspartame consumption is 40 mg/kg of body weight (at least 25 times less than was used in the rat experiments) – and you would need to be a dedicated sweetaholic to get near this threshold as most of us rarely go above 10 mg/kg per day. Despite the weight of evidence and the chemical's approval by such bodies as the Food Standards Agency in the UK and the Food and Drug Administration in the US, there are still numerous websites and articles alleging links between aspartame-containing products and conditions such as leukaemia, asthma, anxiety attacks, depression, migraines, poor concentration and impotency. Time will tell how many of these claims are grounded in scientific truth.

ment and hunger. THC's ability to subvert this system has made it useful in the medical world, helping to diminish nausea and increase appetite in cancer and AIDS patients, decreasing severe pain in rheumatoid arthritis, and reducing both pain and muscular spasms in those with multiple sclerosis (see p.151). However, there are possible dangers associated with the drug. A study into the use of cannabis conducted by a team of scientists from London's Institute of Psychiatry found that up to a quarter of people who begin smoking cannabis in their teenage years are five times more likely to develop psychotic disorders such as schizophrenia (see p.166). This increased vulnerability appears to be linked to the inheritance of a specific variant of the gene that makes **catechol-O-methyltransferase (COMT)**. COMT is involved in the breakdown of neurotransmitters including dopamine – especially within the prefrontal cortex. If a person inherits the variant form of the gene, the functioning of COMT will be altered, affecting dopamine levels within the still-developing brain. The combination of this with the use of THC may be enough to lay the foundations for future mental-health problems.

# Unlocking the brain

The history of human scientific endeavour is largely a mix of curiosity-driven exploration melded with the pursuit of the betterment of mankind – the hunt for knowledge and health. Sometimes, however, the truth one is seeking lies inside the mind of a person determined, for whatever reason, to resolutely hold onto the information in their brain. In such instances, where reasoning and discussion fail, some turn to ethically barren methods that operate outside the judicial system, eliminating free will from the equation: torture. **Physical torture** relies on fear and pain, two of our most basic human responses, to extract information. But people rightly question the validity of information gained under such duress, where the victim is highly motivated to appease their torturer – to tell them what they want to hear. The lure of physical torture is speed of extraction; why use reason to get what you want when threats of oblivion can result in a person gushing with information. A quote from 1883 refers to the observations one Sir James Stephens made of the Indian police at the time:

> "The war against terrorism is a war against those who engage in torture."
>
> Ed Markey, US House of Representatives

> It is far pleasanter to sit comfortably in the shade rubbing red pepper in a poor devil's eyes than to go about in the sun hunting up evidence.

Physical extraction of information has, in more recent times, been joined by a range of brain-specific methods, with a variety of chemicals – never conceived of for the purposes of torture or interrogation – becoming available. Rather than relying on pure pain or fear, interrogators use these drugs to try and get subjects to open up, relax, become compliant and carefree – to reach a point where they *want* to tell you. Here, we'll take a look at how these chemicals came about, what they are and how they work to make a determined mind relinquish its most private thoughts.

## Truth drugs

In Colombia, there's a street drug referred to as **"Devil's Breath"**, which, when administered to an unknowing victim, saps their free will, leaving them in a state in which they become far more compliant to their assailant's wishes whilst retaining no memory of what transpired. The active ingredient in this "zombie drug" is **scopolamine**, an alkaloid drug derived from the nightshade family of plants.

Originally isolated in 1880 by the German chemist Albert Ladenburg (1842–1911), scopolamine went on to become a popular choice for the creation of concoctions designed to help women through childbirth by inducing what was known as a "twilight sleep". In this condition, women entered a state in which, while lucid, their experience of pain was greatly diminished, as was their memory of the experience. It was while observing women in this condition (in Dallas, Texas, in the early 1900s) that one Dr Robert Ernst House observed that, in addition to becoming more sedate, his patients also seemed prone to volunteer information – even in the absence of prompting, they happily divulged details of their lives.

The idea of a "truth drug" was born in 1922, when House decided to expand on his observations of women immersed in the twilight sleep and try scopolamine on the more roguish criminal fraternity. In this first recorded instance of **narcoanalysis**, he arranged to interview two prisoners at the local Dallas county jail, both of whom were thought guilty of their accused misdeeds. Under the influence of scopolamine, both men denied the charges they were accused of and, much to House's delight, found innocent at the conclusion of their trial. This convinced House – and the wider public – that lying was beyond human capability whilst under the drug's influence. Today, however, the law has a less favourable view of such drug-induced verbosity and considers information gained through the use of such drugs inadmissible as evidence in a court of law.

Scopolamine is a "muscarinic receptor antagonist", which deserves a little explanation. Receptor proteins peppering the surface of neurons are often known by the name of the chemical initially found to bind or stimulate them and, in this case, these receptors were found to respond to **muscarine**, a natural compound that can be extracted from certain mushrooms – hence the name. The natural binding partner for these receptors is now known to be the neurotransmitter **acetylcholine** – but when scopolamine is present, it binds to and blocks the receptor (specifically, the M1 muscarinic receptor), preventing acetylcholine from docking. This is generally bad news for the brain and body.

Acetylcholine has widespread effects throughout both the central nervous, autonomic and neuromuscular systems. Scopolamine's ability to cross the blood–brain barrier allows it to gain entry to and disrupt the brain's higher functioning centres responsible for such things as memory (hence the associated amnesia), self-awareness and control. But it was the side effects on the entire nervous system that made it a drug to be wary of and later dropped, ranging from hallucinations to blurred vision, heart palpitations, headache...

## Sodium thiopental

Better known by its trade name **Sodium Pentothal**, this notorious "truth drug" belongs to the barbiturate family of drugs acting on the $GABA_A$ receptors of the central nervous system (as do several other drugs used in this context, such as sodium amytal). This fast-acting, short-lived drug hits the central nervous system, slowing down nerve conduction, dampening the mind, literally making it more difficult to think. As we saw in chapter 6 (p.112), lying takes effort, one has to use the brain to build a fabricated reality. Sodium thiopental significantly ups the effort needed to build falsehoods, making the truth a likelier prospect. However, this does rely on the subject's perception of the truth – if they avidly believe the information in their mind to be truthful, there's simply no lie to tell.

Sodium thiopental first saw the light of day when American chemists, Ernest Henry Volwiler (1893–1992) and Donalee L. Tabern (1900–74) created it for the large pharmaceutical company Abbott Laboratories in the 1930s. Originally developed for use as an anaesthetic, the drug is still widely used today during the induction phase of general anaesthesia. However, its ability to rapidly relax a person to the point where consciousness is abandoned has also made it a chief component of the lethal injection procedure, still widely used throughout the US.

# CHAPTER 10

# The unexplained brain

## Mind over matter and ESP

There is much about the workings of the brain that we still don't understand. Science has come a long way in the last few centuries but it doesn't yet have an answer for everything – for example, as we saw in Chapter 8, our understanding of the causes of mental illnesses is still hazy at best. In this chapter we are going to head beyond the limits of science's current understanding of the brain, delving into controversial areas on the periphery of brain studies to examine phenomena which scientists either can't yet explain or simply don't believe to exist.

The first half of the chapter concerns the mind's ability to influence our physical health, and covers everything from the use of **laughter** to boost the immune system to the use of **hypnosis** to reduce pain. The second half of the chapter ventures further into the realms of what the majority of us would regard as impossible, exploring the belief, held by a surprising number of people, that the mind can perceive things beyond the reach of the traditional five senses through **extra-sensory perception** (ESP).

What science can't explain, it often dismisses as impossible. Alternative therapies are regarded by many scientists as entirely the result of the placebo effect, while ESP is dismissed as simply untrue. But just because we can't explain what is going on during an acupuncture session doesn't mean advances in science won't one day find some credible mechanism for its effects. Equally, the fact that no one has yet managed to reliably reproduce telepathy under lab conditions is not enough to prove categorically that it doesn't exist. Maybe there is some truth in it, but science has not yet developed techniques to record it.

We will take an objective look at all these controversial subjects and, where possible, relay tangible evidence. It is extremely comforting to think we know almost everything there is to know. Well, we don't, and our understanding of the brain has ahead of it one of the longest journeys of all.

# Mind over matter

The concept that the mind is important in the treatment of illness is integral to Chinese medicine, and was for a long time a similarly significant part of the Western medical tradition – it was a central belief of Hippocrates, for example. But modern medicine has largely severed this connection, and the idea that the mind can influence our physical health has long been anathema to our way of thinking about the two. However, times are changing and we are becoming increasingly aware of the link between our mental state and our physical health.

## Is laughter the best medicine?

Few would argue over the personal benefits the sensation of happiness affords – we all enjoy a giggle with friends or indulging in lone activities that elicit joy or relaxing responses, whether reading, listening to music or playing games. But does a happy brain mean a body better able to ward off disease or fight infection?

The Canadian Nova Scotia Health Survey, published in 2009's *European Heart Journal*, followed more than 1700 men and women over ten years to discover if happiness, or "positive affect", had an impact on their risk of heart disease. Each person's affect was determined by subjecting them to standard, scientific assessments of their depressive, hostile or anxious tendencies. What the team, led by William Whang, found was that for every point increase scored on the **positive affect scale**, the risk of heart disease reduced by more than twenty percent. If that's not cause enough for celebration, one of the largest studies ever undertaken to analyse the relationship between "subjective wellbeing" and longevity was published in 2011's *Applied Psychology: Health and Well-Being*. After poring over the data compiled from more than forty other individual studies examining the relationship between either longevity or illness and **perceived wellbeing**, the authors (Ed Diener and Micaela Y. Chan) found that an extra skip in one's step can contribute anything between four and ten years of additional life.

Turning to the **immune system**, studies have found that people taking exams, caring for a relative with Alzheimer's disease or going through a similarly stressful period can take longer to heal wounds and have an increased susceptibility to viral infections such as the common cold. A study by Melissa Rosenkranz and her colleagues at the University of Wisconsin's Laboratory of Affective Neuroscience in 2003 suggested stress may also affect our ability to respond to vaccination. Prior research conducted in their lab, run by Richard Davidson, had discovered that negative emotions like fear and anger seemed to cause higher activity in the **right prefrontal cortex** – the opposite side to that activated by positive thoughts. In this new study, participants were asked to spend a minute thinking about, then five minutes writing about, either an extremely positive or an extremely unpleasant experience they'd encountered in their life. Each immediately received a flu vaccine. Six months later, all participants had their levels of flu-virus antibodies measured – an indication of how successful an immune response they'd mounted. The researchers found that higher activity in the right, "negative-thinking" portion of the cortex correlated quite nicely with lower levels of antibodies. And vice versa – those lucky enough to have been instructed to think happy thoughts had a better immune response.

Dr Esther Sternberg, Director of the Integrative Neural Immune Program at the US's National Institute of Mental Health (NIMH), has suggested a mechanism for the influence of stress on the immune system. When immune cells are fighting an infection, they send signals to the brain inducing "sickness behaviours" – such as a reduced desire to eat, have sex, or even get out of bed – which might help conserve energy for fighting the infection. The signals also activate the hypothalamus, prompting the release of stress hormones such as cortisol. These hormones have the job of shutting down the immune response when it is no longer needed. But if a person is chronically stressed, they will be constantly pumping out these stress hormones, effectively telling their immune cells not to go into battle.

If our state of mind and our immune system are so intimately linked, is it possible we could literally think ourselves better?

Researchers at UCLA's Jonsson Cancer Center are trying to ascertain the health and healing benefits of happiness in their **Rx Laughter** project. Founded in 1998 by Sherry D. Hilber, the project's hypothesis is that comedy can strengthen the immune system so that it is better able to fight illness. Research back in 1985 had suggested that watching a humorous video could boost levels of an immune-system protein called salivary immunoglobulin A, one of our body's first-line defences against infection. Building on this and other research, the project has the dual aim of further investigating this possible link between laughter and the immune system and putting their ideas into practice by determining the most effective material for making seriously ill children laugh, then putting that material to good use. This non-profit organization delivers individualized comedy "treatment programmes" with the aim of diminishing pain and boosting the immune systems in children with serious illnesses such as cancer or AIDS (**Rx Laughter** www.rxlaughter.org).

Professor Leslie Walker, former Director of the Institute of Rehabilitation in Hull has also been carrying out studies to determine precisely how much of an impact the mind can have on the body of a person with cancer. Cancer carries a heavy psychological burden, including long-term stress, depression and "Damocles syndrome", in which a person with cancer is so preoccupied with their uncertain future that they find it difficult to get on with their day-to-day life. It is precisely this type of chronic stress that can cause a weakening of our immune system (according to wide-ranging surveys of the literature) and, potentially, make us less able to fight cancer.

Professor Walker's hypothesis is that, through the use of relaxation and coping mechanisms to combat stress, a patient can strengthen their immune system and stack the odds of survival in their favour. He combines relaxation techniques with the use of "**guided imagery**", in which the patient conjures up, as vividly as they can, an image symbolic of their immune system attacking their cancer. This may seem a little odd, but the effects speak for themselves. In one of Walker's properly controlled studies, participants undergoing this regimen (in combination with traditional treatments) experienced a range of mental benefits including improvements in quality of life. Physical alterations were also evident, with several components of the immune system showing changes thought to be beneficial (for example, an increase in "**natural killer" cells**, which are believed to have anti-tumour activity). However, Walker acknowledges that, so far, there is scant evidence supporting prolonged survival as a consequence of such techniques. In his review of the available studies, six revealed increased longevity, while six did not.

So where does this leave us? Powerful evidence of prolonged survival in serious conditions such as cancer may indeed be currently lacking. But it is clear that there is a link between our state of mind and our immune system. Only further research will reveal whether this link is strong enough to help us in the fight against serious disease.

# Pain

Pain demands attention. Not in the sense that it captures one's attention, but in the sense that the brain must consciously attend to a painful stimulus in order to feel it. Clearly then, if a person can be helped to ignore pain, the sensation should diminish to a more tolerable level, possibly even vanish. This knowledge has long been put into practice in the care of patients undergoing painful medical procedures (see box overleaf). But what if the pain signals could be prevented from ever reaching the conscious part of the brain? Below are three different therapies which aim to reduce our perception of pain in just this way.

## Hypnosis

The hypnotic phenomenon that inspires the most awe is probably the patient who undergoes major surgery without chemical anaesthesia. The history of **hypnoanaesthesia** goes back to the nineteenth century. Back then, surgery was necessarily performed without anaesthetics, simply because they hadn't yet been discovered. As such, when doctors reported carrying out surgery without pain, through the use of what was then known as "animal magnetism" or "mesmerism", there was a great deal of interest. The discovery of chloroform and ether shortly afterwards naturally put an end to further investigation. However, in recent years there has been renewed interest in the possibility of anaesthesia via hypnosis.

In 1996 Elvira Lang and David Spiegel conducted a pilot study into the use of self hypnosis in surgery. Patients due to undergo a variety of invasive procedures were put into two groups. One used hypnosis plus patient-controlled conscious sedation, while the other group used just the sedation. Only four of the sixteen in the hypnotized group, compared to thirteen of the fourteen in the control group, requested medication. And those in the hypnotized group experienced less pain and anxiety than the controls. Lang has since carried out a larger study which reinforced her initial findings.

It has been estimated that as many as ten percent of people could undergo major procedures using hypnoanaesthesia as their sole anaesthetic. Others think the figure would be much lower. The patient certainly needs to be highly responsive to hypnosis for it to work. However, many more people could benefit from the use of hypnosis as an adjunct to chemical anaesthesia. And research has shown that in less extreme cases than surgery, hypnosis can help reduce pain, if not eliminate it altogether.

## Video games and pain

One of the more imaginative video game applications to emerge in recent years is the use of virtual reality (VR) to distract patients from pain. In 1996 Hunter Hoffman of the University of Washington and David R. Patterson of the Harborview Medical Center in Seattle, Washington, came up with the idea of using VR to help severe-burns victims cope with the pain of having their wound dressings changed – considered one of medicine's most painful experiences.

The more a patient focuses attention on their pain, the more painful they perceive it to be. Distraction – for example through music and videos – has long been used to help with painful procedures by luring attention away, leaving less available to process incoming pain signals. However, the fully immersive environment of virtual reality takes this distraction to a whole new level.

The patient puts on a special headset and enters a three-dimensional VR environment called *SnowWorld*. Suddenly, the patient is flying through elaborate icy canyons, populated by snowmen, penguins and robots. To the accompaniment of the sound of soothing music, the patient must fire snowballs at snowmen – the combination of a cold theme, music and a specific task hijacks the brain's attention. While they concentrate on these cold-oriented tasks, their wounds can be cleaned and dressed. They experience a fraction of the pain they would normally suffer and therefore also require fewer drugs.

**You can see a video of SnowWorld in action here:** www.dnatube.com/video/4096/Soldiers-Get-Virtual-Reality-Therapy-for-Burn-Pain

**Above: a patient has his dressing changed while distracted by a virtual reality system. Below: brain scans showing pain-related activity without such distraction (left) and with it (right).**

A study by Dr Christina Liossi from the University of Southampton revealed the pain-reducing benefits of hypnosis on eighty young cancer patients between six and sixteen years of age. In this experiment into **hypnotic analgesia**, some patients received professional hypnotic treatment in addition to their usual anaesthesia, while others received just the anaesthetic. Subsequent to their treatment, each was asked to rate their sensation of pain. Every person who had received hypnosis claimed to experience less pain.

There are numerous theories to explain this hotly debated neurological phenomenon but, thanks to brain-imaging techniques, scientists are now able to monitor the brains of those undergoing hypnosis to see whether brain activity is altered in a way that might explain the pain reduction experienced. A research team from the University of Iowa and the Technical University of Aachen in Germany used functional magnetic resonance imaging (fMRI) to peer directly into the brains of twelve healthy volunteers. The volunteers were subjected to painful heat,

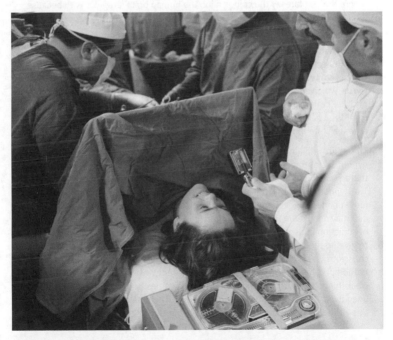

Nineteen-year-old Pierina Menegazzo smiles and jokes during the removal of her appendix in Italy, 1961, after having been "anaesthetized by hypnosis".

# How does hypnosis work?

Hypnosis is, of course, used for many other things than pain relief. And that doesn't just mean embarrassing people on stage in front of their friends. **Hypnotherapy** – the therapeutic use of hypnosis – is used to treat everything from addiction to phobias. But whatever the context, the underlying mechanism is the same: the subject is guided by the hypnotist to respond to suggestions for changes in their thoughts or behaviour.

What is going on in the brain of a hypnotized person? John Gruzelier – Professor of Psychology at Goldsmith's College, University of London – carried out a brain-imaging study that shed some light on this question. Gruzelier's team screened subjects before the study and selected twelve who were classed as "succumbing to hypnotic techniques rather easily" and twelve who were classed as "resistant". All the subjects were asked to complete a standard cognitive exercise called the **Stroop test**, once under normal conditions and once under hypnosis. The Stroop test, named after psychologist John Ridley Stroop, is deceptively simple, usually consisting of lists of colours. What makes it such a brain twister is that the words are written in a different colour from the one the word describes – so the word "blue" may be coloured red, "green" may be yellow, and so on. The task is to ignore the text but say the colour, a job the human brain struggles with because it has to override its immediate, learned response to the text.

Both groups achieved similar scores regardless of their mental state. Before hypnosis, brain activity was similar too, but under hypnosis, the highly susceptible subjects showed increased brain activity in two regions – the **left prefrontal cortex** involved in planning and judgement, and the **anterior cingulate gyrus**, which also plays a role in conflict/error detection. The increased activity of these brain areas implies that these subjects had to work a lot harder to perform the task while hypnotized. This suggests that, during hypnosis, the brain enters a state in which it is less able to reason and detect false information.

This might explain why a hypnotized person may be willing to carry out a stage hypnotist's outrageous suggestions. More usefully, it might explain why hypnotherapy can be so effective in helping a person to give up smoking, for example. The hypnotized brain's difficulty with reasoning and error detection may make it more open to suggestions such as "give up cigarettes". A heavy smoker trying to quit may need more than chewing gum and nicotine replacement, as the craving of addiction is also heavily psychological; the addict must be strongly motivated to give up their vice. In the absence of external influence, the addicted person's consciousness is happy to find new ways to justify its desire to light up. The hypnotherapist, however, may act like a stealth agent, lowering the mind's defences, weakening the left hemisphere's critical faculties and dropping in positive, unequivocal messages: "I *will* stop smoking." The smoker may tell themselves this all the time without truly believing it, but during the session the message may reach a deeper level of penetration, at a more unconscious level.

**Stroop test** www.snre.umich.edu/eplab/demos/st0/stroopdesc.html

sometimes while hypnotized, sometimes while not. While in a hypnotic state, all twelve subjects reported significantly reduced perception of pain. Brain imaging revealed reduced activity in regions involved in our consciously "feeling" pain, such as the **primary sensory cortex** across the top of the brain. However, the researchers found increased activity in other regions, such as the **anterior cingulate gyrus** and the **basal ganglia**. They speculated that these regions could form part of an inhibition pathway that was blocking pain signals from reaching the cortex.

For more information on the use of hypnosis in medicine see **The Hypnotherapy Training Institute of Britain** (www.hypnotherapytraininginstitute.org).

## Acupuncture

Acupuncture belongs to traditional Chinese medicine and has been practised, mainly in the East, for around 2500 years. Its underlying principle is that in a healthy person the life force, or *qi* (pronounced "chee" – there is currently no recognized scientific evidence to support the existence of qi), flows smoothly around the body along pathways known as meridians. If the flow of qi is blocked, or becomes too high or low, we fall ill; acupuncture aims to rebalance this system through the insertion of needles into **acupoints** located throughout the body.

On a typical visit to an acupuncturist, those infamous needles – much finer than a hypodermic needle and just a little wider than a human hair – will be inserted into your skin. The acupuncturist may then twist them manually or pass a small electrical current through them. Beneath the outer, protective layer of our skin lies a profusion of nerves, sensing pain, pressure, temperature and touch, and sending information back to the spinal cord and brain. But does acupuncture actually work: do these needles have any real effect on the brain and nervous system? Could they somehow reduce our perception of pain?

**An acupuncture chart dating from the Ming dynasty.**

## Acupoints

Traditional medicine recognizes more than 2000 acupuncture points located throughout the body. But has science found any evidence that a needle stuck into one of these places will have a greater effect than it would elsewhere? Researchers have found that these acupoints do seem to coincide with specific anatomical structures, including nerves and their bifurcations, blood vessels, ligaments and the suture lines of the skull. Other studies have found that acupoints have higher local skin temperature and lower electrical resistance than points just 3mm away. Brain imaging has also produced some interesting results. Researchers at the University of California, Irvine, have found that stimulating a "vision" acupoint in the foot activated the occipital lobes, which are associated with vision. Stimulating a point just 2cm away did not activate this area. Other researchers have found evidence linking acupoints to areas of the brain associated with language (Broca's area) and hearing. While it would seem that needles, inserted at specific, time-honoured locations around the body, can sometimes affect the brain in specific ways, medicine still regards this area with caution, demanding more rigorous research to fully explain the phenomenon.

One of the biggest problems Western science has with something like acupuncture is that, unlike a drug, it is hard to subject to rigorous scientific method. This has led many sceptics to suggest that the possible benefits of acupuncture are due to the placebo effect – that the treatments themselves offer no physiological benefit whatsoever, but that the patient's belief that they do makes them work.

Testing the contribution of the placebo effect to acupuncture is tricky, as you're either having needles stuck in you or you're not. But a collaboration between Southampton University's Complementary Medicine Research Unit and University College London's Wellcome Department of Imaging Neuroscience has managed to resolve this problem. Taking a group of fourteen people with osteoarthritis, a painful disease, the researchers put each person through a series of three different tests in random order:

▶ they were touched with blunted needles which the subjects knew were incapable of piercing their skin and had no possible therapeutic value

▶ they were fooled into believing they were receiving real acupuncture through the use of dummy needles with collapsible points (like a prop knife in a movie)

▶ they were treated with genuine acupuncture

All the while, the brains of the test subjects were being monitored using imaging equipment. None of the subjects reported decreased pain, but the scientists' findings are interesting nonetheless. They discovered that in the "blunt subjects", only regions of the brain involved in touch were active. In the case of both the "dummy needles" and the genuine needles, the subjects were expecting real acupuncture – this expectation manifested itself as activity in the brain's right **dorsolateral prefrontal cortex** (associated with higher functioning such as working memory), the **anterior cingulate gyrus** (which has numerous roles, including emotional responses) and the **midbrain** (involved in controlling many of our sensory and motor functions). However, in the case of genuine acupuncture, an additional part of the brain was more active than when dummy needles were used, the **insular cortex**, involved in the modulation of pain perception. Although this is just one small study, it does suggest the possibility that acupuncture has a specific effect on a region of the brain involved in pain perception – a demonstrable physiological effect over and above the placebo effect.

So where does the medical profession stand? In 1997, the US National Institute of Health (NIH) published its Consensus Statement on Acupuncture, stating that results to date were hard to interpret, largely due to concerns with experimental design. Since then, the NIH's National Center for Complementary and Alternative Medicine has continued to pursue the scientific truth of acupuncture, funding research into its potential role and effect in everything from migraine to osteoarthritis. Whilst the precise mechanisms underlying this ancient treatment still remain frustratingly elusive, both the US and UK recognize some evidence of acupuncture's effectiveness in treating conditions such as lower back pain.

**What the National Center for Complementary and Alternative Medicine says about acupuncture:** nccam.nih.gov/health/acupuncture/introduction.htm#status

## Magnetic fields

Static magnets have been used for centuries in efforts to relieve pain. In the last forty years, the use of pulsating electromagnetic fields has also been introduced. The usefulness of a pulsating electromagnetic field in bone healing is well established – even NASA conducted its own studies into how specific magnetic fields may be used to prevent muscle atrophy and bone loss during long space flights. But it has also been claimed that it can help relieve the pain associated with osteoarthritis and migraine, among other conditions.

As yet, there is little hard evidence of the beneficial effects of either still magnets or pulsing electromagnetic fields, but this is a growing area of research that is yielding some interesting results. There does appear to be evidence that static magnets are capable of reducing different types of pain, from rheumatic pain to headaches. And a study carried out by researchers at the Perspectivism Foundation in the US has suggested that **extremely low frequency (ELF) magnetic field therapy** can reduce pain in those suffering from osteoarthritis. A group of 176 patients underwent a series of therapy sessions in which they were either subjected to a pulsed electromagnetic field or given a placebo treatment (the magnet was switched off). The volunteers rated their pain levels before and after each session and two weeks later. The reported reduction in pain was 46 percent for the group exposed to the magnetic field, and 8 percent for those in the control group.

Experiments on rats carried out by scientists at the University of Milan have suggested a mechanism by which magnetic fields might cause such a reduction in pain. After prolonged exposure to magnetic fields (over a period of eight months), the rats were found to have altered densities of opioid receptors in their frontal and parietal cortices and hippocampus. This suggests that the brain's pain-dulling opioid network may be responsive to magnetic exposure. Experiments on the land snail *Cepaea nemoralis* by researchers at the University of Western Ontario have given additional support to this theory by demonstrating that the analgesia induced by the magnetic field is reduced in the presence of the opioid antagonist naxolone, or opioid receptor antagonists.

# Extra-sensory perception

Contrary to the available evidence, many people refuse to shake a gut feeling that the brain is somehow capable of seeing beyond the reach of the traditional five senses, into other people's minds, or different times or locations. Belief in extra-sensory perception is surprisingly common – a survey by Gallup in 2005 found that 31 percent of Americans believed in **telepathy**, and 26 percent in **clairvoyance**.

The vast majority of scientists are openly sceptical about the serious study of such phenomena, in the field known as **parapsychology**. This is largely justified, as evidence supporting the existence of paranormal abilities is sparse, controversial or unrepeatable – anathema in the scientific community. However, with only a handful of scientists prepared to develop the means to find hard evidence, the chances of finding it are greatly reduced.

## Telepathy

When we interact with another person, our brain gathers an immense amount of information about them, through body language, or "**paralanguage**". In those vital first moments upon meeting a new person, the vast majority of information we receive comes not from what they say, but from their vocal tones and inflexions, their clothes, posture and facial gestures. The entire body acts like a klaxon, screaming intimate details of our mental state to all and sundry. Remarkably, we barely notice, which is just as well. Were we to consciously process the great volumes of paralanguage flooding in through our senses, we'd barely get past "good morning" before the brain would grind to a halt. But the brain manages very well – the senses relay this information back to the brain, where it is processed at an unconscious, subcortical level. Smells, auditory and visual cues, emotions and memories unite, and the results of this silent rumination are sent streaming to the conscious brain, which responds in the appropriate way. Some are natural masters at this, born negotiators, while others struggle with the simplest of social interactions, failing to "read" those around them. This summed, unconscious knowledge may be called "instinct" or "gut feeling". A non-verbal sense of rightness or wrongness, it is the brain's distilled assessment of a situation or person which functions to increase our chances of survival.

> "We have five senses in which we glory and which we recognize and celebrate, senses that constitute the sensible world for us. But there are other senses – secret senses, sixth senses, if you will – equally vital, but unrecognized, and unlauded."
>
> Oliver Sacks

Some believe there is more to sensing others than pure evolutionary adaptation. Standing in the presence of another human, evaluating their intent and, possibly, their desirability, is one thing. But what about those occasions when we feel we're being watched – only to turn and look directly into the surprised, slightly guilty eyes of someone staring directly at us? In 2005, the journal *Scientific American* published an article about **Rupert's resonance**. This idea, from the mind of British biologist Rupert Sheldrake, intended to explain, among other things, why people often think they know they're being looked at from a distance – even when the person staring lies beyond the limits of their peripheral vision.

Sheldrake proposes that this apparent phenomenon is due to "morphic resonance" – fields of energy (morphs) running between, and shared by,

## Derren Brown and paralanguage

If his claims are to be believed, "psychologist illusionist" Derren Brown is compelling proof of the power of **paralanguage**, and a reminder that even the most incredible feats can be explained away without recourse to the paranormal.

Specifically denying that he is able to read minds, Brown insists in the opening credits of each of his shows that all of his stunts are achieved through a combination of "magic, suggestion, psychology, misdirection and showmanship". In other words, they rely on his ability to manipulate the vast amount of information we give out in the form of paralanguage. Brown would have us believe that he reads the paralanguage of others in order to gauge what they are thinking, and subtly controls their response to him through the use of subliminal messages given out by his own body language.

Over the years, Brown has faked a séance, persuaded religious groups he has special powers, and even got normally respectable members of the public to perform armed robbery. In his most famous stunt, in 2003, he caused uproar in the UK by apparently playing Russian roulette on live television. A volunteer he had chosen from among twelve thousand hopefuls loaded a single shot into a revolver with numbered chambers and then counted from one to six. The idea was that Brown's ability to read paralanguage would allow him to learn from this recitation which chamber held the bullet. Equally, he could have subliminally influenced the volunteer's choice of which chamber to put the bullet in. Either way – if it was not an illusion – the feat was proof of the power of paralanguage. The idea that anyone would take such a risk on their ability to "read" someone in this way is incredible, but previous feats had convinced many viewers that he did have this ability and that it was therefore a genuine feat rather than a trick.

all life that has been and all life that is. Sheldrake claims great success in his defiantly simple experiments, in which a subject, or "staree", tells the experimenter whether or not they are being stared at by a "starer" stationed directly behind them. If the starer stares at their target on an entirely random number of occasions, the staree should guess correctly fifty percent of the time. Should they score significantly higher than this, Sheldrake interprets this as evidence of telepathic behaviour. For there to be a real, demonstrable effect, however, the experimenter needs to ensure factors such as bias and expectation are completely eliminated from the experimental conditions. Other researchers have attempted, unsuccessfully, to repeat Sheldrake's work. He counters this by arguing that their lack of belief in the phenomenon may make it less likely to occur – but this is not an argument ever likely to be accepted in the scientific community.

In 2004, *The British Journal of Psychology* published a meta-analysis (in which a large number of other studies in this field were grouped together and statistically analysed) of available research into "distant intentionality and the feeling of being stared at". The conclusion was that "there are hints of an effect, but also a shortage of independent replications and theoretical concepts". The jury, it seems, is

> "I think the supernatural is a catch-all for everything we don't understand about the vast other parts of life that we cannot perceive."
>
> William Shatner

still out. But studies into this nebulous area continue nonetheless, some of the most recent evidence being collected from a group of Hawaiian healers. The healers, at random time intervals, were invited by the researchers to send their own form of "distant intentionality" (in their case, the intent was related to healing) to recipients isolated within fMRI scanning equipment, capable of detecting patterns of brain activity over time. The healers had chosen their own recipient on the basis that they felt a "special connection". The authors claim to have found increased activity in several brain regions, correlating with the times that the healer sent their intent. Areas that became active include: the cingulate gyrus, involved in a number of functions from controlling autonomic responses to feelings of empathy and pain; the precuneus, part of the parietal lobe that may be involved in self-awareness, among other behaviours; and the frontal lobe, the home of higher functioning and reasoning.

## Clairvoyance

Clairvoyance is the supposed ability to somehow gather information about a place or object beyond the reach of the traditional five senses. To test for clairvoyance, parapsychologists frequently use **Zener cards**. The cards were invented by one of parapsychology's pioneers, **Joseph Banks Rhine** (1895–1980), as a means of measuring ESP in a more scientifically rigorous way which would allow results to be statistically analysed. Each card is printed with either a circle, a plus sign, a square, three wavy lines or a star. There are 25 cards in a pack – five of each design. To test for clairvoyance, the conductor of the experiment goes through the randomly shuffled pack of cards one by one and records both the symbol shown on the card and the test subject's guess. Note that the test subject is concentrating on the card, not attempting to "see through the experimenter's eyes". This procedure requires a number of measures to prevent cheating and ensure that the test subject isn't inadvertently given clues by the body

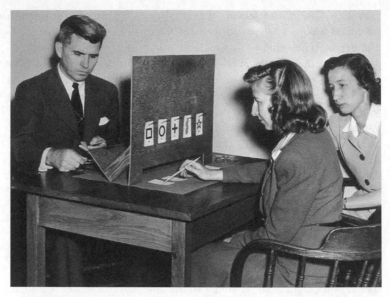

**Joseph Banks Rhine attempts to send messages brain-to-brain in the early days of his clairvoyance experiments.**

language or voice of the experimenter – the two people may even be in entirely different parts of the building.

Because there are five possible symbols, the test subject has a one-in-five chance of guessing each card correctly. Although a person without clairvoyant ability might get lucky in the short term, after several run-throughs their average hit rate would be twenty percent. If some form of clairvoyance is afoot, however, the score should be significantly higher.

Rhine got very excited about some early test subjects who scored exceptionally well. However, flaws were found in his method (a particularly glaring one being that early cards were printed on thin paper which allowed the test subjects to see the symbol through the back of the card), and once Rhine had taken precautions in response to these criticisms he failed to find any further exceptional subjects. Other researchers attempted to duplicate Rhine's results, without success. More recently, the Canadian neurophysiologist Michael Persinger published research in 1987 implicating the brain's **temporal lobes** in clairvoyant ability. In this study, Persinger presented Zener cards to a single test subject (undermining the scientific value of the study) with temporal lobe epilepsy. But before doing so, he exposed the subject's temporal lobes, at the sides of the head,

## Religion and the brain

Is the potential for religious belief hard-wired into the human brain? Like love (see p.191), it is possible to see how religion could have evolutionary benefits. Robin Dunbar at the University of Liverpool has suggested religious belief evolved to encourage us to form more tightly bonded social groups. By sharing a commonality such as religion, early humans would have had a much stronger sense of belonging and community, an essential factor for success. As we have seen, scientists have been trying to explain falling in love in terms of chemicals in the brain. The field of **neurotheology** is trying to do the same for religion.

So what have the neurotheologists come up with so far? Canadian neuro-physiologist Michael Persinger (his work on clairvoyance is discussed opposite and overleaf) has been focusing on religious experiences such as visions or a sense of a divine presence, drawing on insights from the study of **temporal lobe epilepsy** (TLE). The temporal lobes, located towards the sides of the brain's cortex, are involved in processing sound, vision, language and emotion. In the wake of a seizure beginning in the right temporal lobe (responsible for visuo-spatial processing), it seems a proportion of people with TLE are prone to experiences that could be described as religious, such as leaving their body or floating. Persinger has built on these observations, applying magnetic fields to the right hemisphere of non-epileptic test subjects' brains in an attempt to artificially induce religious sensations. In his experiments, eighty percent of subjects experienced the sensation of a "presence" in the room with them.

Persinger argues that by stimulating the right, non-verbal, lobes of the brain (including the temporal and parietal lobes), the magnetic field interferes with the brain's sense of physical self. The normally dominant, talkative left half of the brain attempts to rationalize these altered perceptions by deciding someone else must be present. The person in the midst of all this may choose to call this presence a ghost, a holy spirit or God. Ironically, the other person is themselves – it's simply that the natural balance between the two halves of the brain has been shifted in favour of the normally less dominant right half. If this natural balance were capable of getting out of sync under normal conditions as well, this might explain why some people experience religious visions.

Naturally, such a reductionist approach to religion will frustrate many, and Persinger's work is not without its critics. The obvious criticism is that Persinger's research focuses on an aspect of religion – visions and a sense of God's presence – which is relatively uncommon. Most religious people have never had such experiences. Indeed Christianity, for one, is based on the principle of blind faith – faith without such "proof" of a deity as a vision might provide. Neurotheology is a relatively small and recent field. As yet, it seems, its proponents have not produced evidence likely to make ripples beyond their own scientific circles.

## Professor Karl Friston

*Imaging Neuroscience and Theoretical Neurobiology, Wellcome Trust Centre for Neuroimaging*

**What is your favourite part of the brain and why?** My favourite part of the brain is its (axonal) connections because their delicate architecture is unique, not only in terms of other organs but also in relation to all other biophysical systems. This must point to something quite fundamental about the brain's function and place in the universe.

**What scientific breakthrough helped us to understand the brain the most?** Information theory and statistical physics, because they furnish a principled way to describe neuronal computations.

**What's the next big thing in neuroscience?** A deep and simple understanding of what the brain does (as opposed to how it does it).

to a magnetic field of one, four or seven pulses per second (Hz). The one and seven Hz magnetic fields resulted in no difference from the normal chance success rate of twenty percent. However, when the temporal lobes were subjected to the field of 4Hz, the success rate for predicting the correct card apparently shot up to an astonishing, consistent, fifty percent. One can only speculate why such a potentially revolutionary breakthrough was never pursued.

Actually, clairvoyance was already being seriously explored by some of the most powerful bodies in both the scientific and political worlds, under the guise of **remote viewing** (RV). In 1972 the CIA decided it needed to take a closer look at the potential external threat of psychic phenomena. To do so, it enlisted two respected physicists from California's Stanford Research Institute, Russell Targ and Harold E. Puthoff. After identifying people with an apparent psychic potential, such as artist Ingo Swann from New York (in one test, it is claimed Swann identified an object "sort of like a leaf" hidden inside a box, except that "it seems very much alive" – it was a moth), the project was initially successful enough to secure funding for an advanced eight-month Biofield Measurements Program.

Moving beyond insects, the programme turned to more demanding test conditions. As part of the Scanning by Coordinates programme, or Scanate, remote viewers such as Swann were given geographical coordinates – latitude, longitude, degrees, minutes and seconds. Like a modern GPS system, it seems they were able to both draw detailed maps of the target area and collect sensitive data, such as passwords, from within any building at that site. Not content with planet Earth, they even tested the limits of this unexplained ability in space. Coincident with the

Jupiter probe's fly-by in 1972, Swann attempted to remote view what no human could ever have seen – detailed information about the gas giant from over six hundred million kilometres distant. He received a good deal of information, including details of an icy ring encircling Jupiter. This initially disappointing news suggested to the observers that Swann had got his planets mixed up and was actually viewing Saturn. However, the Jupiter probe later confirmed the presence of this ring. That Swann and others of his kind were apparently able to perform such feats suggests either that they were involved in a conspiracy to promote the widespread belief in ESP, or that their minds really were somehow able to transcend time and space at will.

In 1995, the collected results of the numerous projects were analysed by the American Institutes for Research (AIR). Their final report found the psychics to possess a significant success rate of fifteen percent, a claim disputed by Ray Hyman, Professor Emeritus of Psychology at the University of Oregon and well-known sceptic of parapsychology. Ultimately, AIR recommended that the project, by then known as **Star Gate**, be shut down and all government involvement officially ceased. However, the work continues today in the private sector, under the guise of PSI TECH, a company founded by several of the Star Gate team which, for a fee, provides training in the field of "technical remote viewing".

In 2002, *The Journal of Perceptual and Motor Skills* published research in which Swann's brain was analysed whilst in the act of remote viewing, subsequent to exposure to magnetic fields. The study noted that an unusual pattern of brain activity over the occipital lobes showed a significant correlation with the accuracy of Swann's RV sessions; the authors concluded that there was a neurophysiological basis for his unusual abilities.

**History of the CIA's Remote Viewing Program** www.biomindsuperpowers. com/Pages/CIA-InitiatedRV.html
**PSI TECH** www.psitech.net

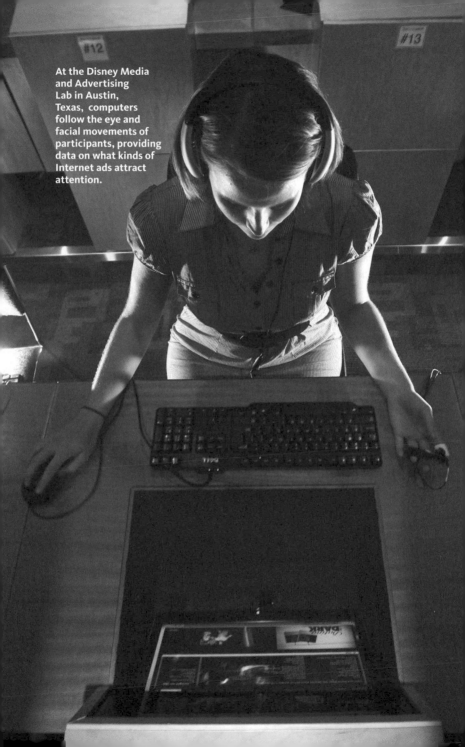

At the Disney Media and Advertising Lab in Austin, Texas, computers follow the eye and facial movements of participants, providing data on what kinds of Internet ads attract attention.

# CHAPTER 11

# The technological brain

## How modern life affects the brain

On 2 June 1896, the British Patent number 12039 was filed on behalf of a young Italian, **Guglielmo Marconi**, giving birth to what we now know as "radio". Prior to this moment, the Earth was a relatively silent place, communication being limited to the written word or voice. In barely more than a century, our species has embraced the notion of electronic communication and entertainment with such zeal that we now spend our every waking moment immersed in one form of technology or another: mobile devices, television, the Internet, video games…

The rapid pace of our **technological evolution** has caused some to question its impact on the modern brain – are we frying our brains whilst we call friends, becoming more violent as we play first-person shooters, turning

At the dawn of modern electronic media: Guglielmo Marconi, inventor.

into passive zombies as we soak up television's persistent signal? In this chapter, we take a look at the impact of modern technology on the brain, examining how modern technology – and the experiences it allows – are affecting the brain. Feel free to tweet.

# Video games...

Video games have been with us for decades – diverting slices of interactive entertainment that began as innocent forays into the worlds of *Pong*, *Pac-Man* and *Space Invaders* in the 1970s. In terms of evolution, however, video games have outstripped every other form of entertainment, with developers today offering up hyper-real, **motion-captured simulations** that can look every bit as real as a top-end movie. Games have never been more immersive, more realistic or more popular.

## ... and violence

*Call of Duty* (*COD*) is one of the most famous video games franchises in existence – even if you have no idea what it means, chances are you will

> **"It's not a toy, it's a freaking grenade!"**
>
> Halo 3

have heard of it. Belonging to a genre of game known as the "**first-person shooter**", it exploits an immersive visual device to create the effect of seeing through the eyes of an onscreen avatar whilst they shoot, jump, fight and run through elaborately designed environments known as "maps". In such games, players from all over the world can meet up with the sole intention of killing an opposing team. In doing so, *COD* players have racked up some formidable statistics, "killing" the entire population of the United States each day and the human population of Earth many times over.

Inevitably, such games have aroused the curiosity of psychologists and neuroscientists, who have suggested that such prolonged, violent behaviour – albeit virtual – can lead to gamers becoming more aggressive within society. The question surrounding video games and violent behaviour has not been helped by recent headlines:

> Video game fanatic hunts down and stabs rival player who killed character online.
>
> *The Daily Telegraph*, 27 May 2010

**Video games, here *Call of Duty 3*, offer an increasingly realistic, first-person experience of extreme violence – but there is still no hard evidence of a link between gaming and real-life violent behaviour.**

Florida mom Alexandra Tobias pleads guilty to murdering baby for crying during her *FarmVille* game.

*Daily News*, 28 October 2010

Playing games engages much of the brain. The emotional, hearing and visual centres are richly engaged – often bombarded – the **parietal lobe** comes into play, affording spatial awareness of the virtual environment, the **motor cortex** tunes in to whatever controlling device is being used, while **memory** becomes vital to retain nuggets of information, navigate vast maps or avoid danger. All the while, the brain's **frontal lobes** are involved in making crucial decisions, affecting one's survival.

But, despite being hotly contested and a rich source of headline news, there is no concrete evidence to support the hypothesis that extensive playing of violent video games leads to long-term increases in aggressive behaviour. In part, this is due to the complexity of the question. The British government took this question very seriously, resulting in the publication of the *Byron Review* in 2008, an extensive independent survey of the scientific literature spanning all forms of digital media, conducted by consultant clinical psychologist Dr Tanya Byron.

The scientific experiment required to fully answer the question "do violent games make people violent?" would be unethical, requiring children to play violent games from a young age and monitoring their behaviour within society. Then there is the question of *perception* – who decides what "violent" actually is? While a parent may look on horrified as their eighteen-year-old son tears bloody holes in screaming victims, research conducted by the British Board of Film Classification (BBFC) suggests their son merely perceives such **digital carnage** as a route to a high score, trophies and a necessary task in order to reach the next level. While a wide-ranging meta-analysis published in *The Journal of Pediatrics* in 2009, concluded: "… studies of media violence effects provided little support for the hypothesis that media violence is associated with **higher aggression**."

Despite the current absence of hard evidence, care should still be taken with young, still-developing brains whose representations of the world – and their place within it – are still maturing. In precisely the same way a parent would not allow their ten-year-old child to watch hour upon hour of violent, adult movies, they should be vigilant about the play duration and associated age rating of video games: in the context of ever more truthful representations of various realities, the excuse "it's just a game" no longer holds water.

**BBFC report** www.bbfc.co.uk/newsreleases/2007/04/playing-video-games-bbfc-publishes-research

## … addiction

The issue of addiction is rarely thrown at familiar forms of entertainment such as say, movies or television, but the more recent introduction of video games has prompted parents and psychiatrists alike to ponder whether or not this medium is capable of dominating their child's mind.

On the face of it, there are grounds to take the concern seriously – many hours spent playing video games, seemingly alone, are hours not spent socializing with real-world friends and family. It's time that could be spent doing physical activity, homework, chores, learning a new skill… However, for **"video game addiction"** to be legitimately classified as a mental disorder within the *Diagnostic and Statistical Manual of Mental Disorders*, there would need to be enough supporting evidence that the activity had achieved such overriding importance within the individual's life that it had detrimental effects on their quality of life (for example, schoolwork and friendships) whilst, should the person be prevented from playing, some form of withdrawal would ensue.

According to the American Psychiatric Association (APA) in 2007:

> The APA defines mental disorders in the *Diagnostic and Statistical Manual of Mental Disorders*. Since the current edition, DSM-IV-TR, does not list "video game addiction," the APA does not consider "video game addiction" to be a mental disorder at this time.

But video games remain under close scrutiny and this may change. Whereas conventional entertainment elicits a spectrum of emotional responses, the entire architecture of the vast majority of video games is built upon notions of fun and reward, key elements making them ripe for activating the brain's reward pathways that play a central role in every other form of addiction. And while video game addiction may be on the fence when it comes to mental disorders, excessive video game-playing behaviour is well recognized: a person playing a game every day for several hours to the detriment of various aspects of their education or social life could be cause for concern.

## ... and "brain training"

What we refer to as "video game technology" is a powerful beast but let's not forget the good it can do. At its core, it allows the human mind and body to engage in experiences beyond its usual range. Whether navigating *Sackboy* through a devilishly warped level in *LittleBigPlanet* or your team of virtual soldiers through a military grade training simulation, the brain is called upon to ensure accurate eye–hand coordination, planning, decision-making, complex strategizing and problem solving.

The ability of games to command the attention of the **central executive** within the frontal cortex has also been exploited within medical environments,

## Tobias Bast
*School of Psychology, University of Nottingham*

**What is your favourite part of the brain and why?** I am very interested in "integrative" parts of the brain that – by virtue of their neuroanatomical connections to other specialized parts of the brain – can bring together different types of information and of mental and behavioural functions. For example, the hippocampus combines different types of information transmitted from the neocortex into memories and can then "translate" these memories into appropriate behaviour by virtue of neuroanatomical connections to brain sites specialized to mediate emotional, motivational, sensorimotor, attentional and other functions.

**What scientific breakthrough helped us to understand the brain the most?** The discovery that the brain is made up of neurons that are arranged into functionally specialized brain areas and that our behaviour and thinking depends on interactions of these specialized brain areas.

**What do you think is the next big thing in neuroscience?** Interactions, interactions! Following the focus on deciphering the specialized functions of distinct brain parts, I feel that there is an increasing interest in putting it all together and to understand how behaviour and thinking are determined by interactions between specialized parts of the brain.

affording distraction from pain, for example (see p.226). But can games make you smarter?

Brain training is big business; the notion that a few minutes of orchestrated fun each day could improve one's brain is highly seductive. But there is a world of difference between tasks that may improve what's known as **"brain fitness"** (the ability to think clearly, plan, focus, learn and so on), and expecting those tasks to boost one's IQ – a property of the brain that actually appears to be stubbornly stable throughout life (p.139). In 2010, one of the world's most respected scientific journals, *Nature*, decided to throw down the gauntlet and determine, using the same rigorous scientific procedures applied to every other scientific hypothesis, whether there was any substance to **"computerized brain-training"**.

The scientists, led by Dr Adrian Owen, were specifically examining:

> … not whether performance on cognitive tests can be improved by training, but rather, whether those benefits transfer to other untrained tasks or lead to any general improvement in the level of cognitive functioning.
>
> *Nature*, June 2010

In other words, does performing these specific types of mental tests lead to general enhancements that will apply to the varied challenges life will throw at us?

In an elegant fusion of popular and hard science, viewers of the BBC television programme *Bang Goes the Theory* – 11,430 of them – were recruited to test the hypothesis, a decent sample size by any scientist's standards. Conducted entirely online, volunteers were initially subjected to a series of benchmark tests, allowing the scientists to acquire data reflecting the group's initial performance on tasks related to verbal short-term memory, spatial working memory, reasoning and paired-associates learning (a form of stimulus–response exercise, often employing words, in which two items are paired: for example, "brain" might be paired with "book").

The volunteers were then split randomly into three groups. Each group performed six training tasks for a minimum of ten minutes per day, three times per week. Group One's tasks placed an emphasis on reasoning, problem solving and planning. Group Two was deliberately set a series of challenges reflecting the content of mass-market brain-training type games – tasks relating to short-term memory, visuo-spatial abilities, attention and mathematics. Group Three was the all-important control group, who, in the absence of any proper cognitive training, spent six weeks answering "obscure questions".

At the end of the six-week training period, each participant was again given the benchmark tests and any change in scores recorded. Critically, the scientists would also be able to determine whether any *transference* had occurred – whether any of the groups showed enhanced ability in tests they had not specifically trained in. On this point the results produced an emphatic "no". All three groups had improved relative to their initial benchmark scores and were better at dealing with their own tasks – even the control group revealed better handling of "obscure questions". But these effects did not work their way over to other, untrained tasks. By way of example, the authors conclude:

> The increase in the number of digits that could be remembered following training on tests designed, at least in part, to improve memory (for example, in Group Two) was three-hundredths of a digit. Assuming a linear relationship between time spent training and improvement, it would take almost four years of training to remember one extra digit. Moreover, the control group improved by two-tenths of a digit, with no formal memory training at all.

# Television

The human brain is drawn to the **narrative form**. As children, bedtime stories are a means of developing imagination and gaining new experiences from the safety of the crib. As adults, we are living narratives, moving through time and memory, recounting our moments on Earth to loved ones and friends. It's unlikely television's early pioneers, amongst them the Scottish engineer John Logie Baird, could have envisaged just how powerful a **storytelling device** they had helped create.

After years of development, the first public broadcasts of moving images across the airwaves began in the late 1920s, spreading rapidly across the globe. The rapidity with which this technology has been embraced by our species is nothing less than breathtaking; bringing advertising, news, entertainment, other cultures and stories straight into our homes – and minds. What possible impact is this ubiquitous slab of technology having on the human brain?

**"Apathetic therapeutic and extremely addictive/The methadone metronome pumping out/150 channels 24 hours a day"**

"Television, the Drug of the Nation", The Disposable Heroes of Hiphoprisy

# The television as storyteller

We're social animals – hard-wired into the fabric of our DNA is the need for companionship. Socialising starts from the moment we're conscious, with parents attending our every helpless need. Family, friends, social networks, telephones, letters, emails – with each leap in technology, humanity seeks new ways to bring our increasingly remote lives closer. Without this primal urge to communicate, to connect and empathize with others, it's highly unlikely we'd ever have evolved beyond our fellow mammals.

**Theory of mind** is the name given to the human capacity to attribute mental states to both oneself and others. Whilst conscious, we are constantly experiencing these mental states – they are the basis of human cognition, or thought – comprised of such elements as our beliefs, desires, intentions… Critically, the brain is also able to recognize the existence of similar mental states within other human beings. This ability, to intro-spectively perceive one's own mind in relation to another, is the founda-tion of successful human social interaction. By being able to understand another person's mental state, it affords us the ability to comprehend their behaviour at any given moment and, importantly, to predict what they might do next. **Empathy** is the name we give to this ability when related more specifically to emotional states – to be aware of and sometimes share another's feelings.

Without this core ability of the brain, stories would be lifeless and flat. Every narrative journey from *Beowulf* to the *Alien* movies has featured at least one central character, a hero whose journey we follow through thick and thin, driven by our neurological empathy for them. Television saturates our minds with heroes. They are the fabric of soap operas, the stars of movies, the underdogs in "talent" shows, the contestants in game shows; they suffer, struggle and strive their way into our minds.

The subtlety and diversity required of the brain to perform the complex task of perceiving and relating to another's mental state is reflected in the range of brain regions increasingly associated with such a task. One area of the brain that seems to be involved is the **prefrontal cortex**, the home of reasoning, planning and personality located at the front of the brain. The **superior temporal sulcus** is found in the temporal lobe (in brain anatomy, a "sulcus" refers to the inward furrows, or folds of the brain, while "gyrus" refers to the outward-facing folds – the combination of sulci and gyri is what gives the brain its rippled appearance). While involved in language processing, another facet of its function appears to be "**gaze processing**" – following another's eyes, allowing us to infer the intentions of another. The **right temporo-parietal junction** has also been associated with theory of mind tasks. Located at the junction of the temporal and parietal lobes, heading towards the rear of the brain, this region helps us locate our body in space and distinguish between our self and others (an ability temporarily lost during "out of body" experiences).

## Surrogates

Is it possible that these characteristics of the human brain equip it to seek out relationships via technology, such as television? The **social surrogacy hypothesis** suggests they might. Humans are, in large part, driven by the need to *belong*, to seek out and cultivate meaningful and fulfilling emotional relationships with others. Success leads to happiness, friendship, understanding and, frequently, children. Alternatively, the opposite of belonging, *loneliness*, leads to feelings of social isolation and, potentially, depression.

The social surrogacy hypothesis suggests television may be one tool the human mind has adopted to ward off such feelings of isolation. Rather than develop relationships with real people, it has been suggested we create one-sided, "parasocial" relationships with characters within the stories on television. In a 2009 study, "Social Surrogacy: How Favored Television Programs Provide the Experience of Belonging", Jaye Derrick and colleagues performed a series of experiments, the results of which provide a fascinating insight into the power of our electronic friend. One part of the study obtained evidence that when people are feeling lonely, they tend to watch a favoured television programme, lessening the sensation of being alone. Remarkably, participants who had been asked to recall an unpleasant experience with a close person (triggering feelings of rejection) then spent more time writing about a favoured show when compared to a show they had little enthusiasm for. The implication being that thinking about a programme one likes is able to **offset feelings of isolation**.

Is this really such a bad thing? Investing emotional time and energy in parasocial, or faux relationships appears to be simply an extension of our innate need to seek out and build relationships. But it is important to maintain a sense of perspective – **parasocial relationships** are entirely unidirectional, offering no lasting friendship, loyalty, companionship or support – they can also be cancelled at any time. Perhaps the rapid rise of **on-demand viewing**, increasingly through mobile technology, has as much to do with keeping our virtual friends by our side as it has to do with our need for freedom of choice.

## How does television affect your brain?

This fifth member of the family has been with us for some time and, despite being an excellent resource crammed full of educational, cultural and informative programming, inevitably – and rightly – some question the value of prolonged exposure to the brain. On average, we spend around four hours a day watching this machine, adding up to around a decade over the course of an average life. Evidence that prolonged television viewing is actively bad for the adult brain is both scant and controversial. By its very nature, watching television is a largely passive and frequently relaxing experience; something we do at the end of a working day to relax, unwind, laugh or forget. Some go as far as to liken the state we enter when watching television as akin to being **hypnotized**. However, the harm television does to an adult appears more to do with the fact that, to watch it, a human must remain sedentary, contributing to poor overall wellbeing.

In 2010, a paper in the *American Journal of Preventive Medicine* reported their findings after taking a look at the association between mental health and what they called "**TV- and screen-based entertainment time**" (TVSE). Their starting point was to return to the 3920 men and women who had participated in the 2003 Scottish Health Survey,

**"The fifth member of the family" (seventh in this case): a late-1950s nuclear family collects around the "cathode-ray nipple".**

## Out of body

Right now, you know where you are. You know if your body is standing or seated, where your body is in relation to your immediate environment – you are one with yourself. **Out-of-body experiences (OBE)** change all that; instead you may perceive your self as being separate from your physical body, an unsettling experience fracturing one's perceived reality. The otherworldly nature of such experiences conjures all manner of explanations, invoking religion, aliens and ghosts – but a deeper understanding of the brain is all that's required.

The body's senses feed the brain an array of information, enabling a person to relate to their environment and their consciousness to build a solid, believable reality. Importantly, this reality is built within the mind and if the sensory information entering is false, or somehow askew, this reality can break down. In 2011, Professor Olaf Blanke of the Brain-Mind Institute, Switzerland, provided an insight into such workings, and mis-workings, of the mind at the annual American Association for the Advancement of Science meeting. Subjects were asked to wear virtual reality goggles showing them a computer-generated image of their own backs, just a few feet in front of them. Both the real volunteers and their virtual projection had their back stroked by a pen. The result was a form of disconnect, causing people to question where "they" really were – an OBE-like experience. The region of the brain involved in such representations of self in relation to others appears to be located where the temporal and parietal lobes meet, the temporo-parietal junction – an area also implicated in studies of theory of mind. In the absence of computer-generated avatars, the implication of such findings is that this region of the brain experiences a temporary malfunction, leading to an OBE.

a wide-ranging health investigation into numerous facets of adult life, including such things as eating habits, physical activity and illness. In the 2010 study, the team zeroed in on the relationship between TVSE and the results gathered from various questionnaires designed to ascertain one's mental health. What they discovered was, when compared to those engaged in TVSE for two or less hours a day, a statistically significant and consistent diminishment of good mental health manifested itself in those engaged in TVSE for four or more hours a day. It's important to point out that this relationship is considered independent, that is, the researchers are not suggesting that watching television and poor mental health are causally linked, simply that these two factors – **sedentary time** spent on screen-based activity and **mental health** – are associated.

Perhaps rather than launching an all-out attack on whether television "is bad for the brain", we should try to get to grips with how it affects our mind and behaviour – an external manifestation of our inner mental state. One interesting experiment to see exactly what goes on inside the brain when we watch visual media was recently conducted in the US. In 2011, a scientific paper revealed what happened when a small group of subjects (seventeen smokers and seventeen non-smokers) were invited to participate in a study in which they would be subjected to fMRI (p.26) whilst watching a portion of *Matchstick Men* (Ridley Scott's 2003 movie featuring con men, one of whom, Roy, suffers from poor mental health). The participants were blissfully ignorant of the study's primary goal – to observe the brain's real-time response to the film's scenes of people smoking, something featuring heavily within the storyline.

When compared to the control group, the team of scientists consistently discovered higher levels of activity in specific regions of the brains of smokers during scenes featuring smoking. The brain regions in question are the **left anterior intraparietal sulcus** (a groove travelling along the parietal lobe) and the **inferior frontal gyrus** (the ridged region of the brain located roughly above the temple). The grooved, parietal region acts as a neural bridge connecting the body's visual perception with movements in space, while the ridged location above the temple has been associated with observation of hand movements. The authors' findings suggest simply watching a fictional narrative containing scenes of smoking is enough to provoke the brains of smokers into action, as if they are unable to stop their mind reaching for nicotine.

These findings provide a clue as to why giving up is so hard – not only is the well-intentioned person struggling with withdrawal from the highly addictive nicotine, every time they see someone smoke, irrespective of whether real or screen-based, their brain literally goes through the motions of smoking. Television programming throws far more at the mind than just scenes of smoking and one can only wonder what the next few years of research will reveal about our brain's response to screen imagery.

## Growing up with television

The adult brain has the capacity to see beyond the veil of television to the truth: television is a **content delivery machine**, serving up slices of information and entertainment. But to a child's still developing mind, with limited capacity to discern between reality and fantasy, or the various shades of morality, it can form a significant component of their reality. In light of television's ability to target ever-younger minds, innumerable studies spanning decades continue to try and fathom the cognitive and

## 3D TV

Suddenly, **3D imagery** seems to have lurched from the domain of B-movie horror to the mainstream. Cinema is increasingly exploiting this extra dimension for the purpose of spectacle, television to enable footballs to appear in one's living room and gaming technology for unprecedented levels of immersive interaction. We're completely familiar with the third dimension – depth – the brain's natural ability to perceive three dimensions in the real world is vital for survival. But the aforementioned mediums are all screen-based, firmly stuck to two dimensions – how do these new technologies trick the brain into thinking there is depth where there is none?

It first helps to understand the basis of how we normally perceive depth. Human eyes sit at the front of the head, several centimetres apart. Their location means that each eye actually captures a slightly different image – you only have to look into the distance and shut each eye in turn to witness this effect. The two images enter the eyes, become a mass of electrical signals that pass down the optic nerve and into the visual cortex at the brain's rear. Once here, the visual cortex seamlessly merges the two images, creating a sense of depth that neither alone could create; this is the essence of stereoscopic vision. So, the key to creating the illusion of 3D from a 2D image source relies on sending slightly different images to each eye. **Polarized glasses** are what most are familiar with from a trip to the cinema. In such glasses, the polarizing filter of one lens is set at right angles to the other, so each lens can only allow light that's been similarly polarized to pass through. Up in the projection room, two projectors simultaneously beam their 3D imagery onto the screen – each image passing through a pair of polarizing filters that match the audience's glasses. The net effect is that matching polarized light passes through each lens causing the eyes to see a different image, hence 3D. Meanwhile, television is making the leap into 3D by exploiting clever autostereoscopic, or glasses-free, technologies capable of displaying slightly differing images to each eye in the comfort of one's home.

behavioural impact of television viewing on young brains. A recommendation from both the American Academy of Pediatrics and Royal College of Paediatrics and Child Health is that children under two years should not watch television at all, allowing more time for play, social interactions, language development – fundamental aspects of **neurological development** and good health.

As we grow, concern has been raised that television can have negative effects on academic prowess and attitudes towards violence, sex or self-image. Despite the literature being mixed, there does appear to be a consensus that the nature of what young people watch can affect their perceptions and behaviour. Indeed, a 2010 review of the effects of media such as television on young people states that the correlation between **media violence** and **aggression** is almost as strong as the link between cigarettes and lung cancer.

There was a time when role models consisted entirely of family and friends, real people helping young minds grow into stable, healthy personalities. Television is capable of great good, acting as an educator and a stimulus for the imagination. It can also feed unrealistic aspirations, glamorize violence and skew a young mind's perceptions of reality. The simplest way to help future generations develop a balanced view of how to conduct themselves within the world is to ensure that what they are consuming is appropriate for their age – limit exposure of the "bad stuff" and encourage a focus on higher-quality programming. Alternately, one could always just turn off the power.

# The Internet

Of all the technologies that have emerged in recent history, the Internet could rightly claim to be the one tech to rule them all. Radio brought our ears sound and television introduced imagery but the Internet is everything, everywhere: sound, vision, information, communication – from embittered bloggers to its unified computing power being harnessed for biomedical research. This globally interconnected, largely democratic, interactive information superstructure is now so commonplace, so familiar to the current generation, it staggers belief that it really only started to emerge in the public's consciousness in the mid-1990s. Initially a largely academic tool for sharing information, today's Internet is all things to all people. What could this information revolution mean for the brain?

Perhaps the reason we've adapted so quickly to the Internet is that its workings echo that of the brain. Traditionally, the brain is thought to work in what's referred to as a top-down, or bottom-up manner – a **hierarchical model of communication** in which information either flows up, from simple to more complex brain circuits, or vice versa. In such a model, the taste of something sweet starts on the tongue, moves through to sensory regions of the brain, which in turn may stimulate the pleasure centre of the brain, signals finally culminating in the highly elaborate cortex, resulting in a groan of delight as we consciously experience pleasure. A city might be said to operate in a similar fashion, the chain of responsibility and power gradually moving up from everyman to government and back again.

Partial map of the Internet based on data from January 2005. Each line is drawn between two nodes, representing two IP addresses – the graphic takes on an almost brain-like pattern of connectivity.

But this might not be the case. In 2010, a paper was published challenging the top-down view of brain organization. The researchers focused on a cubic millimetre of rat brain in a region that was known to be a "**hedonic hot spot**". This tiny cube of mind was located within the **nucleus accumbens**, part of the brain's reward pathway. The elegant setup the scientists used allowed them to inject "tracer" molecules at highly specific points in their chosen brain region. Tracers, as the name suggests, allow scientists to follow the path of a molecule once it's entered a neuron, much like tracking devices in movies being used to follow cars. In their experiment, Richard Thompson and Larry Swanson were able to simultaneously inject two different tracers into exactly the same region – each followed its own path, with one tracer heading towards the source of neuronal signals, and the other towards where those same signals were heading. In doing so, they had constructed a method for revealing how information itself flows within the mammalian brain.

**Mapping the wiring of the human brain using "diffusion MRI": the Human Connectome Project aims to build a complete picture of the brain's functional structure – a daunting task.**

Rather than seeing a **monodirectional flow of information**, as might be expected if the hierarchical model was absolute, the scientists' results revealed that information moves in a complicated series of closed loops, or circuits, between regions previously not known to communicate. In essence, information flow within the brain appears to behave like a vast, distributed network, with no simple **organizational hierarchy** – much like the Internet.

One key advantage of such organization is its robustness. If part of the brain is damaged, such a **distributed network** could afford the brain alternate means of achieving the same goals, such as gradual recovery of language following stroke. From an evolutionary perspective this makes perfect sense, enabling the brain to bypass and reroute information in the event of a neurological catastrophe.

At the start of this century, the human genome was sequenced, liberating our genetic code for all to study – an accomplishment that will continue to reap scientific rewards for decades. Spurred on by advances in science, imaging technology and computing power, scientists are now building a map of the human "**connectome**" – a complete map of the trillions of connections, pathways and circuits that exist within our skulls. It may sound incredible that a high-resolution map of the human mind is on the cards but it's being taken very seriously; the US National Institute of Health invested $40 million in the Human Connectome Project in 2010. Here, one of the scientists involved in the project, Sebastian Seung of MIT, discusses the intimidating complexity of the connectome in a fascinating TED (Technology, Entertainment, Design) talk:

singularityhub.com/2010/10/14/nih-awards-40-million-to-map-the-wiring-of-the-brain

## Is the Internet changing the brain?

Attention, the prefrontal lobe's ability to direct the brain's resources to a particular task, is the cornerstone of thought. In recent years the question of whether the Internet is eroding our ability to focus, to concentrate on a specific train of thought for any significant amount of time, has come to the fore. Writer Nicholas G. Carr is a strong proponent of the view that the Internet is eroding our capacity for deep thought. One concern being, prior to the Internet the mind could settle on a task, whether it be a book or a conversation and explore it deeply, with little distraction. The Internet, with its myriad possibilities, fragments the mind's ability to focus properly, information and choices blossoming and multiplying before our brain, overwhelming it. We no longer think deeply but flit erratically from one branch of information to another, a **cognitive butterfly**. There are, indeed, a near infinite number of routes, diversions and activities one can find on the Internet. The same could be said of the number of books upon entering a library, yet we feel comfortable with this ancient and highly successful form of information-storage device. We are not passive victims of the Internet, a modern **information superstructure**; ultimately, it is simply a tool we can wield – we *choose* how to use it.

Evidence does, however, support the hypothesis that the Internet is capable of changing the structure of the brain, altering how we think. This might sound alarming but it couldn't be more natural – every experience is capable of changing the structure of the mind; it is the foundation of neuroplasticity, the brain's ability to rewire itself, prime examples being our capacity to learn or store memories. Using the Internet is just as likely to alter synaptic pathways within the mind as shopping for groceries.

Dr Gary Small, a professor of psychiatry at the University of California took steps to find out just what's going on inside the brain of people surfing the web, specifically, using a search engine. In his small study, 24 middle-aged and elderly volunteers were asked to perform two tasks while being monitored by fMRI (see p.26), scanning technology that reveals heightened blood flow and, by inference, activity within the brain. In the first task, the volunteers simply read text while their brains were monitored. Small and his team witnessed activity in several brain regions including those dealing with vision (occipital lobe), language and memory (frontal and temporal lobes). Half of the volunteers were actually what Small refers to as Net Savvy, regular users of the Internet, while the other half were Net Naïve, relatively inexperienced web users. And, in this first phase of the study, their brains echoed each other perfectly. However...

In the second phase of the experiment, the volunteers were assigned an Internet search task and this time things were very different. The Net Naïve group's brains appeared as before when they had been reading text, but the Net Savvy group showed a significant jump in activity in additional regions of the brain, including those involved in decision-making, complex reasoning (**prefrontal cortex**), memory (**hippocampus**) and vision. The authors themselves admit to cautious interpretation of their findings but the results do provide compelling evidence that the brains of experienced Internet users have rewired, adapting to the increased need to probe, decide and choose. Intriguingly, Small performed the same test six days later, after the Net Naïve group had been asked to spend an hour a day trawling the Internet. Remarkably, after just five hours of surfing experience, patterns of brain activity in the two groups were far more similar.

# Social networks and the brain

In modern usage, the term "**social network**" has been successfully hijacked by various web and mobile-based forms of communication, such as Twitter and Facebook. For the dwindling numbers for whom these odd words are still meaningless, they represent a social phenomenon of the present day. In essence, they allow connections to form between people; sometimes they are people one actually knows, often they are not. Once connected, "friends" and "followers" can do anything: simply keep in touch, share valuable information or, in the case of Egypt, start a revolution.

But these mechanisms of building and maintaining social groups are merely a recent extension of our innate need to seek out and develop relationships. The healthy human mind is driven to seek out social networks, whether real or virtual – friends, family, peers – we cannot help ourselves. And, once within the direct proximity of a group of people, it's vital that we're able to navigate through the complex labyrinth of emotions, responses and motivations of others to facilitate good relations or sense a threat.

In 2010, a study was performed to try and see if the brains of 58 healthy people might reveal some physical hints as to the origins of our networking behaviour. The group, comprising various ages and both sexes, were quizzed about their own social networks using two pieces of information. The first was simply how many people they each kept regular contact with, providing their network's size. The second related to how the main group of people could be broken down further into smaller, related groups; this provided the scientists with an indication of the network's overall complexity. Each individual then had their entire brain scanned, using MRI, to see if the size of any particular structures within their brains were bigger or smaller and if these size differences in any way correlated with the size and complexity of their social networks (naturally, everybody's brain is a slightly different size, so the scientists took account of this).

The team discovered that those with larger, more complex social networks had a larger **amygdala** (see p.35). This small, almond-shaped structure is thought to play a role in social interactions, for example, interpreting facial expressions, but this research provided strong evidence that our ability to relate to larger, more complex groups is somehow directly tied to the amygdala's size. Whether a larger amygdala makes us better at developing larger networks, or becoming part of larger networks somehow triggers development within the amygdala is unclear but the correlation exists.

Relative to our evolutionary past, where the ability to interpret direct social interactions was paramount, virtual networking is somewhat bereft; there are no facial expressions or gestures to examine, no pheromones to inhale – no one there. Perhaps its popularity relates, in part, to the dispersed nature of modern life. With real friends and families often living large distances apart, web networks may be one mechanism of filling an expanding emotional vacuum; like television, it doesn't really matter if the people are real, as long as they're there.

# Mobile phones

**Mobile technology** has been utterly transformative. In just a few decades, mobile communication devices have become smarter, ubiquitous and a vital accessory throughout the world. But it didn't take long before concerns began to emerge over the potential effects of holding a radio transmitter/receiver so close to the side of one's head; would it cook the brain, or cause cancer?

The sun emits radiation, a torrent of energy composed of differing wave frequencies, or energies. Some energy we experience as visible light, some as warmth and, within the environs of a hospital, the occasional burst of x-rays. Mobile devices exploit the properties of microwave radiation, a branch of the electromagnetic spectrum familiar to most kitchens. So do mobiles heat up the brain? Not really; most of the radiation is absorbed by the skin and other superficial soft tissue, resulting in what scientists deem to be a negligible effect on the brain.

The fear of brain cancer (or "**glioma**", named after the glial cells from which a brain tumour is most likely to originate) due to mobile usage has been an ongoing concern for years and, with upwards of 4.6 billion users globally, that's a lot of potential brains at risk. Cancer is the result of cells within the body dividing when they shouldn't. Our cells are governed by sets of biological rules that tell them when to grow, divide and die. In cancer, these systems fail because of genetic mutation – a cell's DNA is damaged, the result of which happens to be uncontrolled growth and division. Radiation is one cause of DNA damage, for example, too much exposure to ultraviolet radiation, whether from the sun or sunbed, can cause skin cancer. The toxins inhaled during smoking damage the DNA in the nearby lung cells, potentially leading to lung cancer, and so on.

> "Apparently we love our own cell phones but we hate everyone else's."
>
> John Irving Bloom

Several large studies have been conducted in recent years to determine whether we're putting ourselves at risk of cancer whilst idly chatting with our friends or conducting business. In 2006, a Danish long-term study, including no fewer than 420,095 participants "found no evidence for an association between tumour risk and cellular telephone use among either short-term or long-term users". Then in 2010, the Interphone study, spanning 13 countries and more than 5000 participants between the ages of 30 and 59 with a form of brain cancer was published. In an approach referred to as "case-control" each participant with cancer (case) was matched for age, sex and geography with a person free of cancer (control). The scientists then searched for evidence of a correlation between brain cancer and mobile phone usage. While the authors acknowledge more work is required to determine the effects of long-term, heavy mobile usage, they conclude, "no increase in risk of glioma or meningioma was observed", a conclusion that both Cancer Research UK and the World Health Organization currently support whilst maintaining an open mind to new findings as they emerge.

Beyond cancer, there is evidence that bathing the brain in microwave radiation may have other effects. Scientists at the US National Institute of Health published a paper in 2011 containing evidence that regions of the brain close to a mobile phone's antenna became altered following fifty minutes of exposure. The team were measuring glucose metabolism, an indicator of brain activity – higher metabolism suggests more glucose is being used and, therefore, a region of the brain is more active. While the team admits they're currently unsure of the implications of their findings, they did measure statistically significant increases in glucose metabolism in regions of both the prefrontal and temporal cortices, as if glucose metabolism in those regions was somehow being boosted.

Ultimately, time and research will reveal what these devices do to our delicate brains, but currently the hard evidence suggests that the greatest threat from mobiles is not what they do to the structure of our brains, it's how they affect our behaviour. Using a mobile phone whilst driving, fracturing the frontal lobe's attention, means we're significantly more likely to have a serious accident.

# CHAPTER 12

# Future brains

... in man and machine

As we have seen in the previous ten chapters of this book, although brain science has come a long way, we are even now only just beginning to get to grips with how the brain works. There is much still to be learned. But that hasn't stopped us speculating about what might be around the neurological corner. This chapter takes a glimpse at the possible future of the brain. Will the human brain evolve further in the future? Will we take the brain's evolution into our own hands through the use of brain-boosting drugs and implants? And will we ever succeed in building an entirely artificial brain?

## Has the brain stopped evolving?

Or, rather, why should it keep evolving? Why should any part of a human still be evolving? We have managed to shift life's equation greatly in our favour, removing many of the old barriers to survival, such as hunger and disease, which used to mean that only the "fittest" lived long enough to reproduce. Some scientists argue that the modern Western lifestyle now protects humanity from the forces that used to drive evolution. Virtually everyone's genes are now making it to the next generation.

However, others have argued quite the opposite – that, rather than overriding evolutionary pressures, modern society has introduced new pressures. The current driver of human evolution may be the need for intelligence to enable a person to succeed in the "information age". The quantity and complexity of information the brain now deals with on a daily basis is far higher than it was when modern man first appeared around 200,000 years ago. As Christopher Wills of the University of California, San Diego, argues, "There is a premium on sharpness of mind and the ability to accumulate money. Such people tend to have more children and have a better chance of survival." If these trends continue then, rather than sitting back on its laurels, the brain ought to be the key site of future human evolution.

> "The empires of the future are the empires of the mind."
>
> Sir Winston Churchill

Along with humanity's powerful ability to physically manipulate the world to its needs, a defining quality marking us out from the rest of animal life is that we evolved speech and language: the unparalleled use of sound to express to other human beings the thoughts inside our brain. Several hundred thousand years back in our evolutionary past, certain changes occurred to our ancestral DNA that appear to have accelerated us down the path of language, from vocal speech to smartphone Tweets. The stretch of DNA in question contains a gene called FOXP2 – or, Forkhead box protein P2. Under normal circumstances, the protein made by the FOXP2 gene controls the manufacture of other genes critical to normal brain development, in particular, language development (the same gene sequence also appears critical for the development of birdsong, highlighting the conservational elegance of natural selection). Mutations that damage this gene also lead to language impairments, for example, developmental apraxia, a condition in which the person finds it difficult to say their chosen words and may struggle to hit the normal points of inflection and rhythm as they talk. Modern existence places ever higher demands on the ability to successfully communicate, through a variety of channels, suggesting linguistic advancement may be favoured in our species' future.

In 2005 a research team led by Bruce T. Lahn of Howard Hughes Medical Institute at the University of Chicago found genetic evidence that the brain is indeed continuing to evolve. Lahn discovered that two genes involved in controlling brain development had been evolving in very recent times – and are continuing to evolve. The functions of these genes,

**microcephalin** and **ASPM** (abnormal spindle-like microcephaly associated), are not fully known, but both appear to be involved in determining brain size – because if either gene malfunctions, the person is left with microcephaly, a medical condition in which the brain does not develop to full size.

Both genes come in a number of slightly different versions. In both cases, a new class of variants or "alleles" was found to have emerged very recently. The new version of microcephalin appeared around 37,000 years ago, long after the appearance of modern man. New variants of genes come and go all the time, but this one stayed. Not only did it stay, but it spread rapidly throughout the human population, so that around seventy percent of us now possess this variant of the gene. The ASPM variant arrived even more recently, only about 5800 years ago, but it too is spreading quickly through the human population and is currently carried by about thirty percent of us. These time frames are extraordinarily short in evolutionary terms. The speed at which the variant genes have spread through the population implies that they are strongly favoured by natural selection and may endow the carrier with significant evolutionary advantage.

The researchers took the bold step of linking the arrival of these new versions of the genes with landmark steps in human development – microcephalin's with the arrival of human cultural behaviours such as art, music and religion, and ASPM's with the arrival of sophisticated behaviours such as agriculture and written language. As exciting as such a hypothesis is – that somehow these genetic alterations enabled humans to develop more complex brains to cope with a more complex society – correlation is not causation and the parallels between history and our genes may be mere coincidence. What the research does clearly demonstrate, however, is that we are still in a state of "neurological flux" and future brains may well look and function significantly differently from the way our present brain does.

What might this future brain look like? Rather than transform into dome-headed telepaths, it is more likely that evolutionary pressure will favour functional alterations. Perhaps our brains will gradually adapt to need less sleep, allowing us more up-time in our neon-bathed cities. Increasingly rapid cultural and technological advances, particularly in the assimilation and transmission of information, may favour those with brains containing a more powerful working memory, more efficient storage and retrieval mechanisms and a greater degree of intra-cortical connectivity.

Some might argue that the spread of the Internet will reduce the demands placed on the human brain, stalling its evolution. When it's possible to have almost any information appear instantly on one's computer screen, why should the memory or learning capacity of the human brain improve? But the modern Internet is far more than just a knowledge repository. As we saw on p.10, in our distant evolutionary past increased social interaction may have been one of the most significant factors driving increases in our brain size. The rise of communications technology such as the Internet means the potential for interaction with our fellow humans is now greater than ever, via phones, email, blogs, online communities and forums, online gaming, and so on. The need to retain vast numbers of facts may indeed become a thing of the past, but if social networks continue to expand at their current rate it is conceivable that a future brain may be required to juggle many thousands of simultaneous relationships. Could a new era dominated by a dynamic global web of shared conversations, opinions, thoughts and friendships be enough to prompt another leap in brain evolution? For a more detailed look at the interplay between the brain and our increasingly technology-driven lifestyles, see Chapter 11.

## Evolution plus – augmentation

For those unwilling to leave brain improvement to the relatively slow process of evolution, it may soon be possible to take matters into our own hands, boosting the capabilities of the brain through a range of artificial means.

The quest for a better, faster, more efficient human brain has led to the development of **nootropics**, or "smart drugs". These substances act as temporary boosters, accelerating the brain's normal state and improving functions such as concentration, memory and decision-making. We met some of these drugs in Chapter 9 – **caffeine** (see p.193) is a nootropic that is consumed by millions every day, and the US Air Force isn't averse to giving its pilots **Dexedrine** ("go-pills", see p.196) to help keep them alert whilst flying long, expensive missions – but there are many others. Most have been developed to treat neurological disorders such as Alzheimer's disease but a growing number of people with "normal" brain functioning are experimenting with such substances in an attempt to boost their intelligence or memory. **Ritalin**, prescribed to children with ADHD (see p.164), is being used by students hoping to improve exam performance. **Modafinil**, a treatment for narcolepsy (which causes people to suddenly

## Cyborgs

The word "cyborg" conjures malevolent images from the annals of sci-fi history: the Terminator, *Dr Who*'s Cybermen, *Star Trek*'s Borg. Like much science fiction, these stories are grounded in a contemporary fear. We are no longer as afraid of nuclear radiation, or even cloning. What bothers people now is the potential loss of their identity as more and more of their lives come to rely on machines – and the possibility that, as those machines become more intelligent and human-like, they might eventually come to be *our* masters.

The term "cyborg" was coined in 1960 by Manfred E. Clynes and Nathan S. Klyne in their article "Cyborgs and Space". They used the term (short for cybernetic organism) to refer to a human being that had been enhanced with electronics and machinery so that it could survive in hostile extraterrestrial environments. But we don't need to look to outer space for machine-enhanced humans – there are millions already here on Earth.

Taking the broadest definition of the term to mean anyone who uses technology to boost one of their physiological capabilities we are all cyborgs. It may be we use contact lenses or spectacles to improve our eyesight, a hearing aid to boost hearing, or a wristwatch to enhance our awareness of time. The **Internet** also has its place in cybernetic enhancement, acting increasingly as a virtual memory for the species as a whole, and creating a form of "hive mind" as thoughts and opinions from all over the globe pass into its expanding network.

The reason we rarely think of such objects as transforming us into cyborgs is partly their familiarity but mostly the fact that they are *external*. But what happens when the boundary between flesh and machine has been removed? If someone has a **heart pacemaker**, you probably ought technically to consider him a cyborg. And the same goes for those fitted with the **brain implants** used to treat Parkinson's disease (see p.181), **cochlear implants** (see

fall asleep), is being used by people in order to stay awake and alert for days at a time.

There is some evidence that using medicines "off-label" in this way might be worth a try. In 2002 a team from Stanford University led by Jerome Yesavage discovered that **donepezil**, which is used to slow memory loss in Alzheimer's sufferers, improves the memory of the normal population. A group of pilots was put in a flight simulator and taught to perform specific manoeuvres and respond to emergencies. Half received donepezil and half a placebo. When the pilots were tested a month later on the skills they had learned, those who had been given donepezil remembered their training better. However, there is not yet enough research into the effects of the long-term use of such drugs. Perhaps users will develop tolerance p.48), or the **robotic limbs** described on p.57. And there are non-medical examples, too. Some exclusive **nightclubs** now "chip" their members by implanting a small receiver/transmitter under their skin. Scanning the chip not only allows the partying cyborg entry to the club, it also allows them to pay for their drinks.

But what about the future? In the field of cybernetic enhancement, as with much futuristic technology, the ones to watch are probably the **military**. With the money, the resources, the will and a limitless supply of volunteers, should man–machine hybrids appear, they will originate here – as weapons. This may begin with primarily non-invasive technologies allowing augmentation of the senses – contact lenses with an in-built **Head-Up Display** (HUD) allowing detailed information about terrain and enemy positions to be fed directly into a soldier's eyes, for example. And with advances in **nanotechnology** continuing to make inroads in super-strong yet light materials, future soldiers may be in possession of powerful body armour no heavier than a cotton jacket. Add **brain–machine interfacing** (see p.56) to the mix and future cyborgs may end up somewhere between Lee Majors' Six Million Dollar Man and Paul Verhoeven's Robocop.

**A receiver/transmitter shown before being inserted into the arm.**

over time so that, instead of being raised to a higher mental state when they take the drug, they will be reduced to a bovine level in its absence.

Chemical augmentation such as this may one day be as common as taking vitamin supplements. But further down the line we may see far more invasive interventions in the human nervous system.

New-generation implants are already beginning to bring hearing and sight back to those who have lost them. Unlike traditional hearing aids (that amplify ambient sounds and direct them towards the middle ear), **cochlear implants** are surgically installed within the ear. The device acts as a direct interface between sound and the central nervous system, replacing the human parts no longer functioning and directly stimulating the appropriate nerves to send electrical signals to the brain. As for vision, **retinal implants** in the eye directing electrical impulses towards the optic nerve, or implants surgically placed directly within the visual cortex at the back of the brain, are both being explored.

Work on brain implants such as this raises the possibility of **brain–machine interfacing** in the future. Much research is currently going on in this field. In 2003, Professor Miguel A. Nicolelis and his team at Duke University, North Carolina, made a major breakthrough. By interfacing a monkey's brain directly with a computer, they enabled the animal to control the movements of a robotic arm purely by thinking about it. The team implanted electrodes in the brain of a female rhesus macaque monkey and used them to analyse what was going on in her brain as she was taught to grasp a joystick and use it to control a robot arm. The mass of neural data generated was fed into a computer which matched patterns of brain activity with the movements of the monkey's hand. This meant the control of the robotic arm could then be switched over so that the monkey was unknowingly directing it via the computer rather than the joystick. The joystick was then removed. The monkey at first continued to move her arm in midair to control the robot arm. But after only a few days, she realized she didn't need to move her arm at all – she kept her arm at her side and controlled the robot arm via thought alone.

For Nicolelis, the end goal of this research is a new generation of robotic limbs for people suffering from paralysis, governed directly by the user's mind. Further down the line, the signals could be used to directly stimulate the person's own muscles, bypassing the damaged part of the brain or spine. However, the US military, in the form of DARPA (the Defense Advanced Research Projects Agency), which funded Nicolelis's research, has its own long-term aims for the technology. They hope that eventually complex military systems such as aircraft might be controlled by thought alone. As DARPA pursues its aim of preventing soldiers from becoming "the weakest link in the US military", the key driving force behind future "enhancements" to our brains, whether in the form of drugs or surgical procedures, will likely be the military. There is talk of using brain implants to enhance communication between soldiers on the ground, and even of uploading instructions directly into the soldiers' brains.

# Artificial intelligence

Brain enhancement through implants and machine interfacing is one thing, but what about an entirely artificial brain? This is something scientists have been thinking about and working towards since at least the 1950s.

Is there any hope that we will one day manage to build an artificial "human" brain that is genuinely intelligent? This question has divided the artificial intelligence (or "AI") community, and led to the development of two distinct strands, weak (or soft) AI and strong (or hard) AI. Supporters of **weak AI** believe we may manage to create machines that appear to be intelligent, but they will never be truly conscious in the way humans are. **Strong AI**'s position is more optimistic: why shouldn't a machine be able to replicate all the features of the human brain? After all, the brain itself is a machine of sorts – made up of a collection of components including chemicals, cells and so on, and with a power supply in the form of oxygen and glucose. Proponents of strong AI believe it is possible to create a machine that is conscious, self-aware and truly intelligent.

The two strands' different beliefs have led to fundamentally differing goals. While weak AI aims to create a machine that will act as if it is intelligent, strong AI aims to make a machine that genuinely is intelligent.

## Weak AI

Strong AI's ultimate goal may be the holy grail of artificial intelligence, but the less ambitious weak AI has made more tangible progress towards its target, producing some decent results with practical applications. Weak AI is the realm of the "smart machine". Such devices give the impression of intelligence but are no more intelligent than a newspaper is informed.

Spell-checking software is a ubiquitous example of weak AI, but the kings of weak AI are the **chess-playing programs**, such as Fritz and Deep Blue (see box overleaf). These programs do a fine job of regularly outsmarting their opponents; however, they are devoid of intelligence or the will to win, relying on a "brute-force" approach to the game. The relatively vast processing power available allows the machine to analyse every possible move, several moves ahead – it then makes the move it calculates to have the highest probability of success.

Another key application of weak AI is **video games**. These are becoming ever more convincing, so much so that it is now easy to forget that the enemy you face is simply a product of some sophisticated computer-

## Kasparov vs. Deep Blue

It was billed as mankind's greatest challenge – man versus machine in a battle for intellectual supremacy. Could a machine beat the best chess player in the world; was it game over for humans?

Born in Azerbaijan in 1963, Garry Kimovich Kasparov is the greatest chess player in the history of the game. Players of chess are ranked using the Elo points system. Only a handful of players have ever had an Elo over 2800; in 1999, Kasparov achieved a rating of 2851, a score no other human has yet matched. He was the natural choice to stand in the human corner against the machine challenger.

In 1997 Kasparov went head-to-metal against Deep Blue (or rather Deep Blue and its team of programmers) in a six-game match. Using the brute-force approach, Deep Blue was capable of analysing two hundred million positions per second and up to six complete moves ahead (that is, one move each from black and white), compared to a good human player's ability to analyse five. The battle of intellects was really an illusion – IBM's Deep Blue belongs to the "smart machine" category of **weak AI**. Specifically designed to beat Kasparov, it never *thought* as such, but used its processing power to calculate essentially perfect retorts to Kasparov's moves.

Initially, things looked good for Kasparov, who won the first game on 3 May, but the next day the machine retorted with a win. Following this chess bombshell, there followed three draws and a final, swift defeat for Kasparov at the many hands and chipsets of Deep Blue and its team. It was clear, however, that Kasparov found the conduct of IBM's Deep Blue team to be far from honourable, implying human intervention. Kasparov quickly became exhausted, consumed by the idea that he was being manipulated and cheated, while IBM's team looked on impassively and their share price soared. As for Deep Blue, it "retired" after the match, never to play again.

Currently considered two of the most powerful chess engines, following their joint-first placing at the Computer Chess World Championship 2010, are **Rondo** and **Thinker**. Rondo – also known as Zappa – was created by American computer scientist, Anthony Cozzie, while Thinker's code originated in the mind of Canadian, Lance Perkins. According to Cozzie, the Elo rating for the latest iteration of Zappa, Zappa Mexico, is in the region of 3150 while that for Thinker (v5.5) also comes in at over 3100. Given that the best human players on Earth

coding rather than a real creature. During tense confrontations in games such as *Resident Evil IV* it's hard not to gasp in incredulity the first time an enemy does a swift side-step to avoid the laser-sighting you've aimed between their eyes. The impression is of an intelligent entity preserving its life, rather than several lines of programming code that boils down to "if red dot interacts with avatar's head, get dot off head". Similarly, the characters in

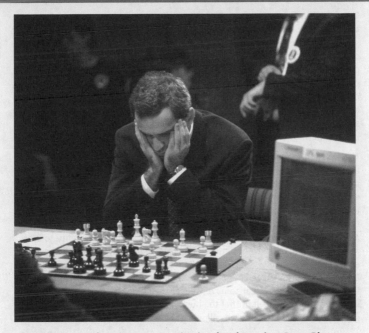

**Garry Kasparov deep in concentration in a battle against Deep Blue.**

are doing supremely well to reach an Elo rating In excess of 2800, machines like these could see the end of human domination of the game within the decade.

When the time arrives and computers consistently beat the best human players, should we be concerned? Not really. Such conquests will merely reveal the onset of a time when technology can challenge the human brain at one specific task.

For the story of the Deep Blue match from Kasparov's perspective, see the documentary *Game Over: Kasparov And The Machine* (2003), directed by Vikram Jayanti.

*The Sims* (see box overleaf) are so intricately programmed that they seem to have wills of their own, with genuine motivations and intelligence.

Computer games get away with this deception because of our difficulty in distinguishing between objects which respond to their environment in a purely reactive manner and ones which are driven from within to perform certain behaviours – that have a will of their own. When we see

## The *Sims* phenomenon

Unleashed in February 2000, *The Sims* is the world's best-selling PC game, created by the American game-design guru Will Wright. The structure of most games relies on fairly straightforward goals – shoot the alien, win the race, checkmate the king – but by the time *The Sims* reached market, it was clear it delivered an entirely different gaming experience. There are no real objectives; players are simply invited to engage in the day-to-day lives of virtual people called "sims". Players create their own characters (shaping the sims appearance and personality traits), designing their homes and running their lives. The sims respond to events in the game independently, but will need the player's intervention to keep their lives on track.

The key to the game's success is the very powerful illusion of a rich social tapestry, of which your characters become an integral part. With each new iteration of the game, the sims become ever more complex and lifelike, the emotional scenarios and interactions richer and more involved. In *The Sims 2*, the characters are driven by more than just virtual hunger or the need to go to the bathroom – they have long-term *aspirations* built into them (such as getting married, attaining wealth or becoming a star). Add to this the ability to store memories of previous events, and the sims are able to develop very believable, emergent behaviours – such as avoiding dogs because they were previously bitten by one. This gives *The Sims* something no other game has – characters that both learn and appear to have wills of their own. Their actions so closely resemble human behaviour that the human player simply fills in the emotional gaps, their capacity for empathy allowing them to see minds behind the pixels.

For the game's programmers, the ultimate goal is to create characters that are driven by such a large range of subtle stimulus/response behaviours that they are indistinguishable from real human beings.

**The Sims** thesims.ea.com

a Venus flytrap engulf a careless fly, it's all too easy to credit the plant with a kind of intelligence, imagining it lying in wait, ready to pounce on the fly at just the right moment. But the plant isn't intelligent – trigger hairs within its specialized leaves are activated by the prey, causing the leaves to spring shut and seize the victim. The plant relies entirely on a reactive mechanism, and so do the characters in video games; it's just that these characters have more reactive mechanisms programmed into them, sometimes mixed with the ability to learn – to store new information which can impact on future behavioural responses.

## Strong AI

It is clear that, for a machine to start to get close to what's going on inside a human mind, it needs to do far more than crunch numbers in the way a chess computer does, or react to its environment in the automated way a *Sims* character does. But what is the missing ingredient? What do we mean by intelligence?

The intelligent behaviour that humans exhibit is born of an innate survival instinct – all life is programmed to behave in a way that promotes its survival; anything without this instinct will die. The key to machine intelligence seems to lie in creating a machine that possesses internal representations of the world and itself within that world that drive its behaviour – what we might call an **artificial consciousness**. This would allow the machine to respond to its environment intelligently, with a sense of purpose, choosing one course of action over another, attempting to increase its probability of survival.

How on Earth should we go about trying to invest a machine with consciousness? Should we try to build a supercomputer capable of processing the sum of all human knowledge in the hope that something resembling intelligence will emerge? Or should we begin by trying to model very simple, insect-like central nervous systems within machines, gradually increasing the complexity of the system until it resembles a human mind? Both these approaches, referred to as **top-down** and **bottom-up** respectively, emerged early on in the history of AI, and both have been pursued by different groups of researchers over the past half-century.

### Top-down: expert systems

Top-down AI attempts to mimic the brain's functions, such as memory and reasoning, using computer programs. It takes the approach that cognition is a high-level phenomenon that is independent of the details of the

## Expert view

*Dr Janaina Mourao-Miranda works at the Centre for Computational Statistics and Machine Learning, University College London. Janaina works at the forefront of machine-learning, a discipline in which hardware and software are being used to both read and interpret the brain's mental landscape. By teaching machines to interpret whether a person's brain scan is indicative of a specific mental illness, she aspires to a time when such approaches will greatly aid clinical diagnosis.*

### What is artificial intelligence – AI?

It's an area of research within computer science that tries to create "intelligent machines". So it's a type of research that is focused on the development of algorithms and computer programs based on, or inspired by, the way the brain works and learns things in a very general way.

### What specific aspect of AI do you work on?

I work specifically with machine-learning approaches – programs that "learn" by discovering automatic regularities in a series of examples. Say we have an input–output relationship and we don't know how to compute that relationship; we don't have a clear mathematical model for it. We give the computer a series of examples – inputs and outputs – and the computer learns those relationships and, once learned, they can be used to make predictions or to classify *new* examples – that's very similar to how we learn things.

For example, when we're kids we learn that a chair is a chair by seeing many chairs, so eventually we know a chair is a chair. But, if we try to describe a chair, like having "four legs" and "an L type of shape", we'll see that there are many chairs that don't fit this framework but they are still chairs; that way of thinking is the inspiration behind my work on machine-learning. We give the computer many examples of a relationship, objects and labels – chairs, photographs of chairs and then labels of chairs and other objects and it learns to generalize to new examples. But what I'm doing is not with chairs but with brain images, brain scans...

### So you're involved in trying to teach machines to learn what particular brain scans mean?

Yes, to find patterns in the brain scans that are characteristic of different cognitive states or different disorders. So we have scans from people with a specific brain disorder versus scans from "normal" people; patterns of brain disorder versus patterns of healthy controls. Each brain scan is a three dimensional image; we then have to transform these scans into a feature vector and we give them labels – they can be cognitive states, normal versus abnormal, for example. We then train the machine-learning algorithm to find the discriminative pattern between the two categories described by the labels, so when we have the brain scan of a new person it's possible to predict if this pattern is closer or more similar to a healthy or abnormal pattern – a clinical application of this work might aid in diagnosis.

## What types of mental illness are you looking at?

Mostly psychiatric, but also neurological disorders, such as depression, schizophrenia, autism, Alzheimer's. We had a group of healthy control people looking at emotional images and depressed patients looking at the same images and we had the brain scans for the two groups. We then trained the machine-learning algorithm with these patterns and labels and we were able to predict if subjects were depressed or not – just by looking at the pattern of brain scans.

## What's exciting you in the field today?

What is very exciting now is that we can train an algorithm to find the differences between scans but we can then have an image from a new subject and make predictions about individual diagnoses. So we're not just saying depressed people have different patterns of brain activity compared to healthy controls but we are saying we've found this associated pattern of activity and we can use this pattern to help classify new subjects.

## Have there been any recent discoveries you've found particularly fascinating?

There have also been some models that go a step further, that try to *generate* either the brain activity or the stimuli the people are looking at. Some researchers have used these techniques to train a machine model to find the relationship between specific stimuli and the brain's response. Then, on a second level of the model they tried to generate brain scans on the basis of the stimuli the people were looking at, or, when given a brain scan, it tried to generate the image that the subject was looking at.

## Does that mean, for example, there could come a time when the algorithm could say this person is looking at a piece of fine art?

Yes, more or less, at least it will be able to say the person is looking at an object or is listening to music. From the clinical side, the cutting edge is prognosis; to predict a patient's response to treatment and follow illness development. In some very recent work, we've been scanning the brains of subjects before they receive treatment, then the group is treated with medication, anti-depressants, for example. Only some of them will respond to the treatment, and we're trying to see if there's any information we can detect in the initial scans that could have been used to predict responsiveness.

## Where do you see the field heading?

Within neuroscience, the models will get much closer to understanding how the brain works and be able to reconstruct the stimulus a subject was either looking at or listening too. And I think from the clinical side there will be greatly improved diagnosis, especially of psychiatric disorders that can be very subjective and difficult to pinpoint, even for the clinicians, because of overlapping symptoms.

## The Turing test

The Englishman Alan Turing (1912–54) was a brilliant mathematician and code-breaker, considered by many to be the father of modern computing. One of his many influential ideas was the **Turing test**.

Originally called the "imitation test" in Turing's key 1950 manuscript *Computing Machinery And Intelligence*, the test is simple in design. An "interrogator" is challenged to decide which of the two unseen entities they are communicating with – by text – is human and which is a machine. If the interrogator guesses incorrectly, the machine has passed the test.

Turing was less interested in the philosophical question "Can a machine think?" than in the practical question "Can a machine fool a human into believing it's a person?" When he published his paper, Turing predicted that, by the year 2000, machines would frequently pass his test. Given the progress he had made in computing, that was a fairly generous amount of time. However, Turing died four years later (by his own hand) and we still do not have machines that can convincingly pass the test.

Since 1990, the **Loebner Prize**, sponsored by New Yorker Hugh Loebner, has been awarded annually for the "most convincing human-like conversation" by a "chatterbot", as contenders are known. One of the frequent winners is A.L.I.C.E., the Artificial Linguistic Internet Computer Entity, created by Richard Wallace. So far, A.L.I.C.E. has won the Loebner Prize three times, in 2000, 2001 and 2004. More recently, the prize went to a chatbot created by Bruce Wilcox in 2010, going by the name, **Suzette**. Suzette has not passed the Turing test but a new bot on the block reached a step closer in 2011. **Cleverbot**, created by British AI scientist, Rollo Carpenter, is the successor to Carpenter's previous chatbot and two times Loebner prize winner, **Jabberwacky**. Cleverbot made its linguistic appearance at the Techniche Festival (The Annual Techno-Management Festival) in India during which it conversed with fifteen individuals over a four-minute period while another fifteen volunteers chatted with humans. Following the chats, which had all been displayed on screens to a viewing audience, both participants and audience – more than 1300 individuals – cast their votes to

underlying mechanism. As such, it doesn't try to mimic the functioning of our neurons, but instead takes an independent approach to achieving cognitive functions. It is essentially trying to achieve artificial intelligence without imitating nature. This seems a perfectly sensible proposition – after all, humans' attempts to achieve flight through imitating the flapping of birds' wings ended in failure, and success only arrived once people cast that example aside and took an independent approach to the problem.

The main type of top-down AI is **expert systems**. These are essentially systems for solving problems and giving advice in specific areas of knowledge. Examples of expert systems include medical diagnosis programs decide who had conversed with a human and who was interacting with silicon. While the human conversations scored 63.3 per cent humanness, Cleverbot scored only 4 percent less, with 59.3 per cent. In this instance, it would seem the gap between human and machine is closing – but we're still not quite at the stage when we can say the Turing test has comfortably been passed.

**User:** Do you read?
**Cleverbot:** Yes. I read.
**User:** What's your favourite book?
**Cleverbot:** Hmmm... *Farenheit 451*.
**User:** What about movies, what's your favourite film?
**Cleverbot:** *Grease*. I love John Travolta!
**User:** I got chills!
**Cleverbot:** That's lovely.

While the above brief exchange reads convincingly, when asked, "What's your favourite part of the brain?", Cleverbot replied, "The New Testament".

One current prediction for when a marriage of hard- and software will convincingly and consistently fool the human mind comes from futurist and polymath Raymond Kurzweil. By examining and extrapolating trends in human technological advancement over decades, Kurzweil has predicted that the year 2029 will see the emergence of machines capable of passing the Turing test.

And what if a machine did pass the test: what has it demonstrated other than a sophisticated ability to engage a human in conversation? It may suggest complex rule-following, but it doesn't suggest true intelligence or intention on the part of the machine. The chatterbot is not trying to fool the interrogator; it is simply responding to the text it receives according to its inbuilt parameters.

**The Alan Turing Home Page** www.turing.org.uk/turing

**A.L.I.C.E. Artificial Intelligence Foundation** www.alicebot.org

**Cleverbot** www.cleverbot.com

and systems offering technical support to customers. To build an expert system, the designers interview people who are expert in the relevant field in order to accumulate a **knowledge base**. They then standardize this knowledge into a set of rules in the form "If X, then Y". An **inference engine** is then created which is able to use these rules to draw conclusions.

Expert systems is the branch of AI that has produced the most useful real-life applications so far. However, they are not yet much like the artificial mind we defined above. An expert system has no sense of itself, no internal representation of the world, no understanding of what it's for. What's more, it may be able to answer questions in a very specialized field, but it can make absurd errors that humans would easily avoid, and is unable to cope with anything outside its own "micro-world" – because it possesses no common sense. The **CYC project** (from "encyclopedia" and pronounced 'psych') was conceived to rectify this, and is the largest experiment yet in top-down AI. Its aim is to accumulate a vast knowledge base containing the whole sum of human common sense, so that future expert systems can be more flexible and less prone to errors. However, most believe that expert systems do not handle data in a way that will work on a much larger scale. It is expected that, before expert-systems technology achieves anything like the common sense that each of us possesses, it will come up against the **frame problem** – its means of accessing and processing information will be unable to handle the huge quantities involved, and it will grind to a halt.

Perhaps, after all, it makes sense to pay attention to how nature handles the problem of dealing with such vast amounts of information. This is exactly what bottom-up AI does.

## From the bottom up: neural networks

Bottom-up AI attempts to replicate the brain's vast, complex network of neurons in the hope that by doing so, what emerges from them – intelligence and consciousness – will also be replicated. In particular, **artificial neural networks** (ANNs) attempt to replicate the way the brain learns, so that intelligence can "evolve" within the system rather than being explicitly programmed in the manner of expert systems. To construct an entire artificial brain in this way would be no mean feat: each of the human brain's one hundred billion neurons is connected to thousands of other neurons, so that there are several hundred trillion such connections (or synapses) in total. However, the neurons themselves are relatively simple units, and we now have a good understanding of how they interact with each other.

As we saw on p.68, the fundamental principle underlying the way our brains learn is known as **Hebbian learning**, after the influential neuropsychologist Donald Hebb. Essentially, his idea was that if one neuron consistently helps stimulate another neuron to fire an action potential, some form of biological change occurs to strengthen the physical connection between those two neurons, ultimately making the chance of one causing the other to fire even greater. And vice versa – if one neuron plays no part in helping a neuron to fire, the connection between them weakens. This deceptively simple principle is the foundation of the brain's **plasticity** – its ability to change over time.

The aim of ANNs is to replicate this method of learning. An ANN consists of a network of artificial neurons, each connected to a number of others in the same way that biological neurons are. This basic system "learns" how to perform a particular task through a tinkering process which gradually alters the strength of the links between the artificial neurons until a pattern of connection weights is established which allows the network to respond correctly to inputs. A famous example of a basic ANN is that created by David Rumelhart and James McClelland at the University of California at San Diego. They trained a set of 920 artificial neurons to be able to correctly form the past tenses of English verbs. This was a serious challenge, since English contains a large number of irregular verbs. The neurons were arranged in two layers, an input layer and an output layer. The researchers presented a root form of the verb to the input layer – for example, "look" – and checked the output of the network against the desired response ("looked"). If the network got it wrong, the researchers tweaked the strength of the connections between neurons to give it a push in the right direction and make it more likely to get it right next time.

# Catherine Hall
*University College London Neuroscience, Physiology and Pharmacology*

**What is your favourite part of the brain and why?** It's not a geographical location, but I really like the whole concept of cortical-subcortical networks – so the idea of circuits of activity rushing from the cortex, through the basal ganglia and back again, becoming progressively more modulated and influencing all the clever cortical stuff, enabling it to reach a threshold to make decisions about what actions to take, what something means, etc. I think this encompasses the concept of the brain being a dynamic network, rather than a bunch of Lego bricks.

**What scientific breakthrough do you think helped us to understand the brain the most?** I don't know if it's the most important, but one of my favourites is Wolfram Schultz's studies showing dopaminergic neurons firing to reward, expectation of reward and a mismatch of expected and delivered reward – a great demonstration of the neural basis of how circuits can be altered to affect behaviour, and what's going on in our heads when we get an unexpected reward!

**What's the next big thing in neuroscience?** I think new technological developments that allow us to measure what lots of neurons are doing while animals are awake and behaving will hugely affect how we understand how neural systems interact with each other. It looks like we'll find that our representations of the world are built up quite differently from how we think at the moment – that what you are actually *doing* has a huge effect on how you encode and perceive your environment.

## Supercomputers and brains

Twice each year, the **TOP500 Project** sorts the super-wheat from the super-chaff in the world of supercomputing. As the title suggests, a supercomputer is one that, at the time it was built, ranked as one of the biggest and fastest computers on the planet. The standard by which these machines are measured is their **FLOPS**, or Floating-point Operations Per Second.

The original supercomputer, the **Cray-1** from 1976, was capable of hitting anywhere between 80 and 240 megaFLOPS (mega being $10^6$). Today, even video game consoles, such as the **PlayStation 3**, can reach in excess of 200 gigaFLOPS ($10^9$). But these are left trailing by the current supercomputers, the fastest of which is currently the Japanese RIKEN Advanced Institute for Computational Science's **K Computer**. Despite still only being half built, the 672 computer racks containing more than 68,000 computer processing units forming the K Computer are capable of 8.162 petaFLOPS ($10^{15}$) – that's more than eight thousand million million FLOPS. As discussed elsewhere, the human brain struggles with such large, abstract numbers; another way to view this value is that in one second the K Computer is capable of performing more calculations than one million times the number of humans on the planet.

So how does the **human brain** compare? The figure that pops up time and again is 100 teraFLOPS ($10^{12}$), barely one third of today's best computer. It's somewhat meaningless, however, to reduce the workings of the brain to mere numbers. No one yet understands precisely how the brain manipulates the information swirling throughout its extraordinary network. On paper, BlueGene may out-FLOP the brain, but all that computing clout is struggling to model the smallest of functional units within a mammalian brain's cortex – just a few cells. It's not necessarily what you've got, but what you do with it that matters.

**The Top 500 Supercomputers** www.top500.org

**The Fujitsu/RIKEN Institute "K Computer": the world's fastest computer as of June 2011.**

Essentially, if a neuron should have fired and didn't, the strength of its connections to the neurons that tried to stimulate it were increased, making it more likely to fire next time. If it did fire and shouldn't have, connections to the neurons that stimulated it were weakened. Over time, the network learned the right answers.

The way the past-tense network learned these verbs is very similar to the way in which children learn them. In particular, it went through a period of over-generalization. Because connections between neurons involved in the regular "-ed" ending were gradually strengthened by the large number of these regular verbs passing through the system, the network began to apply "-ed" to the end of every verb, so that "go" would become "goed". But eventually it was able to tell one verb from another and construct irregular verb forms such as "went".

Just like a child – and unlike an expert system – the past-tense network knows no formal rules of grammar. The rules are implicit in the system rather than explicit. The network also stores information in the same way we believe the human brain does. Thus, the knowledge that enables it to form "wept" from "weep" is not stored in one place, but in the entire pattern of connection weights forged during training. The system does not need to delve deep into some out-of-the-way corner to retrieve it; it is at the tips of its fingers, so to speak. This is what allows ANNs – and the human brain itself – to avoid the frame problem which dogs expert systems.

As we have seen, this past-tense network contained only two layers – an input layer and an output layer. Since then, more complex networks have been built, able to perform tasks that are correspondingly more involved. One application of current ANNs is the conversion of handwriting to text. They are also particularly good at recognizing faces and speech. However, they are still a long way from modelling an entire brain.

A project whose ambition is to do just that is the **Blue Brain Project** at the Brain and Mind Institute in Switzerland. A collaboration between IBM and the École Polytechnique Fédérale de Lausanne (EPFL), the project began in 2005 and is led by Henry Markram.

The project's aim is to build an artificial mammalian brain in the form of a giant **modular neural network** – that is, a neural network composed of a series of connected modules with discrete functions. This approach takes its inspiration from how a biological brain operates – rather than using one large neural network to solve problems, several distinct networks in the brain work together to reach the solution. Groups of connected neurons performing related tasks huddle together, creating

## Steve Grand's *Creatures*

Steve Grand developed *Creatures* while working for games developer Millennium Interactive. It was released in 1996 by Mindscape and was an instant hit, attracting a fan base which has since grown to almost a million enthusiasts worldwide.

This revolutionary computer game was home to the **Norns**, small autonomous beings that hatched from eggs. The player's task was to train the Norns, feed them and teach them to communicate – giving them the skills they needed to survive the intricate world in which they lived. The Norns were motivated by impulses such as boredom (in which case they would find something to do) and hunger (in which case they would find something to eat).

This may seem simple enough, but Grand had created something special with *Creatures*: it was the first commercially available example of **artificial life**, or a-life. Each Norn was built from the ground up from thousands of tiny simulated biological units such as neurons, biochemicals and receptors. The structure and interaction of these units was determined by digital genes. As Grand explains, "Each gene defines something about how a patch of simulated neurons wires itself up, what its neural transfer functions are, how a given chemical influences those neurons or some other part of the body, what chemical reactions take place, and so on." When the Norns bred, these digi-genes were mixed and passed on, as in the organic world. Over time, Norns could develop traits and characteristics of their own, **emergent behaviours** which Grand had never programmed into the game, but which slowly evolved over time.

*Creatures* was much more than just a computer game. A large online community grew up around it, in which players discussed evolutionary trends they had spotted, and tried to unravel the Norns' genome. As Grand claims, this allowed *Creatures* to become "a vast, worldwide scientific experiment in artificial life", and it was an important milestone in its field.

the different neurological structures such as the cortex, hippocampus or cerebellum, which then work in parallel to form a unified whole. Real-time brain scans, such as those from functional magnetic resonance imaging (fMRI), reveal this brilliantly, as simple tasks often result in several parts of the brain becoming active simultaneously. The Blue Brain Project intends to build virtual versions of the various brain structures within a computer, from the ground up, and then mimic their behaviour and interaction.

Using one of the world's most powerful supercomputers, BlueGene, the team's first goal is to model the cellular circuitry of the mammalian **cortex**.

This is a good place to start, since the cortex is the most complex part of our brain, responsible for all higher functions, such as reasoning and attention. As useful as current ANNs are, they are still a way off simulating a brain capable of more than memory and basic learning. To create a machine brain capable of consciousness, for example, it will be necessary to have some form of cortex.

When they have built their detailed digital model of the cortex, the Blue Brain Project researchers intend to use it to run various biological simulations in order to gain insight into such properties as perception, thought and even mental illness. Ultimately, they hope to move beyond the tiny cortical structures to re-create an entire interconnected and functional brain. To bring this dream a large step closer to reality, the project recently joined with twelve other European partners to create the **Human Brain Project**, a bold collaboration aiming to have modelled the complete human brain within ten years. If successful, this virtual brain could provide insights into the precise mechanisms of human thought and intelligence, as well as providing a model system in which to study maladies of the mind, such as mental illness.

> **"The computing power needed is considerable. Each simulated neuron requires the equivalent of a laptop computer. A model of the whole brain would have billions of neurons. Supercomputing technology is rapidly approaching a level where simulating the whole brain becomes a concrete possibility."**
>
> The Blue Brain Project

**The Human Brain Project:** www.humanbrainproject.eu

**The Blue Brain Project:** bluebrain.epfl.ch/page-52744-en.html

## Ghosts in the machine

And what might humans do if we ever manage to create a machine mind smart enough to inhabit a physical body? As technologies advance, it's inevitable that the worlds of robotics and AI will collide. While some may be inspired to pursue the world of "human-like" robots (such as those seen in Alex Proyas's movie based on Isaac Asimov's story, *I Robot*) in an attempt to create empathy between humans and machines, others, such as Andrew Ng (Artificial Intelligence Laboratory, Stanford University) are more focused on the practical details of what intelligent machines can be used for. If successful, Ng and his team will become very popular indeed, as the project, known as **STAIR** (STanford Artificial Intelligence Robot) has set its sights on one of humanity's most tedious chores: tidying up.

While one's immediate response to the notion of such high spec technology ending up in a domestic robot may be a touch of confusion – surely we need such robots to get to Mars, after all – it is the perfect testing ground for interactive AI. The process of tidying demands that we can see our environment, recognize where aspects of it could be improved and then decide how to go about effecting those changes. In other words, it demands dexterity, locomotion, learning, planning and decision-making, all based on sensory input.

> **"If you do not speak English, I am at your disposal with 187 other languages along with their various dialects and sub-tongues."**
>
> Robbie the Robot,
> *Forbidden Planet* (1956)

Sponsored by giants such as Google and DARPA (read, "information-gathering" and "advanced military applications", respectively), amongst others, the academic project's long-term goals are to create a robot that can enter a working office environment, understand speech and perform numerous tasks, from basic tidying and fetching to preparing meals or assembling furniture with tools. In its current prototypic form, STAIR bears little resemblance to a human but it is competent at what it does and, importantly, is learning and improving all the time.

**You can see more about the project and Andrew Ng's research here:**
stair.stanford.edu
www.youtube.com/watch?v=AY4ajbu_G3k

## What does AI mean for us?

Favour has swung back and forth between top-down and bottom-up AI over the years, partly due to increased computing capacity making possible things which were previously impractical, but mainly due to disillusionment. No branch of strong AI has yet lived up to the early optimistic forecasts. However, for many it is still a question of when, not if, we will manage to create true artificial intelligence. Assuming that to be the case, what will be the implications for us, for what it means to be human?

As a species, we have become increasingly precious about our brain in the last millennium. Our sense of self-importance used to be bolstered by the belief that the universe literally revolved around us, until 1542 when Nicolaus Copernicus confirmed we were not even at the centre of the solar system. Similarly, we used to be entranced by the notion of having been created in the image of a god, but thanks to Charles Darwin's elegant theory, we've now been obliged to accept that we're basically smart apes. The only thing we have left to truly distinguish ourselves is our remarkable brain – its extraordinary capacity to perceive, reason, solve and create.

Should true artificial intelligence be created – performing all those functions that we consider unique to humans – it will be a pivotal stage in our cultural evolution, perhaps sinking our long-cherished sense of superiority for good. Indeed, the more radical predictions suggest we may find ourselves, science-fiction-style, actually ceding control to these upstart beings. As Edward Fredkin at MIT's AI Lab suggests, if we manage to create computers whose intelligence greatly exceeds our own, they "might keep us as pets". Whatever the eventual scenario, if we do manage to create artificial intelligence, we will need to recognize that our brain, by itself, may no longer be what sets us apart – and be content with knowing that what we've managed to achieve with it is unique.

# Resources

## Where to find out more

# Books

The *Rough Guide to the Brain* aims to be precisely that, a whistle-stop tour of the main features of your central nervous system. If your appetite's been whetted, then below is a small collection of books to appease that hunger, from excellent general works about the brain to those dealing with some of the more specific facets of the mind covered in various chapters to a full-on textbook for the serious science student.

## Popular science

Igor Aleksander *The World in My Mind, My Mind in the World: Key Mechanisms Of Consciousness In People, Animals And Machines* (Imprint Academic, 2005)
Skilfully and passionately written, the author navigates the reader through some of the most important questions relating to consciousness, irrespective of whether in man, other animals, or machines.

John Morgan Allman *Evolving Brains* (Scientific American Library, 2000)
Their may by a large number of colourful illustrations, but this is as bookish and academic as you'll get. Covering everything from molecular biology to mass extinctions, this comprehensive book will explain to the eager reader (with some basic biological knowledge) how they ended up with such a big brain.

Alan D. Baddeley *Essentials of Human Memory* (Psychology Press, 1999)
Intended as a guide for the general reader, this unashamedly personal book clearly explains the history of the study of memory and how modern approaches and new techniques are unravelling its workings in a clear, informal style.

Rita Carter *Mapping the Mind* (Phoenix, 2003)
Beautifully illustrated, excellently written. Rita Carter's eloquent examination of how the brain's different regions conspire to create the mind guides the general, or informed, reader through various landmarks in our understanding of the brain.

Antonio R. Damasio *Descartes' Error: Emotion, Reason, and the Human Brain* (Penguin Books, 2005)
Using examples from history and his own neurological examinations, Damasio takes the reader on a fascinating exploration of how human reasoning is intimately tied into our ability to experience emotional states.

Ian Deary *Intelligence: A Very Short Introduction* (Oxford Paperbacks, 2001)
The place to start for the person

wanting to know more about the history, study, and significance of intelligence. This excellent, clear, pocket-sized book covers the science, thinking, and disputes of intelligence research with panache.

**Daniel C. Dennett** *Consciousness Explained* (Penguin, 2004)
A highly acclaimed work for both the general readers and professionals. Dennett takes a fun and articulate voyage through the evolution of consciousness, using both neuroscience and modern perspectives on computing to get his fascinating points across. Hard to see your brain in the same light after reading this expansive book.

**Stanley Finger** *Minds Behind the Brain: A History of the Pioneers and their Discoveries* (Oxford University Press, 2000)
This genuinely engaging and thoroughly researched book covers the most important characters and milestones in our understanding of the brain, spanning thousands of years. Full of fascinating stories about those who helped shape our understanding.

**Steve Grand** *Growing Up with Lucy: How to Build an Android in Twenty Easy Steps* (Weidenfield & Nicolson, 2003)
Wit, charm and intelligence abound in this book, which explains artificial intelligence and describes Grand's efforts to create an artificial life form.

**Christian Jarrett** *The Rough Guide to Psychology* (Rough Guides, 2011)
A great introduction to the subject written in a clear, jargon-free style that renders complex concepts easy to understand – very comprehensive, and bang up to date, touching on all aspects of the subject.

**Eric R. Kandel, James H. Schwartz, Thomas M. Jessell** *Principles of Neural Science* (McGraw-Hill, 2000)
For the neuroscience student, this monster of a book is an excellent first stop. Covering every aspect of neuroscience, from molecular biology to anatomy, physiology, and behaviour, this indispensable work achieves for the brain what the dictionary does for language.

**Paul Martin** *Counting Sheep* (Flamingo, 2003)
This easy and captivating book peels back the mystery of what happens to us every night in bed. Covering every aspect of sleep, from its evolution to modern research to the numerous problems of sleep, Martin's anecdote-filled book is a joy.

**Oliver Sacks** *The Man Who Mistook His Wife for a Hat* (Picador, 1986)
A modern classic, this erudite book veers between the fascinating, amusing, and moving. Sacks affectionately recounts his numerous experiences with patients suffering from a range of neurological disorders with quiet sensitivity. The beauty of his approach is that each case is a journey shared by both reader and Sacks, as he carefully observes each case, homing in on their unique, often tragic, malfunction.

**Tom Stafford & Matt Webb** *Mind Hacks: Tips and Tricks for Using Your Brain* (O'Reilly, 2004)
It's impossible to read this fast and furious informal look at the mind's workings for more than five minutes without discovering something amazing. Entertaining and informative.

**Lawrence Weiskrantz** *Consciousness Lost and Found: A Neuropsychological Exploration* (Oxford University Press, 1997)
One of neuropsychology's pioneers

weaves philosophy and the scientific study of brain disorders into his own explanations of the why and how of consciousness. Clear and witty (dense in parts), a good book for those who really want to know more about how brain damage has informed the modern view of consciousness.

## Fiction

**Sebastian Faulks** *Human Traces* (Vintage, 2006)
Two doctors, Thomas Midwinter and Jacques Rebière, explore the human condition while pushing forward our understanding of mental illness in the nineteenth century.

**Ian McEwan** *Saturday* (Vintage, 2006)
The central character of McEwan's contemporary story is neurosurgeon Henry Perowne, and brain surgery and mental illness are recurring themes – alongside global terrorism, ageing and the simple pleasures of life.

**Richard Morgan** *Altered Carbon* (Victor Gollancz, 2002)

What if your entire mind could be "needlecast" – beamed across space – then uploaded into a fresh, cloned version of you (or even a different body)? Morgan's intense, violent, hard-boiled science-fiction epic deals with the implications of such a future with gritty aplomb.

**Robert Louis Stevenson** *The Strange Case of Dr Jekyll and Mr Hyde* (Penguin Popular Classics, 1994)
First published in 1886, Stevenson's classic tale of what becomes of Dr Henry Jekyll as he attempts to polarize man's good and evil personas is a literary metaphor for the left and right hemispheres of the human brain.

**Daniel Tammet** *Born on a Blue Day: A Memoir of Aspergers and an Extraordinary Mind* (Hodder & Stoughton, 2006)
Bridging the gap between personal experience and the perception of others, Tammet offers a rare and fascinating insight into precisely how somebody with Aspergers sees the world around him.

# Websites and podcasts

The Internet may never become self-aware, but it's increasingly becoming the best first place to look for the most up to date information, whatever the topic. The sites below begin by detailing organisations that invest lots of resources in helping to make science accessible for everyone...

## Organizations and societies

**The Royal Society** www.royalsoc.ac.uk
Based in central London, the Royal Society is the UK's oldest, continuous scientific institution (founded 1660). It regularly holds exhibitions, meetings and talks for the general public on all manner of scientific subject matter.

**The Royal Institution** www.ri.ac.uk
Home of the annual "Christmas lectures", the RI is steeped in scientific history. Passionate about creating open dialogue between scientists and the general public, this site tells you what they're up to, from talks to education and research.

**The Wellcome Trust**
www.wellcome.ac.uk

The site of one of the world's largest biomedical charity and source of research funding, the Trust is always looking for new ways to explore the interfaces between science, art and knowledge.

**The Dana Foundation** www.dana.org
A good place to begin for all things brain related. Something for everyone of any age – scientist or not.

**The British Science Association**
www.britishscienceassociation.org
Heavily involved in the promotion and discussion of all scientific subjects, the BSA's site carries extensive information about its UK-wide events (such as their large, annual Festival of Science). There is also an active forum for those wishing to discuss issues online.

**Café Scientifique**
www.cafescientifique.org
By checking this site you'll be able to find the location of your nearest Café Scientifique. These worldwide evenings have successfully modernized the expected format of "science events" by combining a relaxed mix of topical scientific chat with your preferred tipple.

**Cheltenham Festival of Science**
www.cheltenhamfestivals.com
Here you'll find details of all the various festivals held in Cheltenham, including the very popular, annual science festival that uses all manner of approaches to entertain, inform and amaze.

# Science Centres and Museums

**European Collaborative for Science, Industry & Technology (ECSITE)**
www.ecsite.eu

Taking the work out of finding a museum or science centre, whether at home or abroad, this site does all the hard work for you.

**Body Worlds** www.bodyworlds.com
If you've ever wondered what the inside of a human being looks like, but wish to remain on the correct side of the law, visit Gunther von Hagens' Body Worlds exhibition. The regularly updated website will tell you the where and when of upcoming exhibitions and contains useful information for tourists and educators alike.

**The London Science Museum**
www.sciencemuseum.org.uk
Museums have changed a lot since the days of dusty artefacts and the odd interactive button. This site shows you what a modern approach to engaging the mind about science is all about.

# Specialist Organizations

**The National Institute for Health and Clinical Excellence** www.nice.org.uk
An independent umbrella organisation whose remit is to advise and provide guidance in all areas of health. A good place to get the definitive word on health issues appearing in the news.

**PharmWeb** www.pharmweb.net
This powerful portal provides access to country specific pharmaceutical information, discussion groups, drug education and more besides.

**Nobel Prizes** www.nobelprize.org
Not only can you find out about every Nobel Prize ever awarded, you'll find links to the history of the prize plus some decent games that inform whilst entertaining.

## Human Intelligence
www.indiana.edu/~intell
All the major players in the history of intelligence research are here, from Plato to the present day. The Hot Topics section provides quick access to some of the most important questions in intelligence research.

# Mental Health

**Diagnostic and Statistical Manual of Mental Disorders, Fourth Edition** www.behavenet.com/capsules/disorders/dsm4TRclassification.htm
The buck stops here, with the official criteria provided for each of the mental illnesses currently recognized.

**Mind** www.mentalhealth.com
The site of the largest mental health charity in the UK, this is an excellent place to find help, information about conditions and drugs, and local support.

**The National Institute of Mental Health** www.nimh.nih.gov
This US-based site is one main branch of the Department of Health, acting as a conduit and information repository for all matters relating to mental health. Links to many specific organizations can be found here.

# Learning

**British Broadcasting Corporation (BBC)** www.bbc.co.uk/science/
Yes, it's an institution. It also has an excellently informed and well maintained website on scientific subjects, from human evolution to artificial intelligence.

**How Stuff Works** www.science.howstuffworks.com
A wonderfully informal approach to explaining essentially anything you've

ever wondered about the inner workings of, well, "things". Extensive and fun.

**Wikipedia** www.wikipedia.org
More a phenomenon than a resource, this open-source, web-based encyclopaedia contains authoritative and regularly updated information on practically everything.

**Neuroscience for Kids** faculty.washington.edu/chudler/neurok.html
Don't be fooled by the friendly interface, this highly accessible site is an excellent place to start finding out more about the brain. And if you need to stretch your legs, it's also full of brain-related activities.

# Podcasts

These handy downloadable chunks of information are rapidly altering the way we access knowledge. There are dozens of science-based podcasts but, should you get tired reading or surfing the web, any of these are a decent start for the latest in science news.

**Gray Matters** features discussions relating to the brain, such as creativity and neuroethics and can be found through The Dana Foundation's website or through podcasting software.

*New Scientist* podcasts are available for download, featuring interviews and highly accessible information about new breakthroughs in general science.

*Nature* a regular podcast is available from one of the world's most prestigious scientific journals, condensing highlights of the week's publication (frequently using interviews with the contributing scientists) into an informative programme. More for the academic than the general listener.

**NeuroPod** presented by Kerri Smith, this monthly neuroscience podcast (a co-production from *Nature* and the Dana Foundation) weaves the latest news and science into an entertaining programme.

## Blogs

**Mind Hacks** www.mindhacks.com Current, varied and always interesting, this blog comes from Sheffield-based lecturer in Psychology and Cognitive Science, Tom Stafford, and London-based clinical and research psychologist, Vaughan Bell: @ mindhacksblog, @tomstafford and @ vaughanbell.

**Neurophilosophy** www.guardian. co.uk/science/neurophilosophy Now hosted by *The Guardian*'s website, this topical and well-written blog from freelance science writer, Mo Costandi

(@mocost), is "a weblog about molecules, minds and everything in between".

**NeurologicaBlog** www.theness.com/ neurologicablog Penned by Steven Novella (@ stevennovella), both president of the New England Skeptical Society and clinical neurologist based at Yale University's School of Medicine, this blog spans everything from neuroscience to the philosophy of science, all underpinned by rigorous critical thinking.

**TED** www.www.ted.com Where would we be without this vast, free repository of human endeavour. Possibly one of the most inspiring resources the web offers, spanning everything from neuroscience to music and beyond (@tedtalks).

# Film, television and video games

**American Beauty** (Sam Mendes, 1999) A midlife crisis was never so much fun to watch in this beautiful tragic-comedy. Lester Burnham "wakes up" from his mundane existence to rediscover his love of life by way of infatuation, diminished responsibility and a healthy supply of high-grade cannabis from his new neighbour's son.

**American Psycho** (Mary Harron, 2000) A shocking, brutal, and at times amusing peek into the mind of a psychopathic personality.

**Blade Runner** (Ridley Scott, 1982) Scott's sci-noir masterpiece (based on Philip K. Dick's novel) in which rogue

artificial humans, known as replicants, abscond to Earth in search of life and freedom. The film plays heavily on the idea that once a certain level of technology is reached, it would become impossible to tell the difference between real and lab-created human beings. A key piece of equipment used to discriminate between replicants and humans is the Voight-Kampff machine, a polygraph analogue that measures involuntary emotional responses to provocative questions.

**The Cell** (Tarsem Singh, 2000) A spectacular visual treat from director Singh, this sci-fi thriller requires the investigative talents of child psychologist

Catherine Deane (Jennifer Lopez) to enter the mind of a comatose serial killer in an attempt to acquire information that will prevent another victim's death. A relatively ignored but bold film, *The Cell* makes full use of the elaborate set-up to create a rich, believable and darkly menacing mental realm.

**Deus Ex: Human Revolution** (Console version developed by Eidos Montreal, 2011)
A game set in 2027, played as Adam Jensen, the gruff-voiced unwilling recipient of a slew of cybernetic enhancements. The term "game" doesn't do justice to the depth of story, science, or the political and personal turmoil encountered as you strategically weave your way through the experience.

**Eternal Sunshine of the Spotless Mind** (Michel Gondry, 2004)
A beautiful fable set in an imagined present in which selective memory erasure is possible. It serves as a moving reminder of how valuable memories are, whether pleasant or not.

**Fight Club** (David Fincher, 1999)
A powerful exploration of insomnia, psychosis, and what it means to be male in contemporary society.

**Forbidden Planet** (Fred M. Wilcox, 1956)
This curious classic blends science-fiction with Shakespeare's *The Tempest*. Robbie the Robot stars as the imagined future of artificial intelligence, while the darker territories of the human subconscious are wittily explored.

**Harry Brown** (Daniel Barber, 2009)
Playing out of character as a pensioner, Michael Caine delivers a subtle and fiercely compelling performance as the titular Harry Brown, a former Royal

Marine living a quiet, rather lonely, existence in London until his friend and chess companion is slaughtered by a local gang of drug dealers on their housing estate. This beautifully shot film features one of the most astonishing and repulsive turns from actor Sean Harris as heroin dealer and addict, Stretch.

**Inception** (Christopher Nolan 2010)
Another bold, visionary film from the British director, in which Dom Cobb (Leonardo DiCaprio) and a team of accomplices set out to invade the dreams of business magnate, Robert Fischer (Cillian Murphy). A deep, haunting meditation on the nature of dreaming, reality and perception.

**I, Robot** (Alex Proyas, 1999)
Based on the classic novel by Isaac Asimov, the relationship between humans and intelligent machines is explored in this action-intensive murder mystery.

**The Matrix Trilogy** (Andy and Larry Wachowski, 1999, 2003)
The entire nature of perception, consciousness and reality is examined in a world now governed by intelligent machines.

**Memento** (Christopher Nolan, 2000)
This striking first-person-perspective thriller centres on a man, played by Guy Pearce, hunting the killer of his wife in a world shattered by the complete loss of his long-term memory. His only grip on a historical narrative are the notes and Polaroids he leaves peppering his immediate environment and the countless informative tattoos that cover his body.

**My Own Private Idaho** (Gus Van Sant, 1991)
Inspired by Shakespeare's *Henry IV*, this

beautiful film explores the life of Mike, a narcoleptic male prostitute, as he attempts to find his mother.

**Requiem for a Dream**
(Darren Aronovsky, 2000)
No other film more powerfully conveys both the ecstatic heights and hellish, agonizing lows of addiction. Focusing largely on heroin addiction, the film also spreads its net wider, dealing with the idea of addiction in differing guises. Make no mistake, this is a hard watch but it also contains moments of staggering beauty with riveting performances throughout.

**The Social Network**
(David Fincher, 2010)
A dramatic interpretation of how the world's most popular data sharing and assimilation website was born. Featuring an excellent, if not particularly flattering, turn from actor Jesse Eisenberg as Facebook founder, Mark Zuckerburg.

**Trainspotting** (Danny Boyle, 1996)
A revelation when it first appeared, this feat of the imagination somehow manages to make heroin addiction simultaneously hilarious and terrifying. Challenging the then current views about drugs, this driven, bold and energetic movie refused to shy away from the realities of life with heroin, taking the subculture of a bunch of Edinburgh-based addicts by the neck and wringing it relentlessly.

**The Wire** (HBO television drama created by David Simon, broadcast 2002–08)
Set in America's Baltimore, *The Wire* was a series of staggering ambition. Using drugs, and the money and crime it generates, as a recurring theme throughout its five seasons, this series' swooping narrative arcs gave viewers an incredible insight into the social web that glues us all together. Dealers and junkies, media types and politicians, all the characters are utterly believable. A masterpiece.

# Index

# Picture Credits

## Cover images

**Front cover:** Katharine Dowson's *My Soul*, a laser-etched image of the artist's own brain, photographed by Sunderland University Glass and Ceramics Department.

**Inside front cover:** Bipolar neuron – these cells are specialized sensory neurons – they form part of the sensory pathways for smell, sight, taste, hearing and vestibular functions (Corbis/Science Picture Co./Science Faction).

**Back cover:** White matter fibre architecture of the brain. Measured from diffusion spectral imaging (DSI). The fibers are color-coded by direction:
red = left–right; green = anterior–posterior; blue = through brain stem
(Data: Randy Buckner/Visualization: Vaughan Greer/humanconnectomeproject.org).

## Other images
All images public domain except: